Table of Contents

Table of Contents

The American Journey

Active Reading
Note-Taking Guide
Student Workbook

Douglas Fisher, Ph.D.
San Diego State University

 Glencoe

New York, New York   Columbus, Ohio   Chicago, Illinois   Peoria, Illinois   Woodland Hills, California

About the Author

Douglas Fisher, Ph.D., is a Professor in the Department of Teacher Education at San Diego State University. He is the recipient of an International Reading Association Celebrate Literacy Award as well as a Christa McAuliffe award for excellence in teacher education. He has published numerous articles on reading and literacy, differentiated instruction, and curriculum design as well as books, such as *Improving Adolescent Literacy: Strategies at Work* and *Responsive Curriculum Design in Secondary Schools: Meeting the Diverse Needs of Students.* He has taught a variety of courses in SDSU's teacher-credentialing program as well as graduate-level courses on English language development and literacy. He has also taught classes in English, writing, and literacy development to secondary school students.

The McGraw-Hill Companies

Send all inquiries to:
Glencoe/McGraw-Hill
8787 Orion Place
Columbus, Ohio 43240-4027

ISBN-13: 978-0-07-875258-2
ISBN-10: 0-07-875258-2

Printed in the United States of America

7 8 9 QVR 14 13

Table of Contents

Table of Contents

Dear Social Studies Student,

Can you believe it? The start of another school year is upon you. How exciting to be learning about different cultures, historical events, and unique places in your social studies class! I believe that this Active Reading Note-Taking Guide *will help you as you learn about your community, nation, and world.*

Note-Taking and Student Success

Did you know that the ability to take notes helps you become a better student? Research suggests that good notes help you become more successful on tests because the act of taking notes helps you remember and understand content. This *Active Reading Note-Taking Guide* is a tool that you can use to achieve this goal. I'd like to share some of the features of this *Active Reading Note-Taking Guide* with you before you begin your studies.

The Cornell Note-Taking System

First, you will notice that the pages in the *Active Reading Note-Taking Guide* are arranged in two columns, which will help you organize your thinking. This two-column design is based on the **Cornell Note-Taking System**, developed at Cornell University. The column on the left side of the page highlights the main ideas and vocabulary of the lesson. This column will help you find information and locate the references in your textbook quickly. You can also use this column to sketch drawings that further help you visually remember the lesson's information. In the column on the right side of the page, you will write detailed notes about the main ideas and vocabulary. The notes you take in this column

will help you focus on the important information in the lesson. As you become more comfortable using the **Cornell Note-Taking System**, you will see that it is an important tool that helps you organize information.

The Importance of Graphic Organizers

Second, there are many graphic organizers in this *Active Reading Note-Taking Guide*. Graphic organizers allow you to see the lesson's important information in a visual format. In addition, graphic organizers help you understand and summarize information, as well as remember the content.

Research-Based Vocabulary Development

Third, you will notice that vocabulary is introduced and practiced throughout the *Active Reading Note-Taking Guide*. When you know the meaning of the words used to discuss information, you are able to understand that information better. Also, you are more likely to be successful in school when you have vocabulary knowledge. When researchers study successful students, they find that as students acquire vocabulary knowledge, their ability to learn improves. The *Active Reading Note-Taking Guide* focuses on learning words that are very specific to understanding the content of your textbook. It also highlights general academic words that you need to know so that you can understand any textbook. Learning new vocabulary words will help you succeed in school.

Writing Prompts and Note-Taking

Finally, there are a number of writing exercises included in this *Active Reading Note-Taking Guide.* Did you know that writing helps you to think more clearly? It's true. Writing is a useful tool that helps you know if you understand the information in your textbook. It helps you assess what you have learned.

You will see that many of the writing exercises require you to practice the skills of good readers. Good readers *make connections* between their lives and the text and *predict* what will happen next in the reading. They *question* the information and the author of the text, *clarify* information and ideas, and *visualize* what the text is saying. Good readers also *summarize* the information that is presented and *make inferences* or *draw conclusions* about the facts and ideas.

I wish you well as you begin another school year. This *Active Reading Note-Taking Guide* is designed to help you understand the information in your social studies class. The guide will be a valuable tool that will also provide you with skills you can use throughout your life.

I hope you have a successful school year.

Sincerely,

Douglas Fisher

A Note from the Author

Chapter 1, Section 1
Early Peoples

(Pages 16–19)

Reason To Read

Setting a Purpose for Reading Think about these questions as you read:
• How did the first people arrive in the Americas?
• What discovery changed the lives of early Native Americans?

Main Idea

As you read pages 16–19 in your textbook, complete this graphic organizer by filling in the causes and effects of migration to the Americas.

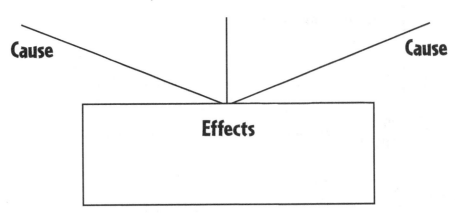

Migration to the Americas

Cause

Cause

Effects

Sequencing Events

As you read, place the following events on the time line:
• **Farming develops in Mexico**
• **Early villages established in Mexico**
• **Last Ice Age ends**
• **Asian hunters enter North America**

♦ 30,000 B.C.   ♦ 10,000 B.C.   ♦ 5,000 B.C.   ♦ 1,000 B.C.

The Journey From Asia *(pages 16–18)*

Scanning

Scan the lesson quickly to get a general idea of what it is about. Use one or two sentences to write that general idea in the spaces below.

Crossing the Land Bridge

_____

_____

In Search of Hunting Grounds

_____

_____

Hunting for Food

_____

_____

Terms To Know

Define or describe the following key terms.

archaeology

_____

_____

artifacts

_____

_____

Ice Ages

_____

_____

migration

_____

_____

nomads

_____

Notes

Academic Vocabulary

Define these academic vocabulary words from the lesson.

expose >

_____

_____

environment >

_____

_____

Settling Down *(pages 18–19)*

Summarizing

Write a summary of each subsection. Make sure that the key point of the section is included in your summary.

Planting Seeds

_____

_____

Early Communities

_____

_____

The Growth of Cultures

_____

_____

Terms To Know

Choose a term from the list below to complete each sentence by writing the term in the correct space.

carbon dating   culture   maize   nomadic

1. The _____ of Native Americans underwent changes when they moved to farming.

2. One of those changes was to abandon their _____ way of life and to live in settled communities instead.

3. _____ , an early form of corn, was an important crop for Native Americans.

4. One technique scientists use for determine the age of artifacts is

_____ .

Academic Vocabulary

Define these academic vocabulary words from the lesson.

community \> _____

_____

_____

complex \> _____

_____

Section Wrap-up

Now that you have read the section, write the answers to the questions that were included in **Setting a Purpose for Reading** *at the beginning of the section.*

How did the first people arrive in the Americas?

_____

_____

What discovery changed the lives of early Native Americans?

_____

_____

Chapter 1, Section 2
Cities and Empires
(Pages 22-26)

Reason To Read

Setting a Purpose for Reading Think about these questions as you read:
- Why did powerful empires arise in the Americas?
- How did the people of each empire of North America adapt to their environment?

Main Idea

As you read pages 22-26 in your textbook, complete this graphic organizer by filling in facts about the religions of these civilizations.

Civilization	Religion
Maya	
Aztec	
Inca	

Sequencing Events

As you read, place the following events on the time line:
- **Aztec establish Tenochtitlán in Mexico**
- **Rise of the Olmec in Mexico**
- **Inca Empire begins to expand**
- **Maya civilization at its height in Central America**

| ◆ 1500 B.C. | ◆ B.C./A.D. | ◆ A.D. 1200 | ◆ A.D. 1400 |

Early American Civilizations (pages 22–23)

Determining the Main Idea

Use the spaces below to write the main idea of this subsection.

Main Idea >

_____

_____

_____

Terms To Know

Use the spaces below to write a sentence that explains the meaning of civilization.

civilization >

_____

_____

Academic Vocabulary

Choose an academic vocabulary word from the list below to complete each sentence by replacing the underlined word. Write the correct term in the space.

enormous   structures   contributions

1. The <u>buildings</u> _____ at Macchu Picchu were carved from the gray granite of the mountaintop.

2. The civilizations of the Americans built <u>huge</u> _____ cities even though they lived in thick jungles and on high mountain-tops.

The Maya (pages 23–24)

Questioning

As you read, ask yourself: what is an important detail? Write one of those details about Mayan cities in the spaces below.

Mayan Cities >

_____

_____

Terms To Know

Match the term in the left column with the correct definition in the right column by writing the letter in the space to the left of the term.

____ **1.** hieroglyphics

____ **2.** theocracy

a. society ruled by religious leaders

b. study of the stars and planets

c. a system of writing that uses symbols or pictures to represent things, ideas, and sounds

Academic Vocabulary

In the spaces below, write three modern examples of each academic vocabulary word.

network
_____
_____
_____

symbol
_____
_____

The Aztec *(pages 24–25)*

Summarizing

Under each heading below, compare the Aztec civilization to the Maya civilization by stating how they were similar and how they differed.

War and Religion
_____
_____

Terms To Know

Look up the following terms in a dictionary and write definitions of them.

causeway
_____
_____

maize
_____
_____

Key Points	Notes
sacrifice >	_____

The Inca (page 26)

Visualizing   *Make a mental picture of the different features of Inca civilization listed below. Draw a sketch of your mental image in the box below each feature.*

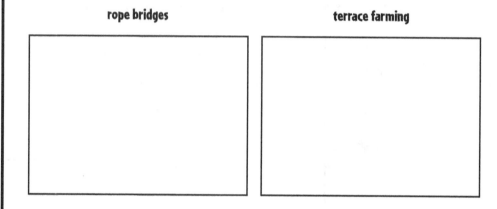

rope bridges   terrace farming

Terms To Know   *Define or describe the following terms.*

quipus > _____

terraces > _____

Academic Vocabulary   *Circle the letter of the word or words that have the closest meaning to the underlined academic vocabulary word.*

1. Some Inca cities were <u>devoted to</u> religious ceremonies.

  a. forbidden from   **b.** incapable of   **c.** set aside for

2. The Inca used *quipus* to keep track of important <u>resources</u>.

  a. people   **b.** property   **c.** messages

Now that you have read the section, write the answers to the questions that were included in **Setting a Purpose for Reading** *at the beginning of the section.*

Why did powerful empires arise in the Americas?

_____

_____

How did the people of each empire adapt to their environment?

_____

_____

Chapter 1, Section 3
North American Peoples

(Pages 28-33)

Reason To Read

Setting a Purpose for Reading Think about these questions as you read:
- What early people lived in North America?
- How did different Native American groups of North America adapt to their environments?

Main Idea

As you read pages 28-33 in your textbook, complete this graphic organizer by filling in information about these cultures.

Culture	Where they lived	How they lived
Anasazi		
Mount Builders		
Inuit		

Sequencing Events

As you read, place the following events on the time line:
- **Hohokam civilizations begins to decline**
- **Cahokia is built**
- **Anasazi build pueblos in North America**
- **First ceremonial mounds built**

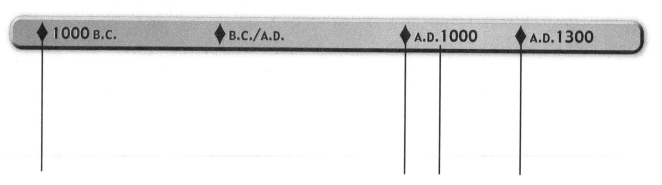

1000 B.C.   B.C./A.D.   A.D.1000   A.D.1300

Early Native Americans (pages 28–31)

Summarizing

Review pages 28–31 and list two key facts about the Mound Builders.

> **The Mound Builders**

_____

_____

Terms To Know

Define or describe the following key terms.

> **pueblos**

_____

_____

> **droughts**

_____

_____

Academic Vocabulary

Use the following academic vocabulary word in a sentence.

> **available**

_____

_____

> **dominate**

_____

_____

Terms To Review

Use this term, which you studied earlier, in a sentence that reflects the term's meaning.

> **culture**
> (Chapter 1, Section 1)

_____

_____

Other Native Americans (pages 31–33)

Inferring

Write a sentence about how Native Americans in the East and the Southeast used the resources available to them. Then, write an inference you can make about the way Native Americans lived.

Peoples of the East and Southeast >

_____
_____
_____

Inference >

_____
_____
_____

Terms To Know

Write a sentence linking each of the following key terms with the Native American peoples of at least one region.

adobe >

_____
_____
_____

nomadic >

_____
_____
_____

federations >

_____
_____
_____

Academic Vocabulary

Write two words that are related to each academic vocabulary word.

region >

_____
_____
_____

temporary >

_____
_____
_____

Notes

Terms To Review

Use each of these terms, which you studied earlier, in a sentence that reflects the term's meaning.

civilization
(Chapter 1, Section 2)

_____

_____

nomad
(Chapter 1, Section 1)

_____

_____

maize
(Chapter 1, Section 1)

_____

_____

Now that you have read the section, write the answers to the questions that were included in Setting a Purpose for Reading *at the beginning of the section.*

What early people lived in North America?

_____

_____

How did different Native American groups adapt to their environments?

_____

_____

Chapter 1, Section 3

Chapter 2, Section 1
A Changing World
(Pages 38–42)

Reason To Read

Setting a Purpose for Reading Think about these questions as you read:
• How did technology make long sea voyages possible?
• What caused great civilizations to flourish in Africa?

Main Idea

As you read pages 38–42 in your textbook, complete this graphic organizer by writing three reasons that Europeans increased overseas exploration.

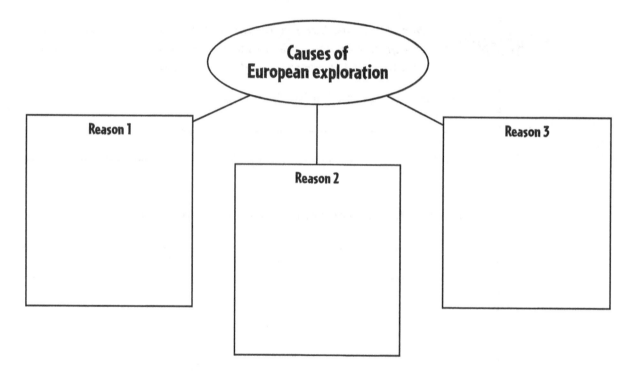

Causes of European exploration

Reason 1

Reason 2

Reason 3

Sequencing Events

As you read, write the correct dates for each of these events:

_____ **Marco Polo travels to China from Italy**

_____ **Mansa Musa makes a pilgrimage to Makkah**

_____ **Renaissance spreads throughout Europe**

Expanding Horizons (pages 38–39)

Connecting — *Describe two important effects about the growth of trade.*

The Growth of Trade

_____

_____

Terms To Know — *Choosing from the list below, write the correct term in the space.*

civilizations   classical   Renaissance

1. The _____ spread from Italy to other European countries.

2. In the 1300s, Italians became interested in the _____ of ancient Greece and Rome.

3. Scholars and artists became interested in the books and artworks of the _____ world.

Academic Vocabulary — *Choose an academic vocabulary word from the list below to complete each sentence by replacing the underlined word. Write the correct term in the space. You may have to change the form of the academic vocabulary word.*

invest   emerge   isolate

1. The Renaissance first <u>appeared</u> _____ in Italy.

2. For many centuries, Europe was <u>separated</u> _____ from other parts of the world.

Powerful Nations Emerge (pages 39–40)

Predicting

Based on what you have read in the lesson so far, predict where you expect that powerful nations emerged.

_____

_____

Academic Vocabulary

Write two words that are related to each academic vocabulary word.

alternative

_____

_____

expand

_____

_____

Terms To Review

Use this term, which you studied earlier, in a sentence that reflects the term's meaning.

region
(Chapter 1, Section 3)

_____

_____

Technology's Impact (pages 40–41)

Monitoring Comprehension

Check how well you have understood what you have read so far by explaining how change in technology contributed to the growth of exploration.

_____

_____

Terms To Know

Define or describe the following key terms.

astrolabe

_____

_____

Key Points	Notes

caravel

_____
_____
_____

technology

_____
_____
_____

Academic Vocabulary

Read the passage below. In the spaces that follow, write a definition of each underlined academic vocabulary word.

The printing press led to the publication of more books, which increased people's access to knowledge and information.

_____
_____
_____

African Kingdoms (pages 41–42)

Connecting

Explain how the growth of wealth and power in Africa was similar to the growth of wealth in Italian cities in the 1300s.

_____
_____

Terms To Know

Choose a term from the list below to complete each sentence by writing the correct form of the term in the correct space.

culture   mosque   architecture   pilgrimage

1. Elements of Islamic _____ like art, learning, and law were adopted by the rulers of Mali and Songhai.

2. Mansa Musa took a long _____ to Makkah, which is a holy city to Muslims.

3. Mansa Musa had an Arab architect build several great _____ at Timbuktu.

Academic Vocabulary

Read each sentence below. Put a checkmark in the space before the phrase that best explains what the underlined academic vocabulary words means in the sentence.

1. The Ghana empire <u>declined</u> when new paths for trade developed outside of the area it controlled.

   _____ lost power   _____ gained power

2. West Africans followed overland <u>routes</u> to trade with people in North Africa and the Middle East.

   _____ empires   _____ paths people followed

Terms To Review

Use this term, which you studied earlier, in a sentence that reflects the term's meaning.

emerge
(Chapter 2, Section 1)

_____

_____

Section Wrap-up

Now that you have read the section, write the answers to the questions that were included in Setting a Purpose for Reading *at the beginning of the section.*

How did technology make long sea voyages possible?

_____

_____

What caused great civilizations to flourish in Africa?

_____

_____

Chapter 2, Section 2
Early Exploration
(Pages 43–49)

Reason To Read

Setting a Purpose for Reading Think about these questions as you read:
• How did Portugal lead the way in overseas exploration?
• What was Columbus's plan for sailing to Asia?

Main Idea

As you read pages 43–49 in your textbook, complete the diagram below.

Explorer(s)	Date(s)	Region
The Vikings		
	1492	
Balboa		
		around the world

Sequencing Events

Match the date in the left column with the correct achievement in the right column by writing the letter in the space to the left of the place.

_____ 1. c. 1000   **a. Columbus lands in the Americas**

_____ 2. 1492   **b. Dias reaches the Indian Ocean**

          c. Magellan begins to circumnavigate the world

_____ 3. 1498   **d. Vikings reach the Americas**

_____ 4. 1519   **e. da Gama reaches India**

Seeking New Trade Routes (pages 43–45)

Sequencing

Place the following developments in the correct order by writing a number from 1 through 5 in the space to the left. Give the number 1 to the earliest development.

_____ **a.** Brazil claimed Portugal

_____ **b.** Center for learning about navigation formed in southern Portugal

_____ **c.** Cape of Good Hope passed

_____ **d.** First Portuguese ships reach India

_____ **e.** Trade established with Gold Coast

Academic Vocabulary

Use each of the following academic vocabulary words in a sentence.

annual >

_____

_____

establish >

_____

_____

Columbus Crosses the Atlantic (pages 45–49)

Clarifying

As you read this lesson, answer the questions to clarify the story of Columbus's voyage.

1. Why did the queen of Spain decide to pay for Columbus's voyages?

_____

_____

2. Where did Columbus think he had landed? What area did he actually reach?

_____

_____

Terms To Know

Define or describe the following terms.

circumnavigate

_____
_____
_____

line of
demarcation

_____
_____
_____

strait

_____
_____
_____

Academic Vocabulary

Circle the letter of the word or words that have the closest meaning to the underlined academic vocabulary word.

1. Before leaving Spain, Columbus incorrectly <u>estimated</u> the distance from Europe to Asia.

   a. drew   **b.** measured   **c.** predicted

2. Columbus needed the help of rulers to <u>finance</u> his expedition.

   a. provide money for   **b.** explain   **c.** justify

Section Wrap-up

Now that you have read the section, write the answers to the questions that were included in **Setting a Purpose for Reading** *at the beginning of the section.*

How did Portugal lead the way in overseas exploration?

_____
_____

What was Columbus's plan for sailing to Asia?

_____
_____

Chapter 2, Section 2

Chapter 2, Section 3
Spain in America

(Pages 51-55)

Reason To Read

Setting a Purpose for Reading Think about these questions as you read:
• How did the great Aztec and Inca empires come to an end?
• How did Spain govern its empire in the Americas?

Main Idea

As you read pages 51-55 in your textbook, complete this graphic organizer by filling in the names of four conquistadors and the regions they explored.

Conquistador	Region Explored

Sequencing Events

As you read, place the following events on the time line:
  • **De Soto crosses the Mississippi River**
  • **Cortés lands in Mexico**
  • **Spain establishes fort at St. Augustine**
  • **Pizarro captures Atahualpa**

◆ 1500   ◆ 1530   ◆ 1560

Spanish Conquistadors (pages 51–53)

Analyzing — *Analyze the information in this lesson by answering the following question.*

How did Spanish rulers benefit from the arrangement they had with conquistadors?

_____

_____

Terms To Know — *Write a sentence using the following terms based on the content in this section.*

conquistador

_____

_____

tribute

_____

_____

Academic Vocabulary — *Write the correct form of the* **boldfaced** *academic vocabulary word in the blank space to complete the sentence. You may have to use another form of the word.*

assist

1. The _____ of some Native American groups helped Cortés defeat the Aztec.

grant

2. By _____ conquistadors the right to keep most of the treasure that they found, Spanish rulers encouraged explorers to seek new sources of wealth.

Spain in North America (pages 53–54)

Determining the Main Idea — *Write down an important idea about Spanish exploration.*

_____

_____

_____

 **Key Points**

 **Notes**

Academic Vocabulary

Use each of the following academic vocabulary words in a sentence that conveys the meaning of the term in the text.

achieve >

_____

_____

_____

encounter >

_____

_____

_____

Terms To Review

Use each of these terms, which you studied earlier, in a sentence that reflects the term's meaning.

establish
(Chapter 2, Section 2) >

_____

_____

_____

conquistador
(Chapter 2, Section 3) >

_____

_____

_____

Spanish Rule *(pages 54–55)*

Summarizing

Write a one-sentence summary of each topic.

Types of Settlements >

_____

_____

Social Classes >

_____

_____

The Plantation System >

_____

_____

Terms To Know

Match the term in the left column with the correct definition in the right column by writing the letter in the space to the left of the place.

_____ **1.** *encomienda*

_____ **2.** mission

_____ **3.** plantation

_____ **4.** presidio

_____ **5.** pueblo

a. town in the Spanish colonies

b. people with Spanish and Native American parents

c. religious settlement in the Spanish colonies

d. large estate where crops were grown

e. fort built by the Spanish, usually near a mission

f. right of conquistadors to demand taxes and labor of Native Americans

Academic Vocabulary

In the space available, define the following academic vocabulary words.

> **convert**

_____
_____

> **export**

_____
_____

Section Wrap-up

Now that you have read the section, write the answers to the questions that were included in Setting a Purpose for Reading at the beginning of the section.

How did the great Aztec and Inca empires come to an end?

_____
_____

How did Spain govern its empire in the Americas?

_____
_____

Chapter 2, Section 4
Exploring North America
(Pages 58–62)

Reason To Read

Setting a Purpose for Reading Think about these questions as you read:
- How did the Protestant Reformation affect North America?
- Why did the activities of early traders encourage exploration?

Main Idea

As you read pages 58–62 in your textbook, complete this graphic organizer by describing the effects.

Exploration of North America

Causes	Effects
Protestant Reformation	
Search for NW passage	
Early trading activities	

Sequencing Events

As you read, write the correct date for each of these events:

_____ **Cabot lands in Newfoundland**

_____ **Luther starts Protestant Reformation**

_____ **Cartier sails up the St. Lawrence River**

_____ **Hudson sails the Hudson River**

A Divided Church (pages 58–59)

Skimming

Review "A Divided Church" and write a one-sentence summary about the topic that follows.

Religious Rivalries in the Americas

_____

_____

_____

Academic Vocabulary

Write the correct form of the boldfaced academic vocabulary word in the blank space to complete the sentence.

establish

1. The _____ of rival colonies by Catholics and Protestants brought Europe's religious differences to the Americas.

reject

2. When he _____ Catholic practices, Luther launched the Protestant Reformation.

Economic Rivalry (pages 59–62)

Analyzing

Review "Economic Rivalry" and write a description about the effects of the Columbian Exchange.

The Columbian Exchange

_____

_____

Terms To Know

Define or describe each of the following terms.

Columbian Exchange

_____

_____

coureurs de bois

_____

_____

Key Points	Notes

mercantilism

_____

_____

_____

Northwest Passage

_____

_____

Academic Vocabulary

In the space available, define the following concepts.

economy

_____

_____

_____

region

_____

_____

Terms To Review

Use each of these terms, which you studied earlier, in a sentence that reflects the term's meaning.

resource
(Chapter 1, Section 2)

_____

_____

route
(Chapter 2, Section 1)

_____

_____

Section Wrap-up

Now that you have read the section, write the answers to the questions that were included in Setting a Purpose for Reading _at the beginning of the section._

How did the Protestant Reformation affect North America?

_____

_____

Why did the activities of early traders encourage exploration?

_____

_____

Chapter 3, Section 1
Early English Settlements

(Pages 70–73)

Reason To Read

Setting a Purpose for Reading Think about these questions as you read:
- What crop saved the people of Jamestown? How?
- How did the colonists receive political rights?

Main Idea

As you read pages 70–73 in your textbook, complete this graphic organizer by describing the economy and government of Jamestown.

Jamestown	Description
Economy	
Government	

Sequencing Events

As you read, place the following events on the time line:
- **Settlers of Roanoke Island vanish**
- **House of Burgesses meets in Jamestown**
- **Colonists settle at Jamestown**
- **Gilbert claims Newfoundland for England**

◆1580   ◆1590   ◆1600   ◆1610   ◆1620

Key Points

Notes

England in America *(pages 70–71)*

Sequencing

Place the following developments in the correct order by writing a number from 1 through 4 in the space to the left. Give the number 1 to the earliest development.

_____ **a.** Raleigh sends first attempt to settle Roanoke.

_____ **b.** White makes return to Roanoke.

_____ **c.** Spanish Armada defeated.

_____ **d.** Newfoundland claimed for Queen Elizabeth.

Jamestown Settlement *(pages 71–73)*

Drawing Conclusions

Answer the following questions about the colony at Jamestown.

1. Did the first settlers choose a good location for their colony? Why or why not?

_____

_____

2. Were the settlers well prepared to start a colony? Why or why not?

_____

_____

3. Was it a good idea to allow people to farm their own land? Why or why not?

_____

_____

4. Was it a good idea to allow people to try to promote families in the colony? Why or why not?

_____

_____

 **Key Points**

 **Notes**

Terms To Know

Define or describe the following terms.

charter

_____
_____
_____

joint-stock company

_____
_____
_____

burgesses

_____
_____

Academic Vocabulary

Write the correct form of the boldfaced *academic vocabulary word in the blank space to complete the sentence.*

invest

1. Each _____ in a joint-stock company bought shares of ownership in the company in the hope of getting a share of profits.

survive

2. Only 60 Jamestown settlers were _____ of the "starving time," when food ran out and there was fighting with Native Americans.

Terms To Review

Use this term, which you studied earlier, in a sentence that reflects the term's meaning.

grant
(Chapter 2, Section 3)

_____
_____

Section Wrap-up

Now that you have read the section, write the answers to the questions that were included in Setting a Purpose for Reading *at the beginning of the section.*

What crop saved the people of Jamestown? How?

_____
_____
_____

How did the colonists receive political rights?

_____
_____

Chapter 3, Section 2
New England Colonies
(Pages 76–80)

Reason To Read

Setting a Purpose for Reading Think about these questions as you read:
• Why did the Pilgrims and Puritans come to America?
• How did the Connecticut, Rhode Island, and New Hampshire colonies begin?

Main Idea

As you read pages 76–80 in your textbook, complete this graphic organizer by explaining why different colonies in New England were settled.

Colony	Reasons the colony was settled
Massachusetts	
Connecticut	
Rhode Island	

Sequencing Events

As you read, put the following events in the correct order by writing the number 1 through 4 in the space to the left. Use the number 1 for the event that occurred first, 2 for the next event, and so on.

_____ **A. Hooker founds Hartford.**

_____ **B. Puritans settle Massachusetts Bay Colony.**

_____ **C. Pilgrims land at Plymouth.**

_____ **D. John Wheelwright founds Exter in New Hampshire.**

Religious Freedom (pages 76–78)

Responding   *After reading each subsection, answer the following questions.*

1. What is religious freedom? Why did the Separatists want it?

   _____

   _____

2. Why did the Separatists who came to America call themselves "Pilgrims"?

   _____

   _____

3. Why did the Pilgrims draw up the Mayflower Compact?

   _____

   _____

4. How did Native Americans help the Pilgrims?

   _____

   _____

Terms To Know   *Match the term in the left column with the correct definition in the right column by writing the letter in the space to the left of the term.*

____ **1.** dissented

____ **2.** persecuted

____ **3.** Mayflower Compact

____ **4.** Pilgrims

____ **5.** Puritans

____ **6.** Separatists

a. people who wanted to leave the Anglican Church to set up their own churches

b. people who wanted to reform the Anglican Church

c. agreement signed by the people who settled at Plymouth

d. disagreed with beliefs or practices of the Anglican Church

e. name given the first settlers at Plymouth

f. punished others for their beliefs

g. treated harshly by others for their beliefs

Academic Vocabulary

Read the sentences below. Put a checkmark in the space before the phrase that best explains what the boldfaced academic vocabulary word means in this passage.

1. Though they were far from their original goal, the Pilgrims settled at Plymouth because winter was **approaching**.

_____ bitter cold

_____ snowy

_____ coming soon

2. The Pilgrims came to Massachusetts, not Virginia, putting them far north of their **target**.

_____ place they left from

_____ place they were going to

_____ bull's-eye

New Settlements (pages 78–80)

Questioning

As you read each subsection, ask yourself: what is an important detail? Write one of those details in the spaces below.

Founding Massachusetts Bay

_____

_____

_____

Growth and Government

_____

_____

_____

Connecticut and Rhode Island

_____

_____

_____

Chapter 3, Section 2

Conflict With Native Americans

_____

_____

_____

_____

Terms To Know

Define or describe each of the following terms.

migration

_____

_____

toleration

_____

_____

Academic Vocabulary

Write two synonyms for each academic vocabulary word. A synonym is a word that means the same or about the same as another word.

conflict

_____

_____

founded

_____

_____

Terms To Review

Use this term, which you studied earlier, in a sentence that reflects the term's meaning.

charter
(Chapter 3, Section 1)

_____

_____

Now that you have read the section, write the answers to the questions that were included in **Setting a Purpose for Reading** *at the beginning of the section.*

Why did the Pilgrims and Puritans come to America?

_____

_____

_____

How did the Connecticut, Rhode Island, and New Hampshire colonies begin?

_____

_____

_____

Chapter 3, Section 3
Middle Colonies

(Pages 82–85)

Reason To Read

Setting a Purpose for Reading Think about these questions as you read:
- Why did the Middle Colonies have the most diverse populations in colonial America?
- Who was America's first town planner?

Main Idea

As you read pages 82–85 in your textbook, complete this graphic organizer by identifying who founded each of these Middle Colonies and identifying the reasons for settlement.

Colony	Founder	Why settlers came
New York		
New Jersey		
Pennsylvania		

Sequencing Events

Match the date in the left column with the correct achievement in the right column by writing the letter in the space to the left of the place.

_____ **1.** 1626

_____ **2.** 1664

_____ **3.** 1642

_____ **4.** 1702

a. New Amsterdam is renamed New York

b. William Penn buys land from Native Americans.

c. Dutch buy Manhattan Island

d. Civil war begins in England

e. New Jersey becomes a royal colony

England and the Colonies *(pages 82–84)*

Interpreting   *Interpret the information you read about New York and New Jersey by answering the following questions.*

1. How did the fight between Puritans and royalists affect the North American colonies?

   _____

   _____

2. Why did the English view New Netherland as a threat?

   _____

   _____

3. Why did Dutch settlers stay in the colony after the English took control of it?

   _____

   _____

4. How did Berkeley and Carteret try to attract settlers to New Jersey?

   _____

   _____

Terms To Know   *Write a sentence using each of the following terms.*

patroons >

_____

_____

proprietary colony >

_____

_____

Academic Vocabulary

Circle the letter of the word or words that have the closest meaning to the <u>underlined</u> academic vocabulary word.

1. The people of New Netherland were very <u>diverse</u>.

    a. Dutch   **b.** religious   **c.** different from one another

2. Wealthy patroons have large <u>estates</u>.

    a. tracts of land   **b.** houses   **c.** numbers of servants

Pennsylvania (pages 84–85)

Analyzing

Answer the following questions.

1. Why was King Charles happy to give Penn so much land?

_____

_____

2. Why did Penn want the land?

_____

_____

3. How did Penn try to attract settlers?

_____

_____

4. How much self-government did the colonists of Delaware have?

_____

_____

Terms To Know

Write sentences using each of these terms. Your sentences should use these terms in the context of this lesson.

pacifists > _____
_____
_____

toleration > _____
_____

Academic Vocabulary

Choose the correct form of the academic vocabulary word and write it in the space to complete the sentence.

functional   functioned   functioning

function > **1.** Delaware _____ as a separate colony from Pennsylvania, although it was supervised by Pennsylvania's governor.

legislating   legislative   legislature

legislate > **2.** Pennsylvania had a _____ assembly that made laws for the people in the colony.

tradition   traditional   traditions

tradition > **3.** Quakers did not follow some customs, or _____, which led other people in England to dislike them.

Section Wrap-up

Now that you have read the section, write the answers to the questions that were included in **Setting a Purpose for Reading** *at the beginning of the section.*

Why did the Middle Colonies have the most diverse populations in colonial America?

_____
_____

Who was America's first town planner?

_____
_____

Chapter 3, Section 4
Southern Colonies

(Pages 86–93)

Reason To Read

Setting a Purpose for Reading Think about these questions as you read:
- How were the Southern Colonies established?
- How did the French and Spanish colonies differ from the English colonies?

Main Idea

As you read pages 86–93 in your textbook, complete this graphic organizer by identifying the main crops of three Southern Colonies.

Colony	Main crop
Maryland	
North Carolina	
South Carolina	

Sequencing Events

As you read, place the following events on the time line:
- **The French found the port of New Orleans**
- **The Spanish found Santa Fe**
- **English settlement of Georgia begins**
- **Bacon's Rebellion starts**

♦ 1600 ♦ 1650 ♦ 1700 ♦ 1750

Coming to America (pages 86–88)

Previewing

Review the subsection called "Coming to America."

1. Look at the map on page 87. What colonies will you read about in this section?

_____

2. According to the map, what crops were important in these colonies?

_____

_____

3. Look at the Read to Learn questions on page 86. What other colonies will you read about in this section?

_____

_____

Terms To Know

Define or describe the following key terms.

indentured servants ›

_____

_____

persecuted ›

_____

_____

Academic Vocabulary

Circle the letter of the word or words that have the closest meaning to the <u>underlined</u> academic vocabulary word.

1. To succeed, Maryland needed <u>capable</u> workers.

    a. skilled   **b.** educated   **c.** wealthy

2. One problem that plagued Maryland was <u>conflict</u> between Protestants and Catholics.

    a. cooperation   **b.** disagreements   **c.** an alliance

Terms To Review

Use each of these terms, which you studied earlier, in a sentence that reflects the term's meaning.

expand
(Chapter 2, Section 1)

_____

_____

_____

persecuted
(Chapter 3, Section 2)

_____

_____

Virginia Expands (pages 88–89)

Reviewing

Reread each subsection and list two key facts.

Virginia Expands

_____

_____

_____

Bacon's Rebellion

_____

_____

_____

Academic Vocabulary

Read the passage below. Put a checkmark in the space before the word or phrase that best explains what each boldfaced academic vocabulary word means.

1. Settlers in western Virginia resented the fact that wealthy planters in the east **dominated** the government.

_____ stayed away from

_____ mostly controlled

_____ avoided paying taxes for

2. Virginia was **founded** before the other Southern Colonies.

_____ established   _____ made a royal colony   _____ financed

Settling the Carolinas (pages 89–90)

Analyzing

Under each heading below, compare the two Carolina colonies by stating how they were similar and how they differed.

Type of colony

_____

Economy

_____

Terms To Know

Write a sentence using each of the following terms.

constitution

_____

_____

proprietary colony

_____

_____

Academic Vocabulary

Write the correct form of the boldfaced academic vocabulary word in the blank space to complete the sentence.

conduct

1. Lacking a good harbor, settlers in northern Carolina had to send their goods to Virginia in order to _____ trade.

process

2. By _____ indigo in certain ways, Carolina plants turned the blue flower into a dye used to color textiles.

Terms To Review

Use each of these terms, which you studied earlier, in a sentence that reflects the term's meaning.

proprietary colony
(Chapter 3, Section 3)

_____

_____

estate
(Chapter 3, Section 3)

_____

_____

Georgia (pages 92–93)

Monitoring Comprehension

Check how well you have understood what you have read so far by answering the following questions.

1. Why was Georgia originally founded?

_____

_____

2. How did Georgia actually develop?

_____

_____

3. What rules of Oglethorpe's did Georgia settlers dislike? What did Oglethorpe do?

_____

_____

Terms To Know

Choose a term from the list below to complete each sentence by writing the term in the correct space.

charter   debtor   proprietor

1. A _____ is someone who owes money to another person.

2. The English king gave a _____ to a group of people to create the colony of Georgia.

Academic Vocabulary

In the space available, define the following academic vocabulary words.

military ⟩ _____

_____

regulate ⟩ _____

_____

Terms To Review

Use this term, which you studied earlier, in a sentence that reflects the term's meaning.

conflict
(Chapter 3, Section 2)

_____

_____

New France (page 92)

Outlining

Complete this outline as you read. The first section of the outline is given.

I. About New France

   A. Economy based on fishing and trapping

   B. Became a royal colony in 1663

II. Down the Mississippi River

   A. _____

   B. _____

III. Growth of New France

   A. _____

   B. _____

   C. _____

Terms To Know

Use the following key term in a sentence.

tenant farmer

_____

_____

Academic Vocabulary

Read the following sentences. In the space below, write in your own words the meaning of the boldfaced academic vocabulary word.

1. French tenant farmers had to pay an **annual** rent to the landholders whose land they farmed.

_____

2. French missionaries tried to **convert** Native Americans to Christianity but they did not try to change their ways of life.

_____

Terms To Review

Use each of these terms, which you studied earlier, in a sentence that reflects the term's meaning.

region
(Chapter 1, Section 3)

_____
_____

convert
(Chapter 2, Section 3)

_____
_____

New Spain *(pages 92–93)*

Synthesizing

Read the lesson on New Spain and then write at least two sentences describing this colony.

_____
_____
_____
_____
_____

Terms To Know

Describe or define missions.

missions

_____
_____

Key Points

Notes

Academic Vocabulary

Write a synonym for each academic vocabulary word. A synonym is a word that means the same or almost the same as another word.

enable

_____

_____

expand

_____

_____

Section Wrap-up

Now that you have read the section, write the answers to the questions that were included in Setting a Purpose for Reading *at the beginning of the section.*

How were the Southern Colonies established?

_____

_____

How did the French and Spanish colonies differ from the English colonies?

_____

_____

Chapter 3, Section 4

Chapter 4, Section 1
Life in the Colonies

(Pages 100–106)

Reason To Read

Setting a Purpose for Reading Think about these questions as you read:
- What was the triangular trade, and how did it affect American society?
- How did the regions in the colonies differ from one another?
- Why did the use of enslaved workers increase in the colonies?

Main Idea

As you read pages 100–106 in your textbook, complete this graphic organizer by describing the differences in the economies of the New England, Middle, and Southern Colonies.

Economic Development		
New England	**Middle Colonies**	**Southern Colonies**

Sequencing Events

As you read, write the correct dates for each of these events:

_____ **Thousands of enslaved Africans are brought to America**

_____ **South Carolina and Georgia have the fastest-growing economies**

_____ **New York City's population reaches 18,000**

New England Colonies *(pages 100–103)*

Scanning

Scan the lesson by reading each subsection quickly to get a general idea of what it is about. Use one or two sentences to write an important idea about colonial trade.

Colonial Trade >

_____

_____

Terms To Know

Define or describe the following key terms.

subsistence farming >

_____

_____

triangular trade >

_____

_____

Academic Vocabulary

Write the correct form of the **boldfaced** *academic vocabulary word in the blank space to complete the sentence.*

immigrate >

1. _____ —people coming to North America from other lands—helped the colonial population grow.

transport >

2. Workers cut down trees and _____ them down rivers to shipyards in coastal towns.

Terms To Review

Use each of these terms, which you studied earlier, in a sentence that reflects the term's meaning.

economy
(Chapter 2, Section 4) >

_____

_____

region
(Chapter 1, Section 3) >

_____

_____

The Middle Colonies (pages 103–104)

Connecting

Write down one similarity and one difference between the economies of the Middle Colonies and the New England Colonies.

Similarity >

_____

_____

_____

Difference >

_____

_____

Terms To Know

Choose a term from the list below to complete each sentence by writing the term in the correct space.

cash crops   diversity   fertile soil   toleration

1. Farmers in the Middle Colonies prospered by growing _____

   _____ .

2. The mix of immigrants from many countries gave the Middle Colonies

   great _____ .

3. The need to work and get along together led to _____
   of other people's differences.

Academic Vocabulary

Write two words that are related to each academic vocabulary word.

culture >

_____

_____

method >

_____

_____

The Southern Colonies (pages 104–105)

Determining the Main Idea

Review pages 104–105 and write down the main idea.

Main Idea

_____

_____

_____

Terms To Know

Write a sentence using each of the following key terms.

indentured servants

_____

_____

plantation

_____

_____

Academic Vocabulary

Choose an academic vocabulary word from the list below to complete each sentence by replacing the underlined word. Write the correct term in the space. You may need to change the spelling of the academic vocabulary word.

convince   involve   rely

1. Working in rice paddies <u>consisted of</u> _____ difficult labor under unpleasant conditions.

2. Many plantation owners in the Southern Colonies <u>depended</u>

_____ on enslaved Africans to do the farm work.

Terms To Review

Use each of these terms, which you studied earlier, in a sentence that reflects the term's meaning.

cash crop
(Chapter 4, Section 1)

_____

_____

community
(Chapter 1, Section 1)

_____

_____

Slavery (page 106)

Inferring

Write two facts about the lives of enslaved Africans and then write an inference you can make from those facts. An inference is a conclusion you make from the facts.

_____

_____

_____

_____

Terms To Know

Define or describe the following key terms.

overseers

_____

_____

_____

slave code

_____

_____

Academic Vocabulary

Read the following sentences. In the space below, write in your own words the meaning of the boldfaced academic vocabulary word.

1. Eventually, the North and South came to war over the issue of slavery.

_____

_____

2. Slaves could be whipped even when they only committed **minor** offenses.

_____

_____

Now that you have read the section, write the answers to the questions that were included in Setting a Purpose for Reading *at the beginning of the section.*

What was the triangular trade, and how did it affect American society?

_____

_____

How did the regions in the colonies differ from one another?

_____

_____

Why did the use of enslaved workers increase in the colonies?

_____

_____

Chapter 4, Section 2
Government, Religion, and Culture

(Pages 108–113)

Reason To Read

Setting a Purpose for Reading Think about these questions as you read:
- Why did the Navigation Acts anger the colonists?
- Who had the right to vote in colonial legislatures?

Main Idea

As you read pages 108–113 in your textbook, complete this graphic organizer by identifying the three types of English colonies.

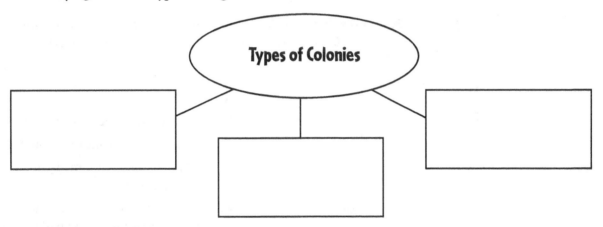

Types of Colonies

Sequencing Events

As you read, place the following events on the time line:
- **Harvard College is established**
- **Benjamin Franklin publishes** *Poor Richard's Almanack*
- **Great Awakening sweeps through the colonies**
- **College of William and Mary is founded**

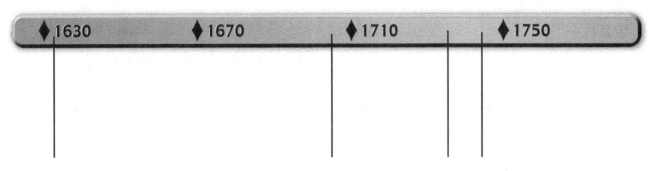

♦1630   ♦1670   ♦1710   ♦1750

English Colonial Rule (pages 108–109)

Identifying Cause and Effect

Answer the following questions to identify the causes and effects of changes in the English government in the late 1600s.

Cause	Action	Effect
_____ _____ _____	Parliament forced out James and gave the throne to William and Mary.	_____ _____ _____
England viewed the colonies as an economic resource.	_____ _____ _____	_____ _____ _____

Terms To Know

Match the term in the left column with the correct definition in the right column by writing the letter in the space to the left of the term.

_____ **1.** English Bill of Rights

_____ **2.** export

_____ **3.** import

_____ **4.** mercantilism

_____ **5.** Navigation Acts

_____ **6.** smuggling

a. economic theory

b. law that guaranteed basic rights

c. to send goods to another country

d. buy goods that were made in another country

e. law that guaranteed colonists' rights to trade with any nation

f. trading illegally

g. guaranteed right

h. law that limited colonists' right to trade

Academic Vocabulary

Circle the letter of the word or words that have the closest meaning to the underlined academic vocabulary word.

1. Charles II <u>restored</u> royal rule when he took the English throne.

    a. ended   **b.** returned to   **c.** rejected

2. The English Bill of Rights was an important <u>document</u> for all citizens.

    a. bill   **b.** essay   **c.** legal paper

Colonial Government (pages 110–111)

Skimming

Skim each subsection to identify the colonies that belonged to each of the three types.

_____

_____

_____

_____

Terms To Know

Choose a term from the list below to complete each sentence by writing the term in the correct space.

charter colonies   proprietary colonies   royal colonies   buffer colonies

1. In _____ , individuals or groups owned the colony and controlled the government.

2. In _____ , the English government ruled directly by naming a governor and council.

3. In _____ , settlers elected their own governors and members of the legislature.

Terms To Review

Use each of these terms, which you studied earlier, in a sentence that reflects the term's meaning.

establish
(Chapter 2, Section 4)

_____

_____

charter
(Chapter 3, Section 4)

_____

_____

An Emerging Culture (pages 112–113)

Analyzing

Analyze the information in this section by answering the following question.

How did the Great Awakening affect people?

_____

_____

Terms To Know

Match the term in the left column with the correct definition in the right column by writing the letter in the space to the left of the term.

____ **1.** apprentices

____ **2.** indentured servants

____ **3.** literacy

a. people who worked without wages for a set period of time in exchange for having their passage to America paid for

b. the ability to read and write

c. the strict definition of a term

d. learning assistants

Academic Vocabulary

*Answer the following questions to interpret the **boldfaced** academic vocabulary words.*

1. What does it mean to say that "The family formed the **foundation** of colonial society"?

_____

_____

2. What does the statement "Married women were considered under their husbands' **authority** and had few rights" mean?

_____

_____

Now that you have read the section, write the answers to the questions that were included in **Setting a Purpose for Reading** *at the beginning of the section.*

Why did the Navigation Acts anger the colonists?

_____

_____

Who had the right to vote in colonial legislatures?

_____

_____

Chapter 4, Section 3
France and Britain Clash

(Pages 116–119)

Reason To Read

Setting a Purpose for Reading Think about these questions as you read:
- How did wars in Europe spread to the American colonies?
- What was the purpose of the Albany Plan of Union?

Main Idea

As you read pages 116–119 in your textbook, complete this graphic organizer by describing the events that led to conflict in North America.

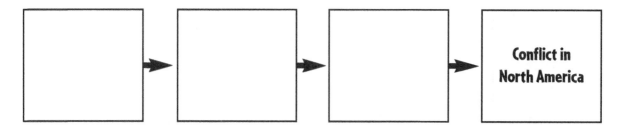

Sequencing Events

As you read, put the following events in the correct order by writing the number 1 through 3 in the space to the left. Use the number 1 for the event that occurred first, 2 for the next event, and so on.

_____ **A. New England troops seize Fort Louisbourg from France.**

_____ **B. George Washington sent to Ohio country to protest French actions.**

_____ **C. Benjamin Franklin proposed Albany Plan of Union.**

British-French Rivalry *(pages 116–118)*

Clarifying

Answer the following questions about the conflict between the British and French.

1. What river valley did both British colonists and French traders want to control?

_____

2. Why did the French have better relations with many Native Americans than the British did?

_____

_____

Academic Vocabulary

Write the academic vocabulary word in the blank space that best completes the sentence.

dominated   organized   advanced

The Iroquois, the strongest power, _____ the area around the Great Lakes.

American Colonists Take Action *(pages 118–119)*

Predicting

Read the title of the lesson and the first two paragraphs under the title. Predict what you think will happen, explaining why. Then read the rest of the lesson and decide whether your prediction was correct or not.

_____

_____

_____

Terms To Know

Write a sentence using the term militia *that explains what the term means.*

_____

_____

Academic Vocabulary

Circle the letter of the word or words that has the closest meaning to the underlined academic vocabulary word.

1. "The French told me that it was their <u>design</u> to take possession of the Ohio."

   a. drawing   **b.** pattern   **c.** plan

2. Washington gained fame when his account of the fight in Ohio was <u>published</u>.

   a. broadcast   **b.** made public   **c.** written

Section Wrap-up

Now that you have read the section, write the answers to the questions that were included in **Setting a Purpose for Reading** *at the beginning of the section.*

How did wars in Europe spread to the American colonies?

_____

_____

What was the purpose of the Albany Plan of Union?

_____

_____

Chapter 4, Section 4
The French and Indian War

(Pages 121-125)

Reason To Read

Setting a Purpose for Reading Think about these questions as you read:
- How did British fortunes improve after William Pitt took over direction of the war?
- How did Chief Pontiac unite his people to fight for their land?

Main Idea

As you read pages 121-125 in your textbook, complete this graphic organizer by describing the effects these events had on the conflict between France and Britain.

Turning point	Effect
Pitt takes charge	
Quebec falls	

Sequencing Events

As you read, place the following events on the time line:
- **French forces driven out of Fort Duquesne**
- **French and Indian War begins**
- **Proclamation of 1763 established**
- **British forces capture Quebec**

◆ 1750   ◆ 1755   ◆ 1760   ◆ 1765

The British Take Action (pages 121–124)

Outlining

Complete this outline about the early stages of the conflict as you read.

Early Stages

    A. _____

    B. _____

    C. _____

Terms To Know

Write a sentence that explains the meaning of these key terms.

alliances >

_____

_____

_____

militia >

_____

_____

Academic Vocabulary

Choose an academic vocabulary word from the list below to complete each sentence by replacing the underlined word or words. Write the correct term in the space. You may have to change the form of the word to fit the sentence.

abandon   intervene   survive

1. Washington led those of Braddock's soldiers who <u>did not die</u>

_____ the attack back to Virginia.

2. When Fort Duquesne was surrounded, the French had to <u>leave</u>

_____ it.

3. When the British thought that the French threat had grown too

strong, they decided to <u>take an active part</u> _____
and send troops to North America.

The Fall of New France *(page 124)*

Reviewing

Review the subsection entitled "The Treaty of Paris" and list two key facts about the treaty.

_____

_____

_____

Academic Vocabulary

Choose one of the academic vocabulary words from the list below to complete each sentence by replacing the underlined word or words. Write the correct term in the space. You may have to change the form of the word to fit the sentence.

assemble   reinforce   grant

1. The British army <u>gathered</u> _____ on the Plains of Abraham, ready to fight.

2. The French tried to <u>strengthen</u> _____ its army in Canada by sending more troops.

Trouble on the Frontier *(page 125)*

Monitoring Comprehension

Check how well you have understood what you have read so far by explaining what happened after the French and Indian War.

_____

_____

_____

Terms To Know

Find these words in the section. Write a definition of each of these terms based on your reading.

alliance _____

_____

speculators

Section Wrap-up

Now that you have read the section, write the answers to the questions that were included in Setting a Purpose for Reading *at the beginning of the lesson.*

How did British fortunes improved after William Pitt took over direction of the war?

_____

_____

How did Chief Pontiac unite his people to fight for their land?

_____

_____

Chapter 5, Section 1
Taxation Without Representation

(pages 132-135)

Reason To Read

Setting a Purpose for Reading Think about these questions as you read:
- Why did the British face problems in North America after the French and Indian War?
- Why did the American colonists object to new British laws?

Main Idea

As you read pages 132-135 in your textbook, complete this graphic organizer by describing why the colonists disliked these policies.

British action	Colonists' view
Proclamation of 1763	
Sugar Act	
Stamp Act	

Sequencing Events

As you read, place the following events on the time line:
- **Townshend Acts tax colonial imports**
- **George Grenville becomes prime minister**
- **Parliament enacts Stamp Act**
- **Parliament passes Sugar Act**

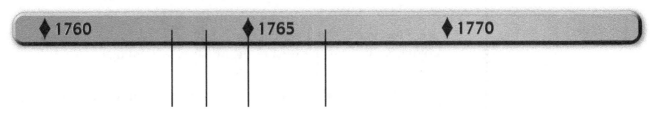

Relations with Britain (pages 132–134)

Identifying Cause and Effect

As you read the lesson, answer the following questions to identify the causes and effects of changes in the English government in the late 1600s.

Cause	Action	Effect
British government is concerned about conflict between colonists and Native Americans in lands beyond the Appalachian Mountains.	_____ _____ _____	_____ _____ _____
_____ _____ _____	Parliament passes Sugar Act and authorizes writs of assistance.	_____ _____ _____

Terms To Know

Read the following sentences. Choose the correct term from this lesson to complete the sentence by circling the term.

1. The British government used the (Proclamation of 1763, writs of assistance) to try to crack down on smuggling.

2. To raise money from colonists, Parliament passed the (Income Act, Sugar Act) in 1764.

3. The British government wanted to raise (debts, revenues) in the colonies.

Academic Vocabulary

Choose an academic vocabulary word used in this lesson from the list below to complete each sentence by replacing the underlined word. Write the correct term in the space. You might need to change the form of the word.

finance   prohibit   violate

1. The Proclamation of 1763 <u>banned</u> _____ the colonists from moving west of the Appalachian Mountains.

2. The colonists felt that this rule and other actions of the British government <u>went against</u> _____ their rights.

 **Key Points**

 **Notes**

Terms To Review

Read each sentence below. In the spaces that follow, explain the meaning of the word you studied earlier.

documents
(Chapter 4, Section 2)

1. Writs of assistance were legal documents that allowed British officials to search for illegal goods.

_____

smuggling
(Chapter 4, Section 2)

2. The British wanted to crack down on the amount of smuggling in the colonies.

_____

The Stamp Act (page 134)

Summarizing

As you read page 134, write a one-sentence summary about protesting the Stamp Act.

_____

_____

Terms To Know

Match the term from this lesson in the left column with the correct definition in the right column by writing the letter in the space to the left of the term.

_____ **1.** boycott

_____ **2.** Declaratory Act

_____ **3.** effigy

_____ **4.** nonimportation

_____ **5.** repeal

_____ **6.** resolution

_____ **7.** Sons of Liberty

_____ **8.** Stamp Act

_____ **9.** Stamp Act Congress

a. British law placing a tax on the colonies
b. formal expression of opinion by an organized group of people
c. protest a law by demonstrating
d. rag figure burned to protest actions
e. British law that stated Parliament's right to tax the colonies
f. meeting of colonial leaders in New York
g. formally cancel an earlier law
h. referring to agreement to not ship goods to other countries
i. referring to agreements to not buy goods from other countries
j. refuse to buy
k. Virginia group that protested the Stamp Act
l. group formed in Boston to protest British tax law

 **Key Points**

 **Notes**

Academic Vocabulary

Write two synonyms for the following academic vocabulary word from this lesson.

consent >

_____

Terms To Review

Write the correct form of the word you studied earlier in the blank space to complete the sentence.

burgesses
(Chapter 3, Section 1) >

1. The members of the colonial assembly in Virginia were called

_____ .

legislate
(Chapter 3, Section 3) >

2. Colonists said that the only fair tax was one passed by their own

assemblies or _____ .

tradition
(Chapter 3, Section 3) >

3. The colonists said that the Stamp Act broke the long _____
that they enjoyed of self-government.

New Taxes *(page 135)*

Predicting

Read the lesson "New Taxes." Then use the spaces below to predict how you think the British government will react to the protests over the Townshend Acts.

_____

_____

_____

_____

Terms To Know

Define or describe the following key terms from this lesson.

Daughters of Liberty >

_____

_____

 **Key Points**

 **Notes**

Townshend Acts ⟩ _____

Academic Vocabulary

In the space available, define the following academic vocabulary word from this lesson.

levy ⟩ _____

Section Wrap-up

Now that you have read the section, write the answers to the questions that were included in Setting a Purpose for Reading *at the beginning of the section.*

Why did the British face problems in North America after the French and Indian War?

_____

_____

Why did the American colonists object to new British laws?

_____

_____

Chapter 5, Section 2
Building Colonial Unity
(pages 136–139)

Reason To Read

Setting a Purpose for Reading Think about these questions as you read:
- Why did Boston colonists and British soldiers clash, resulting in the Boston Massacre?
- How did the British government try to maintain its control over the colonies?

Main Idea

As you read pages 136–139 in your textbook, complete this graphic organizer by describing how the Intolerable Acts change life for colonists.

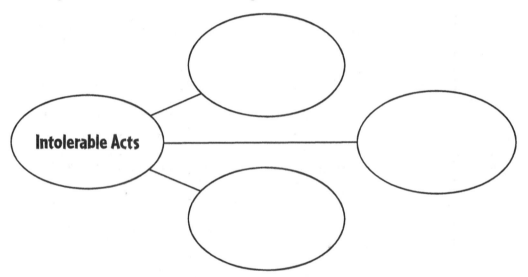

Intolerable Acts

Sequencing Events

As you read, put the following events in the correct order by writing the number 1 through 5 in the space to the left. Use the number 1 for the event that occurred first, 2 for the next event, and so on.

_____ **A. Boston Tea Party occurs.**

_____ **B. Samuel Adams sets up a committee of correspondence.**

_____ **C. Boston Massacre takes place.**

_____ **D. Parliament passes the Intolerable Acts.**

_____ **E. Hancock's ship *Liberty* seized.**

Trouble in Boston *(pages 136–137)*

Monitoring Comprehension

Check how well you understood what you read in this lesson by answering the following question.

1. What happened at the Boston Massacre?

_____

_____

2. How did the colonists respond to the Boston Massacre?

_____

_____

Terms To Know

Use the spaces that follow to write sentences using the terms in this lesson.

Boston Massacre

_____

_____

committee of correspondence

_____

_____

_____

propaganda

_____

_____

Academic Vocabulary

Explain what the means academic vocabulary word occupy *means in the following sentence about colonists' views towards the British:*

"Now they had sent an army to <u>occupy</u> colonial cities."

_____

_____

 **Key Points**

 **Notes**

Terms To Review

Choose a term you studied earlier from the list below to complete each sentence by replacing the underlined word. Write the correct term in the space. You will not use all the terms.

boycott (Chapter 5, Section 1)   encounter (Chapter 2, Section 3)

repeal (Chapter 5, Section 1)   dissent (Chapter 3, Section 2)

1. After the Boston Massacre, Parliament decided to <u>cancel</u> _____ most of the Townshend Act taxes to try to calm the colonies.

2. Each <u>meeting</u> _____ between the colonists living in Boston and the British soldiers stationed there caused tension.

3. When the tea tax was left in place, the colonists continued to <u>refuse to buy</u> _____ that product.

A Crisis Over Tea (pages 138–139)

Questioning

As you read these pages, ask yourself: what is an important detail? Write one of those details in the spaces below.

A Crisis Over Tea ⟩ _____

_____

Terms To Know

Choose a term from the list below to complete each sentence by writing the term from this lesson in the correct space. You will not use all the terms.

Boston Tea Party   Boston Massacre   Coercive Acts

Stamp Act Congress   Sugar Act   Tea Act

1. The _____ let the East India Company sell goods at prices much lower than colonial merchants could.

2. The _____ made the British realize they were losing control of the colonies.

3. To punish Boston, Parliament passed the _____.

Academic Vocabulary

Circle the letter of the word or words that have the closest meaning to the underlined academic vocabulary word from this lesson.

1. The colonists <u>maintained</u> that the Coercive Acts took away their rights as British citizens.

    a. argued   **b.** denied   **c.** wrote

2. The Coercive Acts marked a new approach to British <u>policy</u> in the colonies.

    a. official action   **b.** insurance matters   **c.** political debate

Terms To Review

Use the following term you studied earlier in a sentence.

isolate
(Chapter 2, Section 1)

_____

_____

Section Wrap-up

Now that you have read the section, write the answers to the questions that were included in Setting a Purpose for Reading *at the beginning of the section.*

Why did Boston colonists and British soldiers clash, resulting in the Boston Massacre?

_____

_____

How did the British government try to maintain its control over the colonies?

_____

_____

Chapter 5, Section 3
A Call to Arms

(pages 141-145)

Reason To Read

Setting a Purpose for Reading Think about these questions as you read:
• What happened at the Continental Congress in Philadelphia?
• How did the colonists meet British soldiers in the first battle?

Main Idea

As you read pages 141-145 in your textbook, complete this graphic organizer by listing six events leading to the Battle of Bunker Hill.

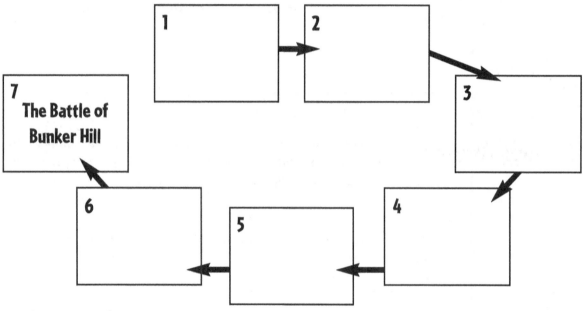

Sequencing Events

Match the date in the left column with the correct achievement in the right column by writing the letter in the space to the left of the date.

_____ 1. September 1774

_____ 2. April 1775

_____ 3. May 10, 1775

_____ 4. June 17, 1775

a. Ethan Allen captures Fort Ticonderoga

b. Parliament passes Coercive Acts

c. Gage has several thousand British soldiers in and around Boston

d. First Continental Congress meets

e. Battle of Bunker Hill is fought

f. Boston Tea Party

The Continental Congress (pages 141–142)

Responding

Check your understanding of this lesson by answering the following questions.

What were the Suffolk Resolves? What did the Congress do about them?

_____

_____

_____

Academic Vocabulary

Read each sentence below. Put a checkmark in the space before the phrase that best explains what the boldfaced academic vocabulary word from this lesson means in this passage.

1. Some of the delegates who came to the Continental Congress wanted to **challenge** British control of the colonies.

_____ dispute _____ end _____ strengthen

2. The delegates **drafted** a statement of grievances.

_____ agreed to _____ talked about _____ wrote

Terms To Review

Use each of the following terms you studied earlier in a sentence.

establish
(Chapter 2, Section 2)

_____

_____

militia
(Chapter 4, Section 3)

_____

_____

The First Battles (pages 142–144)

Visualizing

Read the material on Lexington and Concord and try to picture one scene from the battles in your mind. Then write three sentences describing what you think took place.

_____

_____

_____

_____

More Military Action (pages 144–145)

Visualizing

Imagine that you were a Patriot soldier who took part in the Battle of Bunker Hill. Write a diary entry describing the end of the battle.

_____

_____

_____

Terms To Know

Match the term from this lesson in the left column with the correct definition in the right column by writing the letter in the space to the left of the term.

____ **1.** Bunker Hill

____ **2.** Fort Ticonderoga

____ **3.** Loyalist

____ **4.** Patriot

a. colonist who wanted American independence

b. battle near Boston that produced heavy British casualties

c. battle near Lake Champlain that was an American victory

d. colonist who wanted to avoid fighting

e. colonist who wanted the British to stay in control

Academic Vocabulary

Define or describe the academic vocabulary word revolution *used in this lesson.*

revolution

_____

_____

Terms To Review

Use the spaces provided to explain the meaning of the academic vocabulary word assemble, *which you studied in Chapter 4, Section 4, in the following sentence:*

"The next day the redcoats crossed the harbor and <u>assembled</u> at the bottom of Breed's Hil."

_____

_____

Section Wrap-up

Now that you have read the section, write the answers to the questions that were included in Setting a Purpose for Reading *at the beginning of the section.*

What happened at the Continental Congress in Philadelphia?

_____

_____

How did the colonists meet British soldiers in the first battle?

_____

_____

Chapter 5, Section 4
Moving Toward Independence

(pages 147–151)

Reason To Read

Setting a Purpose for Reading Think about these questions as you read:
• What happened at the Second Continental Congress?
• Why did the colonists draft the Declaration of Independence?

Main Idea

As you read pages 147–151 in your textbook, complete this graphic organizer by describing the parts of the Declaration of Independence.

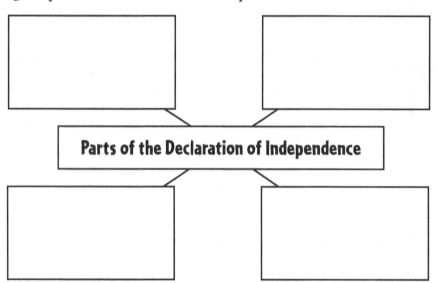

Parts of the Declaration of Independence

Sequencing Events

As you read, write the correct date for each of these events:

_____ **Second Continental Congress begins meeting**

_____ **Paine publishes *Common Sense***

_____ **The British leave Boston to Washington**

_____ **The Second Continental Congress accepts the Declaration of Independence**

Colonial Leaders Emerge (pages 147–150)

Determining the Main Idea

Write down the main idea of this lesson and at least three details that support that idea.

_____

_____

_____

_____

Terms To Know

Read the following sentences. Choose the correct term from this lesson to complete the sentence by circling the term.

1. The (Independence Committee, Second Continental Congress) began meeting in Philadelphia in May 1775.

2. This group created the (American Army, Continental Army) to fight against the British.

3. It also issued an appeal to the British for peace called the (Olive Branch Petition, Plea for Peace).

4. A (document, petition) is a formal request that someone take an action.

5. Thomas Paine wrote a pamphlet called (*Common Sense, Independence Now*) that inspired many Americans.

Academic Vocabulary

Write two synonyms for each of these academic vocabulary words from this lesson.

acquire _____

communicate _____

The Colonies Declare Independence (pages 150–151)

Evaluating

Read the Declaration of Natural Rights in the Declaration of Independence (second, third, and fourth paragraph on page 154 of your textbook). Select what you think is the single most important idea and explain how that idea affects your life today.

_____

_____

_____

_____

Terms To Know

Define or describe the following key terms from this lesson.

Declaration of Independence >

_____

_____

preamble >

_____

_____

Academic Vocabulary

Choose an academic vocabulary word from this lesson from the list below to complete each sentence by replacing the underlined word. Write the correct term in the space. You might have to change the form of the word.

debate   instruct   portion

principle   revolution   emerge

1. Jefferson based his arguments in the Declaration of Independence on

what he thought were some universal <u>standards</u> _____ .

2. In the spring, colonists in North Carolina <u>directed</u> _____
their delegates to vote in favor of independence.

3. The American war for independence is called a(n) <u>rebellion</u>

_____ because it changed the government in the
British colonies.

4. The delegates to the Congress <u>argued over</u> _____ whether or not to declare independence.

5. Some delegates pointed out that a large <u>share</u> _____ of colonists did not want independence.

Now that you have read the section, write the answers to the questions that were included in Setting a Purpose for Reading *at the beginning of the section.*

What happened at the Second Continental Congress?

_____

_____

Why did the colonists draft the Declaration of Independence?

_____

_____

Chapter 6, Section 1
The Early Years

(pages 162–168)

Reason To Read

Setting a Purpose for Reading Think about these questions as you read:
- Why did some Americans support the British?
- How did the Battle of Saratoga affect the British plan for New England.

Main Idea

As you read pages 162–168 in your textbook, complete this graphic organizer
by describing British and American advantages and disadvantages in the spaces
provided.

	Advantages	**Disadvantages**
British		
American		

Sequencing Events

As you read, place the following events on the time line:
- **Burgoyne surrenders at Saratoga**
- **Patriots capture Hessians at Trenton**
- **British win victories at Brandywine and Paoli**

♦1776   ♦1777   ♦1778

The Opposing Sides (pages 162–165)

Scanning

Scan the section by reading the headings and looking at the map on page 165. Then write down three topics you think will be covered in this subsection.

_____

_____

_____

_____

Terms To Know

Read the following sentences. Choose the correct term from this lesson to complete the sentence by circling the term.

1. The British used hired soldiers, or (mercenaries, regulars), to strengthen their forces.

2. Many of these hired soldiers were called (Germans, Hessians), after their homeland.

3. The Congress relied on (drafted, recruited) soldiers.

4. Some colonists remained (hostile, neutral), unwilling to take a side in the fight.

Academic Vocabulary

Circle the letter of the word or words that have the closest meaning to the underlined academic vocabulary word from this lesson.

1. Many colonists did not want to <u>transfer</u> much power to the Congress.

   a. change   **b.** give   **c.** withhold

2. Some women <u>accompanied</u> their husbands who entered the army.

   a. came along with   **b.** criticized   **c.** rejected

 **Key Points**

 **Notes**

Terms To Review

Match the term you studied earlier, in the left column, with the correct definition or description, in the right column, by writing the letter in the space to the left of the term.

_____ **1.** conflict
(Chapter 3, Section 2)

_____ **2.** Patriot
(Chapter 5, Section 3)

_____ **3.** region
(Chapter 1, Section 3)

a. area or section of a country

b. colonist who wished to stay part of Britain

c. disagreement or fight

d. settlement of a dispute

e. colonist who wanted independence

Fighting in New York (pages 166–167)

Synthesizing

Read the lesson and then write two sentences describing the fighting in New York and the result of the fighting.

_____

_____

_____

People To Meet

Read the following sentences. Choose the correct person from this lesson to complete the sentence by circling the name of the person.

1. The Patriot (Nathan Hale, Thomas Paine) was captured by the British and hanged for spying.

2. General (Thomas Gage, William Howe) led the British in their victory in the Battle of Long Island.

Patriot Gains (page 167)

Analyzing

Analyze the information in this section by answering the following question.

Why did Washington's attack at Trenton surprise the British?

_____

 **Key Points**

 **Notes**

Terms To Review

In the space available, define the following academic vocabulary word that you studied earlier.

estimate
(Chapter 2, Section 2)

_____

_____

A British Plan for Victory *(pages 167–168)*

Clarifying

As you read this lesson, answer the following question to clarify the information about the British plan for victory in 1777.

What was the British plan?

_____

_____

_____

Places To Locate

From the list below of sites of battles discussed in this lesson, choose the one where the British were forced to surrender nearly 6,000 soldiers. Circle the correct battle site.

Bennington   Brandywine   Fort Stanwix   Saratoga

Section Wrap-up

Now that you have read the section, write the answers to the questions that were included in Setting a Purpose for Reading *at the beginning of the section.*

Why did some Americans support the British?

_____

_____

_____

_____

How did the Battle of Saratoga mark a turning point in the war?

_____

_____

_____

_____

Chapter 6, Section 2
The War Continues

(pages 172–176)

Reason To Read

Setting a Purpose for Reading Think about these questions as you read:
- Why did other nations help the Patriots?
- How did Washington's troops survive the winter at Valley Forge?
- What challenges did Americans face at home as a result of the war?

Main Idea

As you read pages 172–176 in your textbook, complete this graphic organizer by describing how each person helped the Americans fight for independence.

Person	Contribution
Lafayette	
Pulaski	
Von Steuben	
De Miralles	

Sequencing Events

Match the date in the left column with the correct achievement in the right column by writing the letter in the space to the left of the date.

_____ 1. Winter 1777–1778

_____ 2. February 1778

_____ 3. 1779

_____ 4. 1780

_____ 5. 1781

a. Spain declares war on Britain

b. France and U.S. form an alliance

c. Spanish capture British fort at Pensacola

d. Americans gain victory at Trenton

e. Americans gain victory at Saratoga

f. Patriot troops suffer at Valley Forge

g. Spanish capture British fort at Mobile

Gaining Allies *(pages 172–175)*

Determining the Main Idea

Write down the main idea of this lesson.

Main Idea ❯ _____

_____

_____

Terms To Know

Look up the following terms from this lesson in a dictionary and write definitions of them.

desert ❯ _____

_____

_____

inflation ❯ _____

_____

Academic Vocabulary

Choose an academic vocabulary word from this lesson from the list below to complete each sentence by replacing the underlined word. Write the correct term in the space.

commit   survive   contribute

1. Before Saratoga, the French secretly gave money to the Americans, but

they would not <u>obligate</u> _____ themselves to an alliance.

2. Some useful people came from Europe to America to <u>give</u> _____

their effort—and in some cases their lives—to the Patriot cause.

Terms To Review

Use each of the following terms you studied earlier in a sentence.

challenge
(Chapter 5, Section 3) ❯ _____

_____

policy
(Chapter 5, Section 2) ❯ _____

_____

Life on the Home Front (pages 175–176)

 **Connecting**

As you read the lesson, fill in some details about each group to describe how the war affected women, Loyalists, and African Americans.

Women	Loyalists	African Americans

Academic Vocabulary

Write two synonyms for each academic vocabulary word from this lesson.

radical

_____

_____

similar

_____

_____

Section Wrap-up

Now that you have read the section, write the answers to the questions that were included in Setting a Purpose for Reading *at the beginning of the section.*

Why did other nations help the Patriots?

_____

_____

How did Washington's troops survive the winter at Valley Forge?

_____

_____

What challenges did Americans face at home as a result of the war?

_____

_____

Chapter 6, Section 3
The War Moves West and South

(pages 177-182)

Reason To Read

Setting a Purpose for Reading Think about these questions as you read:
- How did the war involve Native Americans?
- How did a new kind of fighting develop in the South?

Main Idea

As you read pages 177-182 in your textbook, complete this graphic organizer by describing the significance of key battles in the West and South.

Key Battle	Significance
Vincennes	
Camden	
Kings Mountain	
Guilford Courthouse	

Sequencing Events

As you read, place the following events on the time line:
- **George Rogers Clark captures Vincennes second time**
- **British troops take Charles Town**
- **Patriots defeat British at Cowpens**

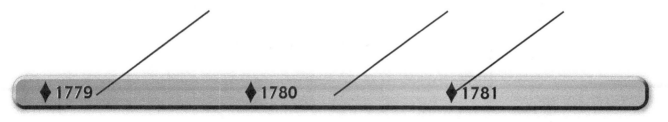

◆1779   ◆1780   ◆1781

War in the West *(pages 177–178)*

People To Meet

Match the person from this lesson in the left column with the correct description in the right column by writing the letter in the space to the left of the person.

_____ **1.** Joseph Brant

_____ **2.** George Rogers Clark

_____ **3.** Henry Hamilton

a. British commander at Detroit

b. Virginia militia commander

c. officer in the Continental Army

d. Native American chief

Terms To Review

Put a check mark in the box next to the word or words that have the closest meaning to **militia,** *a term that you studied in Chapter 4, Section 3.*

_____ people who promised to be ready to fight in a minute

_____ Continental Army

_____ force made of citizen soldiers

Glory at Sea *(pages 178–179)*

Inferring

Read the lesson and then answer the question to make an inference about what you read.

How would you describe John Paul Jones's character? Why?

_____

_____

Terms To Know

Define or describe the following terms from this lesson.

blockade _____

_____

privateers _____

_____

Academic Vocabulary

Write the correct form of the academic vocabulary word from this lesson in the blank space to complete the sentence.

approximate

1. Congress hoped to have <u>roughly</u> _____ 2,000 privateers to help in the fight against the British.

equip

2. Each of these ships had to be <u>fitted</u> _____ with guns so they could fight at sea.

Terms To Review

Read the passage below. Put a checkmark in the space before the phrase that best explains the meaning of the term **maintain,** *which you studied in Chapter 5, Section 2.*

Several states decided to <u>maintain</u> their own small fleets of warships during the Revolutionary War.

_____ bouy _____ keep in service _____ seize

Struggles in the South (pages 179–182)

Evaluating

As you read the lesson, find the information to answer the following question and write your answer in the space provided.

Why did the Patriots gain support in the South after Kings Mountain?

_____

_____

Terms To Know

Define or describe the following key terms from this lesson.

guerrilla warfare

_____

_____

 **Key Points**

 **Notes**

 **Academic Vocabulary**

Read the following sentences. In the space below, write in your own words the meaning of the boldfaced academic vocabulary word from this lesson.

1. In 1778, the British decided to **concentrate** their efforts in the South.

_____

2. The British **sustained** heavy losses in some battles in the Carolinas.

_____

3. When Cornwallis moved his troops to Virginia, the war in the South entered a new **phase**.

_____

Terms To Review

Use the following term you studied earlier in a sentence.

neutral
(Chapter 6, Section 1)

_____

_____

Section Wrap-up

Now that you have read the section, write the answers to the questions that were included in Setting a Purpose for Reading *at the beginning of the section.*

How did the war involve Native Americans?

_____

_____

What new kind of warfare developed in the South?

_____

_____

Chapter 6, Section 4
The War Is Won
(pages 183–187)

Reason To Read

Setting a Purpose for Reading Think about these questions as you read:
- How did George Washington change his military strategy?
- Why did the Americans win the Revolutionary War despite many disadvantages?

Main Idea

As you read pages 183–187 in your textbook, complete this graphic organizer by listing the reasons why the Americans were able to defeat the British in the Revolutionary War.

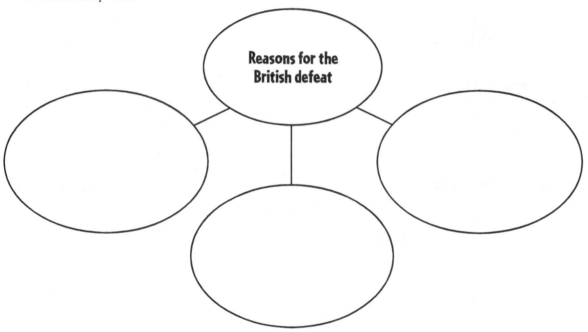

Reasons for the British defeat

Sequencing Events

As you read, write the month and year each of these events took place:

_____ French troops arrive in colonies

_____ Washington advances toward British at Yorktown

_____ Cornwallis surrenders at Yorktown

_____ Congress approves preliminary peace treaty

_____ Treaty of Paris is signed

Victory at Yorktown (pages 183–185)

Outlining

Complete this outline about the siege of Yorktown.

The Siege of Yorktown

A. _____

B. _____

Academic Vocabulary

Circle the letter of the word or words that have the closest meaning to the underlined academic vocabulary word from this lesson.

<u>Likewise</u>, the soldiers in different areas of Cornwallis's lines around Yorktown suffered many wounds from the fearful fire.

a. in the opposite way   **b.** in the same way   **c.** later

Independence (pages 185–187)

Questioning

As you read each subsection, ask yourself: what is an important detail? Write one of those details in the spaces provided about the topics.

Why the Americans Won

_____

_____

_____

The Influence of the American Revolution

_____

_____

_____

Terms To Know

Read the following sentences. Choose the correct term from this lesson to complete the sentence by circling the term.

1. American fighters took advantage of fighting on their own land to stage (ambushes, barrages) that surprised the British.

2. In April 1783, Congress voted to (decline, ratify) the peace treaty.

3. The (Treaty of London, Treaty of Paris) was signed in September 1783, officially ending the Revolutionary War.

Academic Vocabulary

Use each of the following academic vocabulary words from this lesson in a sentence.

assign

_____

_____

_____

preliminary

_____

_____

Section Wrap-up

Now that you have read the section, write the answers to the questions that were included in Setting a Purpose for Reading *at the beginning of the section.*

How did George Washington change his military strategy?

_____

_____

_____

Why did the Americans win the Revolutionary War despite many disadvantages?

_____

_____

_____

_____

Chapter 7, Section 1
The Articles of Confederation

(pages 192–198)

Reason To Read

Setting a Purpose for Reading Think about these questions as you read:
- How did the weakness of the Articles of Confederation lead to instability?
- How did Congress deal with the western lands?

Main Idea

As you read pages 192–198 in your textbook, complete this graphic organizer by listing the powers you think a national government should have.

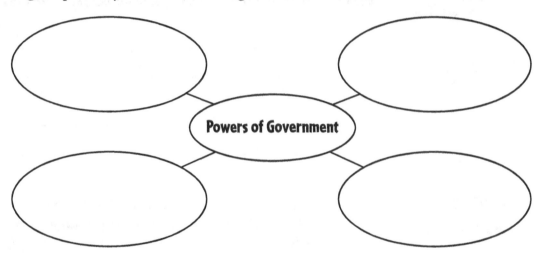

Powers of Government

Sequencing Events

As you read, write the correct dates for each of these events:

_____ **All states approve Confederation government**

_____ **Spain closes Mississippi River to American shipping**

_____ **Congress passes ordinance organizing western lands**

_____ **Congress sends John Adams to London to negotiate settlement**

_____ **Northwest Ordinance is passed**

Thirteen Independent States (pages 192–193)

Drawing Conclusions

Draw conclusions about the thirteen state governments by answering the following questions.

1. What led the people writing state constitutions to limit the powers of governors?

   _____

   _____

2. Why did they have frequent elections for the state legislatures?

   _____

Terms To Know

Define or describe the following key terms from this lesson.

bicameral >

   _____

   _____

constitution >

   _____

   _____

Academic Vocabulary

Circle the letter of the word or words that have the closest meaning to the underlined academic vocabulary word from this lesson.

1. The leaders who wrote the state constitutions wanted to <u>restrict</u> the powers of the state governments.

   a. eliminate   **b.** expand   **c.** limit

2. Connecticut and Rhode Island <u>retained</u> their original charters as state constitutions.

   a. avoided using   **b.** kept   **c.** replaced

Forming a Republic (pages 193–195)

Monitoring Comprehension

Check how well you understood what you read in this lesson by answering the following questions.

1. What powers did the Congress have under the Articles of Confederation?

_____

_____

2. What weaknesses did the Confederation government have?

_____

_____

Terms To Know

Look up the following terms from this lesson in your text and write definitions for them.

Articles of Confederation >

_____

_____

republic >

_____

_____

Academic Vocabulary

Read each sentence below. Put a checkmark in the space before the word or phrase that best explains what the boldfaced academic vocabulary word from this lesson means in this passage.

1. Most people **assumed** that the new central government would not be very powerful.

_____ believed as a basic idea   _____ protested   _____ urged

2. Still, a central government was needed to **coordinate** all the activities needed to carry out the war effort.

_____ bring together   _____ locate   _____ make less expensive

Key Points

Notes

New Land Policies (pages 195–196)

Summarizing

As you read pages 195–196, write a one-sentence summary about the Ordinance of 1785.

_____

_____

_____

Terms To Know

Write a sentence that explains the meaning of ordinance, a term from this lesson, in the spaces below.

_____

_____

Trouble on Two Fronts (pages 197–198)

Skimming

Skim the section by reading the text under each heading quickly to get a general idea of what it is about. Use one or two sentences to write that general idea in the spaces below:

_____

_____

_____

Terms To Know

Explain what depreciate, a term from this lesson, means.

depreciate

_____

_____

 **Key Points**

 **Notes**

 **Terms To Review**

Match the term you studied earlier, in the left column, with the correct definition or description, in the right column, by writing the letter in the space to the left of the term.

_____ **1.** contribute
(Chapter 6, Section 2)

_____ **2.** finance
(Chapter 2, Section 2)

_____ **3.** portion
(Chapter 5, Section 4)

_____ **4.** region
(Chapter 1, Section 3)

a. to provide money for

b. to tax

c. geographical area with similar features

d. to give to

e. part of something

f. take away from

Section Wrap-up

Now that you have read the section, write the answers to the questions that were included in Setting a Purpose for Reading *at the beginning of the section.*

How did the weaknesses of the Articles of Confederation lead to instability?

_____

_____

_____

_____

_____

How did Congress deal with the western lands?

_____

_____

_____

_____

_____

Chapter 7, Section 2
Convention and Compromise

(pages 199–205)

Reason To Read

Setting a Purpose for Reading Think about these questions as you read:
- How did the Constitutional Convention break the deadlock over the form the new government would take?
- How did the delegates answer the question of representation?

Main Idea

As you read pages 199–205 in your textbook, complete this graphic organizer by describing how each individual played a role in creating the new plan of government.

Individual	Role
Edmund Randolph	
James Madison	
Roger Sherman	

Sequencing Events

Match the date in the left column with the correct achievement in the right column by writing the letter in the space to the left of the date.

_____ **1. January 1787**

_____ **2. May 1787**

_____ **3. June 1787**

_____ **4. September 1787**

a. Paterson presents the New Jersey Plan for changing the Articles of Confederation

b. Delegates meet to revise Articles of Confederation

c. Delegates sign draft of Constitution

d. Delegates approve Three-Fifths Compromise

e. Shays's Rebellion ended

Economic Depression *(pages 199–201)*

Skimming

Skim the section by reading the text under each heading quickly to get a general idea of what the section is about. Use one or two sentences to write that general idea in the spaces below:

_____

_____

_____

Terms To Know

Read the following sentences. Choose the correct term from this lesson to complete the sentence by circling the term.

1. Virginia passed a law that made (enslavement, manumission) of African Americans easier.

2. Shays's (Convention, Rebellion) showed the deep worries of farmers.

3. The number of unemployed workers rose during the (depression, economic growth) that followed the Revolutionary War.

A Call for Change *(page 201)*

Predicting

Quickly read through the lesson. Then predict what you think will happen as a result of the call for change. Write your prediction in the spaces below.

_____

_____

_____

People To Meet

Put a checkmark next to the name of the people from this lesson who were active in the movement to fix the Articles of Confederation.

_____ John Adams   _____ Alexander Hamilton

_____ Thomas Jefferson   _____ James Madison

_____ George Washington

The Constitutional Convention (pages 202–203)

Interpreting

Interpret the information you read about the early stages of the Constitutional Convention by answering the following questions.

1. How did the government under the Virginia Plan differ from the government under the Articles of Confederation?

_____

_____

2. Why did the small states object to the Virginia Plan?

_____

_____

Terms To Know

Match the term from this lesson in the left column with the correct definition in the right column by writing the letter in the space provided.

_____ **1.** Father of the Constitution

_____ **2.** New Jersey Plan

_____ **3.** proportional

_____ **4.** Virginia Plan

a. equal regardless of size

b. corresponding to size

c. name given to James Madison

d. name given to George Washington

e. proposal to change the government in a major way

f. proposal to only revise the Articles of Confederation

Compromise Wins Out (pages 203–205)

Connecting

Define the word compromise *in your own words, then answer the questions that follow.*

Compromise is _____

Think of a time when you compromised. What did you give up? What did you gain? _____

_____

How did the agreement you finally reached differ from the initial idea?

_____

_____

Terms To Know

Use the spaces below to restate your definition of the term compromise, *a term in this lesson. Then answer the question below those spaces.*

_____

_____

Draw lines to link the important compromise to the issue it settled.

Great Compromise   representation of enslaved persons

Three-Fifths Compromise   representation of states

Academic Vocabulary

Write the academic vocabulary word from this lesson in the blank space that best completes the sentence the sentence.

defined   assembled   revised   varied

1. The delegates _____ at the Constitutional Convention debated basic issues about the form of the new government.

2. The Constitution carefully _____ the powers of the new national government.

3. In the final plan, the number of seats each state had in the lower

house _____ according to population.

Now that you have read the section, write the answers to the questions that were included in* Setting a Purpose for Reading *at the beginning of the section.

How did the Constitutional Convention break the deadlock over the form the new government would take?

_____

_____

_____

_____

_____

How did the delegates answer the question of representation?

_____

_____

_____

_____

_____

Chapter 7, Section 3
A New Plan of Government

(pages 207–213)

Reason To Read

Setting a Purpose for Reading Think about these questions as you read:

• What are the roots of the Constitution?
• How did the Constitution limit the power of government?

Main Idea

As you read pages 207–213 in your textbook, complete this graphic organizer by explaining how the system of checks and balances works.

	Has check over which branches of government:	Example
President		
Congress		
Supreme Court		

Sequencing Events

As you read, place the following events on the time line:

• **Locke's *Two Treatises on Civil Government* is published**
• **Montesquieu writes *The Spirit of Laws***
• **English Bill of Rights protects the people's rights**
• **Constitutional Convention assembles in Philadelphia**

◆1680　　　◆1720　　　◆1760　　　◆1800

Roots of the Constitution (pages 207–208)

Outlining   *Complete this outline as you read the lesson. The first subsection has been done for you.*

    I. Careful Study

        A. European political development

        B. Attitudes toward British traditions

    II. British System of Government

        A. _____

        B. _____

        C. _____

        D. _____

Terms To Know   *Read the following sentences. Choose the correct term from this lesson to complete the sentence by circling the term.*

1. The (Magna Carta, Bill of Rights) placed limits on the power of English kings back in 1215.

2. The Constitution was based on many political ideas that came from the movement called the (Enlightenment, Reformation).

3. One idea that became part of the Constitution was that all people had certain (human rights, natural rights).

The Federal System (pages 208–209)

Reviewing   *Reread each subsection and list two key facts from each.*

_____

_____

_____

_____

Chapter 7, Section 3

Terms To Know

Define or describe federalism, *a term from this lesson.*

federalism

_____

_____

The Organization of Government *(pages 209–211)*

Clarifying

As you read the lesson, give examples of the powers of the three branches of the federal government.

_____

_____

_____

_____

Terms To Know

Match the term from this lesson in the left column with the correct definition or description in the right column by writing the letter in the space to the left of the term.

_____ **1.** articles

_____ **2.** checks and balances

_____ **3.** Electoral College

_____ **4.** executive branch

_____ **5.** judicial branch

_____ **6.** legislative branch

a. group that chooses the president and vice president

b. Congress

c. led by president

d. Supreme Court and other courts set up by Congress

e. parts of the Constitution

f. state governments

g. system that balances power within the government

h. system that protects rights of individuals

The Constitutional Debate *(pages 211–212)*

Connecting *Answer the following questions to compare the Federalists and the Antifederalists.*

1. How well organized were the two groups?

_____

_____

2. What were the chief fears of each side? What did each side want as a way of preventing those fears from coming true?

_____

_____

Terms To Know *Define or describe the following key terms from this lesson.*

Federalists >

_____

_____

Antifederalists >

_____

_____

Adopting the Constitution *(page 213)*

Connecting *Answer the following questions to link the material in this lesson to the previous one.*

1. Which group did Patrick Henry belong to, Federalists or Antifederalists?

_____

2. What weakness in the Constitution had to be fixed before Virginia agreed to approve it?

_____

_____

 **Key Points**

 **Notes**

Terms To Know

Define or describe the following key term from this lesson.

amendment

_____

_____

Section Wrap-up

Now that you have read the section, write the answers to the questions that were included in Setting a Purpose for Reading *at the beginning of the section.*

What are the roots of the Constitution?

_____

_____

_____

_____

_____

How did the Constitution limit the power of government?

_____

_____

_____

_____

_____

Chapter 8, Section 1
The First President

(pages 258-262)

Reason To Read

Setting a Purpose for Reading Think about these questions as you read:
- What actions were taken to launch the new government?
- How did Hamilton propose to strengthen the economy?

Main Idea

As you read pages 252-258 in your textbook, complete this graphic organizer by listing the actions taken by Congress and Washington's first administration.

Actions	
Washington	**Congress**

Sequencing Events

As you read, place the following events on the time line.
- **Bill of Rights added to the Constitution**
- **Washington takes the oath of office**
- **George Washington is elected president**

◆1789   ◆1790   ◆1791   ◆1792

April 6, 1789
April 30, 1789

December, 1791

President Washington *(pages 258–260)*

Reviewing

Review pages 258–260 and list a key fact about the Bill of Rights.

_____

_____

_____

Terms To Know

Read the following sentences. Choose the correct term from this lesson to complete the sentence by circling the term.

1. The first ten amendments to the Constitution are known as the (Bill of Rights, First Articles).

2. Congress passed the (Courts Act, Judiciary Act) to create the first national court system.

3. One of Washington's concerns was that everything he did set new (precedents, traditions).

Academic Vocabulary

Circle the letter of the word or words that have the closest meaning to the underlined academic vocabulary word from this lesson.

1. During Washington's term, people decided that the most <u>appropriate</u> way of addressing the president was as "Mr. President."

   a. honorable   **b.** praising   **c.** suitable

2. Some people wanted a <u>uniform</u> national legal system. Others wanted state courts to have power as well.

   a. inconsistent   **b.** special; unique   **c.** standardized

Financial Problems *(pages 260–261)*

Outlining

Complete this outline as you read the lesson. The first subsection has been completed.

I. A Major Problem

    A. Washington has Hamilton deal with economic policies.

    B. Hamilton's major problem is increasing national debt.

II. Hamilton's Plan

    A. _____

    B. _____

III. Opposition to the Plan

    A. _____

    B. _____

IV. Compromise Results in a Capital

    A. _____

    B. _____

Terms To Know

Define or describe the following key terms from this lesson.

bond _____

_____

national debt _____

_____

Building the Economy *(page 262)*

Summarizing

As you read each subsection, write a one-sentence summary.

The Fight Over the Bank >

_____

_____

_____

Tariffs and Taxes >

_____

_____

Terms To Know

Read the following sentences. Choose the correct term from this lesson to complete the sentence by circling the term.

1. Hamilton wanted to place a (tariff, limit) on imported goods to help American manufacturing industries grow.

2. Jefferson and Madison both thought the creation of a national bank was (constitutional, unconstitutional).

Academic Vocabulary

Read the sentence below. Put a checkmark in the space before the phrase that best explains what the academic vocabulary word vision, from this lesson, means in this passage.

Jefferson and Hamilton had different <u>visions</u> of the kind of society America should have.

vision >

_____ objects seen   _____ sights   _____ views about

 Key Points

 Notes

 Section Wrap-up

Now that you have read the section, write the answers to the questions that were included in Setting a Purpose for Reading *at the beginning of the section.*

What actions were taken to launch the new government?

_____

_____

_____

How did Hamilton propose to strengthen the economy?

_____

_____

_____

Chapter 8, Section 2
Early Challenges

(pages 263–266)

Reason To Read

Setting a Purpose for Reading Think about these questions as you read:
- How did the federal government assert its power in the West?
- How did the United States try to stay out of European conflicts?

Main Idea

As you read pages 263–266 in your textbook, complete this graphic organizer by listing results of these government actions during the early Republic.

Government action	Result
Treaty of Greenville	
Proclamation of Neutrality	
Jay's Treaty	
Pinckney's Treaty	

Sequencing Events

As you read, put the following events in the correct order by writing the number 1 through 5 in the space to the left. Use the number 1 for the event that occurred first, 2 for the next event, and so on.

_____ **A. Proclamation of Neutrality declared**

_____ **B. Pinckney Treaty allows American shipping on the Mississippi River**

_____ **C. Battle of Fallen Timbers takes place**

_____ **D. French Revolution starts**

_____ **E. Tax on whiskey results in Whiskey Rebellion**

The Whiskey Rebellion (pages 263–264)

Questioning

As you read the lesson, ask yourself: what are two important details? Write those details in the spaces below.

_____

_____

_____

Terms To Know

Use the spaces below to define the Whiskey Rebellion, *a term in this lesson.*

_____

_____

Struggle Over the West (page 264)

Identifying Cause and Effect

As you read the lesson, answer the following questions to identify the causes and effects of conflicts in the Northwest during this period.

Cause	Action	Effect
	Washington sends an army under St. Clair to the Northwest Territory.	
The British join with Native Americans to try to win control of the Northwest Territories.		

Terms To Know

Match the term from this lesson in the left column with the correct definition in the right column by writing the letter in the space to the left of the term.

____ **1.** Battle of Fallen Timbers

____ **2.** Treaty of Greenville

a. fight that Arthur St. Clair lost

b. fight that Anthony Wayne won

c. agreement in which Native Americans gave up most of present-day Ohio

d. agreement in which British give up their claims to present-day Ohio

Problems With Europe *(pages 264–266)*

Analyzing

Analyze the information in this lesson by answering the following questions.

1. How did the British respond to raids on their ships?

_____

_____

2. Why did people oppose Jay's Treaty?

_____

_____

Terms To Know

Match the term in the left column with the correct definition in the right column by writing the letter in the space to the left of the place.

____ **1.** impressment

____ **2.** Jay's Treaty

____ **3.** neutrality

____ **4.** Proclamation of Neutrality

____ **5.** Pinckney's Treaty

a. agreement with the British that got British troops off American soil

b. agreement with the Spanish that let Americans use the Mississippi River

c. Washington's announcement that the U.S. would not take sides in the war between France and Britain

d. policy of staying out of a fight

e. seizing Americans and forcing them into the British navy

Washington's Farewell (page 264)

Inferring *Answer the question to make an inference about what you read.*

How many terms in office did many presidents after Washington limit themselves to? Why?

_____

_____

_____

Terms To Review *Choose a term you studied earlier from the list below to complete each sentence by replacing the underlined word. Write the correct term in the space using the correct form of the word.*

precedent (Chapter 8, Section 1)   charter (Chapter 3, Section 1)

publish (Chapter 4, Section 3)   petition (Chapter 5, Section 4)

1. Washington created many <u>examples</u> _____ for later presidents, including the tradition of only serving two terms.

2. His Farewell Address was <u>printed</u> _____ in a newspaper for all Americans to read.

Section Wrap-up *Now that you have read the section, write the answers to the questions that were included in* **Setting a Purpose for Reading** *at the beginning of the section.*

How did the federal government assert its power in the West?

_____

_____

How did the United States try to stay out of European conflicts?

_____

_____

Chapter 8, Section 3
The First Political Parties
(pages 267–272)

Reason To Read

Setting a Purpose for Reading Think about these questions as you read:
- How did political parties get started and what positions did they support?
- How did John Adams and Thomas Jefferson become candidates of opposing parties in the election of 1796?

Main Idea

As you read pages 267–272 in your textbook, complete this graphic organizer by listing the differences between the Federalists and the Democratic-Republicans.

Issue	Federalists	Democratic-Republicans
Role of federal government		
Interpretation of the Constitution		

Sequencing Events

Match the date in the left column with the correct achievement in the right column by writing the letter in the space to the left of the date.

_____ **1.** 1796

_____ **2.** 1797

_____ **3.** 1798

_____ **4.** 1800

a. U.S. and France agree to a treaty

b. United States and Britain sign the Jay Treat.

c. John Adams becomes president

d. Adams and Jefferson nominated for president by different parties

e. The threat of war led Congress to pass the Alien and Sedition Acts

 **Key Points**

 **Notes**

Opposing Views *(pages 267–270)*

Determining the Main Idea *Write down the main idea of this lesson and at least three details that support that idea.*

_____

_____

_____

_____

_____

Terms To Know *Read the following sentences. Choose the correct term from this lesson to complete the sentence by circling the term.*

1. The (Federalists, Republicans) believed in a strong central government.

2. In the election of 1796, the parties gathered in meetings called (caucuses, conventions) to choose their nominees.

3. The (Federalists, Republicans) had their strength mostly in the South.

4. Another name for the Democratic-Republicans was the (Democrats, Republicans).

5. During the 1790s, leaders became more (even-handed, partisan).

President John Adams *(pages 270–272)*

Clarifying *As you read this lesson, answer the following questions to clarify the information about the Adams administration.*

1. Why did Congress pass the Aliens and Sedition Acts?

_____

_____

2. Why did the Federalists turn against Adams?

_____

_____

Terms To Know

Define or describe the following terms from this lesson.

nullify

_____
_____
_____

sedition

_____
_____
_____

states' rights

_____
_____
_____

Virginia and Kentucky Resolutions

_____
_____

Terms To Review

Choose a term you studied earlier from the list below to complete each sentence by replacing the underlined word. Write the correct term in the space using the correct form of the word.

principle (Chapter 5, Section 4)   violate (Chapter 5, Section 1)

resolution (Chapter 5, Section 4)   repeal (Chapter 5, Section 1)

1. The legislatures of Virginia and Kentucky both passed a <u>declaration</u>

_____ stating that the Alien and

Sedition Acts could not be legally enforced.

2. These declarations said that the laws <u>went against</u> _____

the Constitution.

3. The states claimed the authority to take these steps based on the <u>idea</u>

_____ of states' rights.

Now that you have read the section, write the answers to the questions that were included in **Setting a Purpose for Reading** *at the beginning of the section.*

How did political parties get started and what positions did they support?

_____

_____

_____

How did John Adams and Thomas Jefferson become candidates of opposing parties in the election of 1796?

_____

_____

_____

Chapter 9, Section 1
The Republicans Take Power
(pages 278–281)

Reason To Read

Setting a Purpose for Reading Think about these questions as you read:
• How was the election deadlock of 1800 resolved?
• How did John Marshall strengthen the Supreme Court?

Main Idea

As you read pages 278–281 in your textbook, complete this graphic organizer by identifying ways Republicans tried to reduce the role of government.

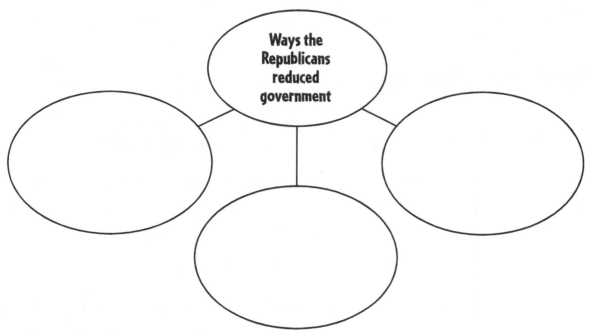

Ways the Republicans reduced government

Sequencing Events

As you read, put the following events in the correct order by writing the number 1 through 4 in the space to the left. Use the number 1 for the event that occurred first, 2 for the next event, and so on.

_____ **A.** Jefferson inaugurated

_____ **B.** Congress passes Judiciary Act of 1801

_____ **C.** Twelfth Amendment is ratified

_____ **D.** Jefferson and Adams run against each other for president

Key Points

Notes

The Election of 1800 (pages 278–279)

Scanning

Scan pages 278–279 by reading the headings. Then write down two topics you think will be covered in this lesson.

_____

_____

_____

Terms To Know

Define or describe the following key term from this section.

laissez-faire

_____

_____

Jefferson's Policies (page 280)

Interpreting

Interpret the information you read about Jefferson's policies by answering the following questions.

1. Why did Jefferson put an end to the Alien and Sedition Acts and the Naturalization Act?

   _____

   _____

2. What role did Jefferson think the national government should play?

   _____

   _____

Terms To Know

Define or describe customs duties, *a term from this lesson.*

_____

_____

Jefferson and the Courts *(pages 280–281)*

Sequencing

As you read, put the following events in the correct order by writing the number 1 through 6 in the space to the left. Use the number 1 for the event that occurred first, 2 for the next event, and so on.

_____ **a.** Jefferson is inaugurated.

_____ **b.** Marshall rules in *Marbury* v. *Madison*.

_____ **c.** Jefferson tells Madison not to deliver judicial commissions.

_____ **d.** Adams appoints judges.

_____ **e.** Congress passes Judiciary Act of 1801.

_____ **f.** Marbury tries to get the Court to get his commission.

Terms To Know

Define or describe judicial review, *a term from this lesson.*

judicial review > _____

_____

Academic Vocabulary

Circle the academic vocabulary word that best completes the sentence.

presidents   precedence   presumption

In *Gibbons* v. *Ogden*, Marshall argued that federal law takes _____ over state law in matters related to transportation between states.

Terms To Review

Read each sentence that follows. In the spaces, explain the meaning of the boldface term or academic vocabulary word you studied earlier.

judicial branch
(Chapter 7, Section 3)

1. Jefferson came into conflict with the Federalists over control of the **judicial branch**.

_____

_____

nullify
(Chapter 8, Section 3)

2. Marshall said that only the federal courts could **nullify** a law.

_____

_____

Now that you have read the section, write the answers to the questions that were included in Setting a Purpose for Reading *at the beginning of the section.*

How was the election deadlock of 1800 resolved?

_____

_____

_____

How did John Marshall strengthen the Supreme Court?

_____

_____

_____

Chapter 9, Section 2
The Louisiana Purchase
(pages 282–285)

Reason To Read

Setting a Purpose for Reading Think about these questions as you read:
- How did the United States expand in the early 1800s?
- How did Lewis and Clark lead an expedition to explore the Louisiana Territory?

Main Idea

As you read pages 282–285 in your textbook, complete this graphic organizer by describing the areas that Lewis and Clark and Zebulon Pike explored.

Explorer	Region explored
Meriwether Lewis and William Clark	
Zebulon Pike	

Sequencing Events

Match the date in the left column with the correct event in the right column by writing the letter in the space to the left of the date.

_____ **1.** 1802

_____ **2.** October 1803

_____ **3.** July 1804

_____ **4.** 1804–1806

_____ **5.** 1805–1807

a. The Spanish release Pike

b. Lewis and Clark explore Louisiana Territory

c. Pike explores upper Mississippi River and present-day Colorado

d. Napoleon tries to retake Santo Domingo

e. U.S. Senate approves Louisiana Purchase

f. Burr kills Hamilton in duel

g. French expelled from Santo Domingo

Western Territory (pages 282–283)

Visualizing

Imagine you are a member of the Lewis and Clark or Zebulon Pike expedition exploring unknown territory in the Far West. Write a journal entry describing a day's activities and sights.

_____

_____

_____

Terms To Know

Write a sentence explaining what is meant by Conestoga wagons, a term in this lesson.

Conestoga wagaons

_____

_____

Academic Vocabulary

Circle the letter of the word or words that have the closest meaning to the <u>underlined</u> academic vocabulary word from this lesson.

1. The Louisiana Territory was a huge <u>area</u>.

   a. amount of land   **b.** valley   **c.** wasteland

2. Jefferson <u>confirmed</u> that the French had gotten control of the Louisiana Territory from Spain.

   a. believed   **b.** learned the truth   **c.** pretended

3. The Conestoga wagon was a useful <u>vehicle</u> for many pioneers.

   a. boat   **b.** carriage   **c.** means of transportation

The Nation Expands (pages 283–285)

Previewing

As you read pages 283–285, answer the following questions.

1. Read the main heading of this section. What will it be about?

_____

2. Look at the map on page 284. What areas were explored by Lewis and Clark? by Pike?

_____

_____

3. Read the last heading in the section. What two political leaders will be discussed?

_____

_____

Terms To Know   *Find the following terms from this lesson and write descriptions or definitions of them.*

Louisiana Purchase >

_____

_____

secede >

_____

_____

Places To Locate   *Write the correct place from this lesson in the space to complete the sentences below.*

1. Lewis and Clark and Pike started their expeditions from (New Orleans, St. Louis), a city on the Mississippi River.

2. Lewis and Clark explored along the (Missouri River, Red River).

 **Key Points**

 **Notes**

 **Section Wrap-up**

Now that you have read the section, write the answers to the questions that were included in **Setting a Purpose for Reading** *at the beginning of the section.*

How did the United States expand in the early 1800s?

_____

_____

_____

What route did the Lewis and Clark expedition follow?

_____

_____

_____

Chapter 9, Section 3
A Time of Conflict

(pages 288–294)

Reason To Read

Setting a Purpose for Reading Think about these questions as you read:
- Why did Tecumseh build a confederacy among Native American nations?
- Why did the War Hawks want to go to war?

Main Idea

As you read pages 288–294 in your textbook, complete this graphic organizer by describing in the box the actions the United States took in each of these situations.

	Demand for tribute
	Attack on *Chesapeake*
	Tecumseh's confederation

Sequencing Events

As you read, place the following events on the time line:
- **Madison asks for declaration of war against Britain**
- **Congress passes Embargo Act**
- **Battle of Tippecanoe**

♦1804   ♦1808   ♦1812

Americans in Foreign Seas (pages 288–289)

Reviewing

Reread pages 288–289 each subsection and identify a key fact about each of the following topics.

Merchant Ships

_____

_____

War With Tripoli

_____

_____

Terms To Know

Define or describe this key term from this lesson.

> tribute

_____

_____

Academic Vocabulary

Read the sentence below. Put a checkmark in the space before the word or words that best explain(s) what the boldfaced academic vocabulary word from this lesson means in this passage.

Despite the dangers of sea travel in the early 1800s, many Americans depended on trade over the seas to earn a living.

_____ because _____ even though _____ as a result of

Freedom of the Seas (pages 290–291)

Connecting

Answer the following questions to connect events described in this lesson with earlier events.

1. What British action towards American seamen outraged many Americans in both the Washington and Jefferson presidencies?

_____

_____

 **Notes**

2. How did Washington try to solve the problem? What did Jefferson do?

_____

_____

Terms To Know *Read the following sentences. Choose the correct term from this lesson to complete the sentence by circling the term.*

1. Jefferson tried to use a(n) (blockade, embargo) to hurt Britain by cutting off its trade.

2. Jefferson's (Embargo Act, Nonintercourse Act) cut off trade between the United States and all countries.

3. The later (Embargo Act, Nonintercourse Act) cut off trade with Britain and France and their colonial possessions.

4. Americans wanted to maintain their (natural rights, neutral rights) to trade without getting involved in the war between Britain and France.

War Fever (pages 291–294)

Responding *As you read the lesson, answer the following questions.*

1. What lands did the War Hawks want?

_____

_____

2. Why did the British decision to stop seizing American sailors not prevent war between Britain and the United States?

_____

_____

Terms To Know

Match the term from this lesson in the left column with the correct definition in the right column by writing the letter in the space to the left of the term.

_____ **1.** Battle of Tippecanoe

_____ **2.** nationalism

_____ **3.** War Hawks

a. people strongly in favor of a war

b. people strongly opposed to a war

c. fight that killed Tecumseh

d. fight that weakened Tecumseh's forces

e. feeling of intense loyalty to the country

f. favoring one state or region over the central government

Academic Vocabulary

Read the following sentences. In the space below, write in your own words the meaning of the boldfaced academic vocabulary word from this section.

1. As more American settlers poured into the Northwest Territories, some Native Americans renewed their **contacts** with the British.

_____

2. In 1812, Madison decided that war with Britain was **inevitable**.

_____

Section Wrap-up

Now that you have read the section, write the answers to the questions that were included in **Setting a Purpose for Reading** *at the beginning of the lesson.*

What was Tecumseh's goal in building a Native American confederacy?

_____

_____

_____

Why did the War Hawks want war with Great Britain?

_____

_____

_____

Chapter 9, Section 4
The War of 1812

(pages 296–300)

Reason To Read

Setting a Purpose for Reading Think about these questions as you read:
- How did the British seize and set fire to Washington, D.C.?
- Why did Andrew Jackson fight a battle after the war was over?

Main Idea

As you read pages 296–300 in your textbook, complete this graphic organizer by describing each battle's outcome.

Battle	Outcome
Lake Erie	
Washington, D.C.	
New Orleans	

Sequencing Events

As you read, write the correct dates for each of these events:

_____ **British put the torch to Washington, D.C.**

_____ **Francis Scott Key is inspired to write "The Star-Spangled Banner"**

_____ **Battle of the Thames**

_____ **United States declares war on Britain**

_____ **Battle of Lake Erie**

_____ **Treaty of Ghent ends war**

War Begins (pages 297–298)

Outlining

Complete this outline as you read page 297.

Naval Battles

    A. _____

    B. _____

    C. _____

Terms To Know

Choose a term from this lesson from the list below to complete each sentence by writing the term in the correct space. You will not use all the terms.

battleships   Horseshoe Bend   frigates   the Thames

1. Tecumseh was killed and his confederacy shattered at the Battle of

_____ .

2. The U.S. Navy had three of the fastest _____
of the time, including the *Constitution*.

3. The Creeks, Native Americans of the South, were defeated at the Battle

of _____ .

Academic Vocabulary

Read the passage below. Put a checkmark in the space before the phrase that best explains what the academic vocabulary word consist, *from this lesson, means in this passage.*

After reductions made to cut government spending, the American army
<u>consisted</u> of fewer than 7,000 troops.

_____ controlled   _____ included   _____ were commanded by

The British Offensive (pages 298–299)

Questioning

As you read "The British Offensive" ask yourself: what is an important detail? Write one of those details about the attack on Washington, D.C.

_____

_____

Terms To Know

Match the term from this lesson in the left column with the correct description in the right column by writing the letter in the space to the left of the term.

____ **1.** Battle of New Orleans

____ **2.** Battle of Plattsburgh

____ **3.** Hartford Convention

____ **4.** Treaty of Ghent

a. secured northern border

b. document that ended the War of 1812

c. document that urged Madison to end the war

d. meeting that produced list of suggested changes to the Constitution

e. meeting that called for end to the war

f. fought after the war had ended

g. allowed British to capture Washington, D.C.

Academic Vocabulary

Read the passage below. Put a checkmark in the space before the phrase that best explains what the academic vocabulary word proceed, *from this lesson, means in this passage.*

"They proceeded, without a moment's delay, to burn and destroy everything in the most distant degree connected with the government."

_____ advanced   _____ retreated   _____ denied

Now that you have read the section, write the answers to the questions that were included in Setting a Purpose for Reading *at the beginning of the section.*

How did the British seize and set fire to Washington, D.C.?

_____

_____

_____

_____

Why did Andrew Jackson fight a battle after the war was over?

_____

_____

_____

_____

Chapter 10, Section 1
Economic Growth

(pages 306–311)

Reason To Read

Setting a Purpose for Reading Think about these questions as you read:
- How did the Industrial Revolution begin in the United States?
- How did the United States change as it became more economically independent?

Main Idea

As you read pages 306–311 in your textbook, complete this graphic organizer by describing in the ovals changes brought about by the Industrial Revolution.

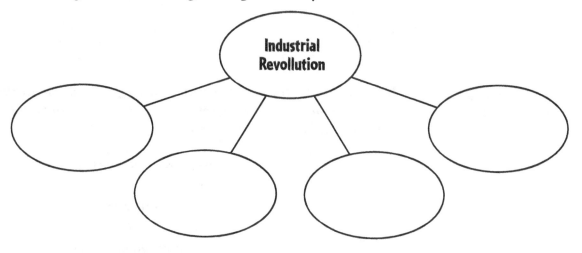

Industrial Revollution

Sequencing Events

As you read, place the following events on the time line:
- **Lowell sets up first textile plant in Massachusetts**
- **Eli Whitney invents the cotton gin**
- **Congress enacts patent law**
- **Congress establishes Second National Bank is chartered**

♦1790   ♦1807   ♦1810   ♦1820

The Growth of Industry (pages 306–308)

Outlining

Complete this outline as you read pages 306–308.

The Industrial Revolution in New England

A. _____

    1. _____

    2. _____

    3. _____

    4. _____

B. _____

    1. _____

    2. _____

Terms To Know

Match the term from this lesson in the left column with the correct definition in the right column by writing the letter in the space to the left of the term.

_____ **1.** capital

_____ **2.** capitalism

_____ **3.** cotton gin

_____ **4.** free enterprise

_____ **5.** Industrial Revolution

_____ **6.** patent

a. protection of legal rights of an inventor

b. period of worker and owner conflict in industry

c. money invested in a business

d. machine used to make textiles

e. system based on business owner's opportunity to earn profit

f. machine used to clean seeds out of cotton

g. period of changes in how goods were made

h. system based on competition, profit, private property, and economic freedom

i. right of competitors to make a product following another person's design

Analyzing

Complete the following sentence.

For the North the **Industrial Revolution** was revolutionary because it

_____

_____

Academic Vocabulary

Circle the letter of the word or words that have the closest meaning to the underlined academic vocabulary word from this lesson.

1. A good labor supply and the availability of water power were two <u>elements</u> that made New England the region where the Industrial Revolution came to the United States.

   a. technologies　　**b.** factors　　**c.** inclusions

2. Inventors wanted to have the <u>sole</u> right to profit from their inventions for a period of time.

   a. only　　**b.** shared　　**c.** temporary

New England Factories *(pages 308–309)*

Inferring

Answer the following questions to make inferences about this lesson.

1. Why would the British want to keep the workings of industrial machinery secret?

   _____

   _____

2. What effect would the factory system have on transportation costs? Why?

   _____

   _____

3. How were goods probably made before interchangeable parts came into use?

   _____

Terms To Know

Use the spaces below to explain how each of these ideas improved manufacturing.

factory system >

_____
_____
_____

interchange-
able parts >

_____
_____

Agriculture Expands *(page 309)*

Summarizing

As you read the lesson, write a one-sentence summary about agriculture expanding.

_____
_____
_____
_____

Economic Independence *(pages 310–311)*

Predicting

Read the lesson and then answer the questions to make some predictions about what you read.

1. What do you think will happen when the charter of the Second Bank of the United States nears its end? Why?

_____
_____

2. As industrial growth increases, what do you think will happen to cities? Why?

_____
_____

Terms To Know

Define or describe the following key terms from this lesson.

corporation

_____

_____

Second Bank of the United States

_____

_____

stock

_____

_____

Terms To Review

Choose the term from the list below that best completes each sentence by writing the correct term in the space. You may have to change the form of some of the terms.

charter (Chapter 3, Section 1)   recruit (Chapter 6, Section 1)

bond (Chapter 8, Section 1)

1. The government can raise money by selling _____ .

2. Congress _____ the Second National Bank so it could loan money to businesses to help them grow.

Section Wrap-up

Now that you have read the section, write the answers to the questions that were included in Setting a Purpose for Reading *at the beginning of the section.*

How did the Industrial Revolution begin in the United States?

_____

_____

_____

How did the United States change as it became more economically independent?

_____

_____

_____

Chapter 10, Section 2
Westward Bound

(pages 314–319)

Reason To Read

Setting a Purpose for Reading Think about these questions as you read:
- How did land and water transportation improve in the early 1800s?
- How did settlements in the West affect the nation's economy and politics?

Main Idea

As you read pages 314–319 in your textbook, complete this graphic organizer by describing why each was important to the nation's growth.

	Significance
National Road	
Robert Fulton	
Erie Canal	

Sequencing Events

As you read, put the following events in the correct order by writing the number 1 through 4 in the space to the left. Use the number 1 for the event that occurred first, 2 for the next event, and so on.

_____ **A.** First section of National Road opens.

_____ **B.** Erie Canal opens.

_____ **C.** Congress approves funding for National Road.

_____ **D.** Fulton's *Clermont* steams to Albany.

Moving West *(pages 314–317)*

Questioning

As you read pages 314–317, write one detail about each of the listed topics.

Population Growth >

_____

_____

Roads and Turnpikes >

_____

_____

River Travel >

_____

_____

Terms To Know

Read the following sentences. Choose the correct term from this lesson to complete the sentence by circling the term.

1. The first steamboat, the (*Albany Special, Clermont*) traveled up the Hudson River from New York City to Albany.

2. Private companies built (paved roads, turnpikes), which they paid for by charging travelers tolls.

3. Every ten years, the government carries out a (census, poll) to count all the people in the country.

4. Congress paid to build the (National Road, National Turnpike) from Maryland to Illinois.

Canals *(pages 317–318)*

Determining the Main Idea

Write down the main idea of this subsection and at least three details that support that idea.

_____

_____

_____

_____

_____

Terms To Know

Use the following key terms from this lesson in a sentence.

canal

_____

_____

Erie Canal

_____

_____

_____

locks

_____

_____

Academic Vocabulary

Read the sentence below. Put a checkmark in the space before the phrase that best explains what the academic vocabulary word link, *from this lesson, means in this passage.*

De Witt Clinton wanted to <u>link</u> New York City to the Great Lakes.

_____ add   _____ chain   _____ connect

Western Settlement (page 319)

Connecting — *As you read the lesson, complete the following chart to compare and contrast two waves of westward migration.*

	First Wave	Second Wave
When did it occur?		
What states were formed?		

Section Wrap-up — *Now that you have read the section, write the answers to the questions that were included in* Setting a Purpose for Reading *at the beginning of the section.*

How did land and water transportation improve in the early 1800s?

_____

_____

_____

_____

_____

How did settlements in the West affect the nation's economy?

_____

_____

_____

_____

_____

Chapter 10, Section 3
Unity and Sectionalism

(pages 321–327)

Reason To Read

Setting a Purpose for Reading Think about these questions as you read:
• Why did sectional differences grow in the 1820s?
• What effect did the Monroe Doctrine have on foreign policy?

Main Idea

As you read pages 321–327 in your textbook, complete this graphic organizer by naming issues that divided the nation.

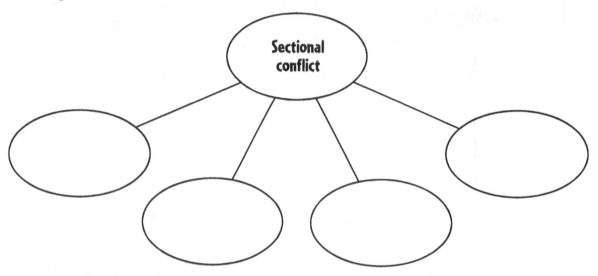

Sequencing Events

Match the date in the left column with the correct description in the right column by writing the letter in the space to the left of the date.

_____ **1.** 1816

_____ **2.** 1817

_____ **3.** 1819

_____ **4.** 1820

_____ **5.** 1823

_____ **6.** 1824

a. Monroe Doctrine issued

b. Missouri Compromise passed

c. Clay explains the "American System"

d. Monroe elected president for first term

e. Mexico wins its independence from Spain.

f. Adams-Onís Treaty gains Florida for United States

g. Jackson invades Florida

h. Rush-Bagot Treaty provides for disarmament on Great Lakes

The Era of Good Feelings (pages 321–322)

Inferring

Read this lesson and then write an explanation of why this period was called the Era of Good Feelings.

_____

_____

_____

_____

_____

Terms To Review

Use each of the following terms, which you studied earlier, in a sentence.

Federalist
(Chapter 8, Section 3)

_____

_____

margin
(Chapter 7, Section 3)

_____

_____

Sectionalism Grows (pages 322–324)

Analyzing

Answer the following questions to analyze the growing trend toward sectionalism.

1. What role did slavery play in the growth of sectional feeling?

_____

_____

2. What role did sectionalism play in the question of Missouri statehood?

_____

_____

Terms To Know

Choose a term from this lesson from the list below to complete each sentence by writing the term in the correct space. Note that you will not use all the terms.

state sovereignty	Missouri Compromise
nationalism	sectionalism

1. The _____ of 1820 settled the issue of which states would be allowed to enter that Union that year.

2. Calhoun supported the idea of _____ .

3. Growing _____ was an important factor in the politics of Monroe's presidency.

Academic Vocabulary

Circle the letter of the word or words that have the closest meaning to the underlined academic vocabulary word from this lesson.

1. The Era of Good Feelings seemed to be a <u>period</u> of harmony, but there were problems beneath the surface.

   a. area   **b.** presidency   **c.** time

2. Disagreements over slavery produced <u>intense</u> discussions.

   a. long   **b.** strong   **c.** wrong-headed

Terms To Review

Write two words or phrases that are related to **tariff**.

> **tariff**
> (Chapter 8, Section 1)

_____

_____

The American System (pages 324–325)

Drawing Conclusions

Answer the following questions to draw conclusions about this lesson.

1. Why would Clay expect that people from every section would support his "American System"?

_____

_____

2. Why did many people in the South not support the American System?

_____

_____

Terms To Know

Read the following sentences. Choose the correct term from this lesson to complete the sentence by circling the term.

1. In (*McCulloch* v. *Maryland*, *Marbury* v. *Madison*), the Supreme Court ruled that states could not tax the national bank because it had been set up by the federal government.

2. In (*Gibbons* v. *Ogden*, *Calhoun* v. *Clay*), the Supreme Court ruled that states could not pass laws that got in the way of Congress's right to regulate interstate commerce.

3. The (American System, Clay System) had three parts: a protective tariff, funding for internal improvements, and a national bank that could help businesses grow.

Academic Vocabulary

Read the passage below. Put a checkmark in the space before the phrase that best explains what the academic vocabulary word controversy, *from this lesson, means in this passage.*

The Second National Bank remained an object of <u>controversy</u>.

_____ agreement   _____ argument   _____ improvement

Foreign Affairs (pages 325–326)

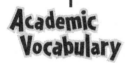

Clarifying

As you read this lesson, answer the following questions to clarify the information about American foreign policy.

1. Why did the United States want better relations with Britain?

_____

_____

2. Why did Secretary of State John Quincy Adams not want to reprimand Andrew Jackson for taking the Spanish forts in Florida?

_____

_____

Terms To Know

Match the term from this lesson in the left column with the correct definition in the right column by writing the letter in the space to the left of the term.

_____ **1.** Adams-Onís Treaty

_____ **2.** Convention of 1818

_____ **3.** court martial

_____ **4.** demilitarized

_____ **5.** disarmament

_____ **6.** Rush-Bagot Treaty

a. treaty with Britain over fishing rights

b. agreement with Britain about Great Lakes

c. trial by a military court

d. removal of weapons

e. agreement with Spain over Florida and Spanish territorial boundaries

f. trial by a civilian court

g. agreement with Spain about navigation rights on Mississippi River

h. without armed forces

i. agreement with Britain about northern boundary of Louisiana Territory

Academic Vocabulary

Write the correct form of the academic vocabulary word from this lesson in the blank space to complete the sentence.

remove > In 1817, the United States and Britain agreed to the _____ of weapons from the Great Lakes.

Copyright © by The McGraw-Hill Companies, Inc.

Latin American Republics *(pages 326–327)*

Sequencing

As you read, put the following events in the correct order by writing the number 1 through 5 in the space to the left. Use the number 1 for the event that occurred first, 2 for the next event, and so on.

_____ **a.** Mexico wins its independence.

_____ **b.** Most of South America has gained independence from Spain.

_____ **c.** Brazil gains its independence from Portugal.

_____ **d.** Rebellion begins against Spain in Mexico.

_____ **e.** Monroe Doctrine issued.

Terms To Know

*Write a sentence describing the **Monroe Doctrine**, a term in this lesson.*

_____

_____

Section Wrap-up

*Now that you have read the section, write the answers to the questions that were included in **Setting a Purpose for Reading** at the beginning of the section.*

Why did sectional differences grow in the 1820's?

_____

_____

_____

_____

What effect did the Monroe Doctrine have on foreign policy?

_____

_____

_____

_____

Chapter 11, Section 1
Jacksonian Democracy
(pages 334–349)

Reason To Read

Setting a Purpose for Reading Think about these questions as you read:
• Why was the nation's sixth president chosen by the House?
• What political changes came under President Jackson?

Main Idea

As you read pages 334–339 in your textbook, complete this graphic organizer by describing the political parties in 1828.

	Candidate	**Views**
Democratic Republicans		
National Republicans		

Sequencing Events

As you read, write the correct dates for each of these events:

_____ No candidate wins electoral majority in four-candidate race for president

_____ Congress passes "Tariff of Abominations"

_____ Jackson wins presidency

_____ Democrats hold first nominating convention

_____ Congress passes Force Bill

The Election of 1824 (pages 334–335)

Monitoring Comprehension

Check how well you understood what you read in this lesson by answering the following questions.

1. Why was Crawford a weak candidate even though he had received the party's nomination?

_____

_____

2. Why was the 1824 election decided by the House of Representatives?

_____

_____

3. Why was Adams unpopular as president?

_____

_____

Terms To Know

Choose a term from this lesson from the list below to complete each sentence. Write the term in the correct space. You might not use all the terms.

"corrupt bargain"	"criminal pact"	dark horse
favorite son	majority	plurality

1. Having a _____ means winning more than half the votes in an election.

2. Adams was charged with making a _____

_____ to gain the presidency.

3. Three of the candidates in 1824 represented local interests, making them _____ candidates.

4. Jackson won a _____ of electoral votes.

The Election of 1828 *(pages 335–336)*

Interpreting

Interpret the information you read about the election of 1828 by answering the following questions.

1. What groups supported the Democrats? What groups supported the National Republicans?

_____

_____

2. What features of this campaign became permanent parts of elections?

_____

_____

Terms To Know

Define or describe the following terms from this lesson.

landslide ＞ _____

_____

mudslinging ＞ _____

Terms To Review

Define or describe the following terms, which you studied earlier.

desert
(Chapter 6, Section 2) ＞ _____

_____

states' rights
(Chapter 8, Section 3) ＞ _____

_____

Jackson as President (pages 336–337)

Determining the Main Idea

Write down the main idea of this lesson and at least three details that support that idea.

_____

_____

_____

_____

_____

Terms To Know

Read the following sentences. Choose the correct term from this lesson to complete the sentence by circling the term.

1. Jackson used an approach called the (favorite son, spoils) system to fill jobs in the federal government.

2. Before 1832, candidates were chosen by party officials, who got together in meetings called (associations, caucuses).

3. In the 1830s and 1840s, more people gained (balloting, suffrage), or the right to vote.

4. Jackson worried that the government had become a (bureaucracy, tyranny), in which unelected officials make decisions.

5. In 1832, the Democrats held the first (nominating convention, presidential primary) to choose their candidate for president.

The Tariff Debate (pages 338–339)

Summarizing

As you read pages 338–339, write a one-sentence summary about these topics.

The Webster-Hayne Debate

_____

_____

The Nullification Crisis

_____

_____

Terms To Know

Choose a term from this lesson from the list below to complete each sentence by writing the term in the correct space. You will not use all the answers.

Anti-Tariff Act   Force Bill   Nullification Act

1. The South Carolina law saying it would not pay the tariffs it disliked

   was called the _____ .

2. Jackson ended the crisis by getting a lower tariff passed and also by

   getting Congress to pass the _____ ,which
   said that he could use military power to make states obey the law.

Academic Vocabulary

Write the correct form of the academic vocabulary word from this lesson in the blank space to complete the sentence.

consumed   consumers   consumption

1. The tariff helped protect American manufacturers from foreign

   competition but meant that _____ had
   to pay higher prices.

                                        revise   revision

2. A _____ to the tariff bill helped end the
   Nullification Crisis.

Terms To Review

Choose a term you studied earlier by circling the correct term from the pair in parentheses.

1. Some Southerners thought the South should (secede, unite) because they were unhappy with some federal laws.

2. The high (tariff, debt) on imported goods was popular with manufacturers, who mostly lived in the Northeast.

3. Calhoun and others argued that states could (nullify, approve) federal laws that they felt were unconstitutional.

Section Wrap-up

Now that you have read the section, write the answers to the questions that were included in Setting a Purpose for Reading *at the beginning of the section.*

Why was the nation's sixth president chosen by the House of Representatives?

_____

_____

_____

_____

_____

What political changes came under President Jackson?

_____

_____

_____

_____

_____

Chapter 11, Section 2
Conflicts Over Land

(pages 341–345)

Reason To Read

Setting a Purpose for Reading Think about these questions as you read:
- How were Native American peoples forced off their lands in the Southeast?
- How did President Jackson defy the Supreme Court?

Main Idea

As you read pages 341–345 in your textbook, complete this graphic organizer by describing what happened to each group of Native Americans as the United States expanded.

	Description
Cherokee	
Sauk/Fox	
Seminole	

Sequencing Events

As you read, place the following events on the time line:
- **Congress creates Indian Territory**
- **Cherokee driven from their homes**
- **Congress passes Indian Removal Act**

♦1830   ♦1833   ♦1836   ♦1839

Moving Native Americans (pages 341–344)

Connecting

As you read the lesson, answer the following questions to identify the causes and effects of the removal of the Cherokee.

Cause	Action	Effect
_____ _____ _____	Congress passes Indian Removal Act.	_____ _____ _____
The Cherokee sue the government and take their case to the Supreme Court.	_____ _____ _____	_____ _____ _____

Terms To Know

Define or describe the following terms from this lesson.

Indian Removal Act > _____
_____
_____

relocate > _____
_____
_____

Trail of Tears > _____
_____

Terms To Review

Read the passage below. Put a checkmark in the space before the phrase that best explains the meaning of the term authority, which you studied in Chapter 4, Section 2.

The Supreme Court ruled that only the federal government, not the states, had the <u>authority</u> to deal with Native Americans.

_____ desire   _____ power   _____ skill

Native American Resistance (pages 344–345)

Responding   *Read the lesson and then answer the questions.*

1. Why does the text say that the Seminole were more successful than the Sauk and Fox in resisting removal to the West?

   _____

   _____

2. How did the Five Civilized Tribes live in Oklahoma?

   _____

   _____

Terms To Know   *Define or describe the term* guerrilla tactics *from this lesson.*

   _____

   _____

Section Wrap-up   *Now that you have read the section, write the answers to the questions that were included in* Setting a Purpose for Reading *at the beginning of the section.*

How were Native American peoples forced off their lands in the Southeast?

   _____

   _____

   _____

   _____

How did President Jackson defy the Supreme Court?

   _____

   _____

   _____

   _____

Chapter 11, Section 3
Jackson and the Bank

(pages 348–351)

Reason To Read

Setting a Purpose for Reading Think about these questions as you read:
• Why did Jackson want to destroy the Bank of the United States?
• How did the Whigs come to power in 1840?

Main Idea

As you read pages 348–351 in your textbook, complete this graphic organizer by describing the steps that Andrew Jackson took that put the Bank of the United States out of business.

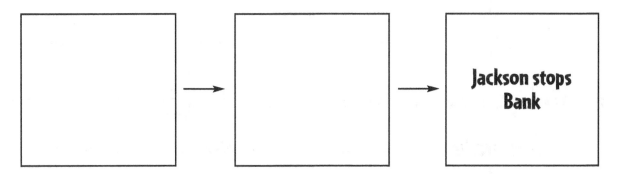

| | | **Jackson stops Bank** |

Sequencing Events

As you read, place the following events on the time line:
• **Economic depression strikes**
• **Jackson refuses to sign charter renewing Bank**
• **Jackson challenges renewal of Bank charter**
• **Polk elected president**

♦ 1830   ♦ 1836   ♦ 1840   ♦ 1845

Key Points  Notes

War Against the Bank (pages 348–349)

Reviewing

Review pages 348–349 and list two key facts about the war against the National Bank.

_____

_____

Terms To Know

Define or describe the following key terms.

Panic of 1837 >

_____

_____

veto >

_____

_____

The Whigs Come to Power (page 349)

Responding

As you read the lesson, answer the following questions.

1. Why did the Whigs show Harrison in front of a log cabin?

_____

_____

2. How did the Whigs portray Van Buren?

_____

_____

Terms To Know

Define or describe the following term from this lesson.

log cabin campaign >

_____

_____

 *Now that you have read the section, write the answers to the questions that were included in* Setting a Purpose for Reading *at the beginning of the section.*

Why did Jackson want to destroy the Bank of the United States?

_____

_____

_____

_____

_____

How did the Whigs come to power in 1840?

_____

_____

_____

_____

_____

Chapter 12, Section 1
The Oregon Country
(pages 356–360)

Reason To Read

Setting a Purpose for Reading Think about these questions as you read:
• Why did large numbers of settlers head for the Oregon country?
• How did the idea of Manifest Destiny contribute to the nation's growth?

Main Idea

As you read pages 356–360 in your textbook, complete the time line by listing key events that occurred.

♦ 1819	♦ 1825	♦ 1836	♦ 1846

Sequencing Events

As you read, identify the year in which each of these events occurred:

_____ **John Jacob Astor organizes American Fur Company**

_____ **Spain sets northern border of California in Adams-Onís Treaty**

_____ **Russia gives up its claim to land south of Alaska**

_____ **Whitmans build mission in Oregon**

_____ **Population of Americans in Oregon reaches 5,000**

_____ **Treaty with Britain divides Oregon with United States and fixes northern border**

Rivalry in the Northwest (pages 356–358)

Clarifying

As you read this lesson, answer the following questions to organize information about the Northwest.

1. What countries claimed the Oregon country in the early 1800s?

_____

_____

2. Why did the United States and Britain need an agreement for joint

occupation of Oregon? _____

_____

Terms To Know

Define or describe the following key terms.

joint occupation >

_____

_____

mountain men >

_____

_____

rendezvous >

_____

_____

Settling Oregon (page 358)

Questioning

As you read each subsection, ask yourself: what is an important detail? Write one of those details in the spaces below.

The Whitman Mission >

_____

_____

_____

_____

> The Oregon Trail

_____

_____

_____

Terms To Know

Read the following sentences. Choose the correct term from this lesson to complete the sentence by circling the term.

1. The vehicles people used to carry their goods to the Pacific Northwest were called (Pullman cars, prairie schooners).

2. Those who left the United States for the Pacific Northwest were called (emigrants, aliens).

3. The route settlers took to the Pacific Northwest was called the (Oregon Trail, Pacific Trail).

The Division of Oregon (pages 359–360)

Outlining

Complete this outline as you read the lesson. The first section has been completed.

I. Population Growth

    A. Destination of most settlers: Willamette Valley

    B. Population growth there from 1840 to 1845

II. Expansion of Freedom

    A. _____

    B. _____

III. Manifest Destiny

    A. _____

IV. "Fifty-four Forty or Fight"

    A. _____

    B. _____

    C. _____

V. Reaching a Settlement

 A. _____

Academic Vocabulary

Choose a term from the list below to complete each sentence by writing the correct term in the space.

inevitable (Chapter 9, Section 3)   significant (Chapter 7, Section 2)

specific (Chapter 7, Section 3)

1. Many Americans believed that it was _____ that the United States would spread to the Pacific Ocean.

2. Oregon became a(n) _____ issue in the 1844 Presidential campaign.

Section Wrap-up

Now that you have read the section, write the answers to the questions that were included in Setting a Purpose for Reading at the beginning of the section.

Why did large numbers of settlers head for the Oregon country?

_____

_____

_____

_____

How did the idea of Manifest Destiny contribute to the nation's growth?

_____

_____

_____

_____

Chapter 12, Section 2
Independence for Texas

(pages 362-368)

Reason To Read

Setting a Purpose for Reading Think about these questions as you read:
- Why did problems arise between the Mexican government and the American settlers in Texas?
- How did Texas achieve independence and later become a state?

Main Idea

As you read pages 362-368 in your textbook, complete this graphic organizer by listing key events that occurred in Texas in the boxes.

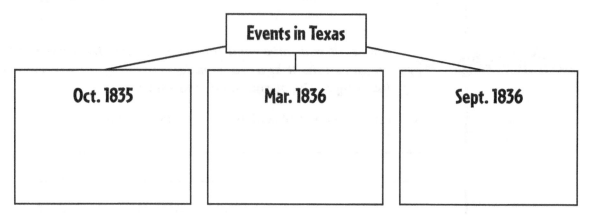

Sequencing Events

Match the date in the left column with the correct event in the right column by writing the letter in the space to the left of the date.

_____ **1.** 1819

_____ **2.** 1821

_____ **3.** 1823

_____ **4.** 1830

a. Moses Austin receives land grant from Spain to settle in Texas

b. Mexico passes law allowing slavery in Texas

c. Spain drops any claim to Texas

d. Mexico passes first of three colonization laws affecting Texas

e. United States drops any claim to Texas

f. Mexico passes last colonization law affecting Texas

g. Mexican order bans all immigration to Texas from United States

A Clash of Cultures (pages 362–365)

Analyzing *Analyze the information in this section by answering the following questions.*

1. Why did the Spanish grant large tracts of land to people willing to settle Texas?

_____

_____

2. Why was Mexico's 1830 decree about settling in Texas a problem?

_____

_____

Terms To Know *Match the term from this lesson in the left column with the correct definition in the right column by writing the letter in the space to the left of the term.*

____ **1.** decree

____ **2.** empresario

____ **3.** Old Three Hundred

____ **4.** Tejanos

a. person given a land grant to promote settlers

b. Mexicans who lived in Texas

c. first settlers of Texas

d. official order

e. first settlers in Austin's colony

f. proclamation

g. Mexican name for Americans who came to Texas

Academic Vocabulary *Read each sentence below. Put a checkmark in the space before the phrase or words that best explains what the boldfaced academic vocabulary word from this lesson means in this passage.*

1. Davy Crockett of Tennessee won notice for his frontier skills, his sense of humor, and the shrewd common sense he often **displayed** in politics.

_____ showed through actions   _____ signaled in code

_____ urged in others

 Notes

2. The Spanish wanted to give **grants** of land to people who would bring more settlers to Texas.

_____ gifts   _____ large expanses   _____ rental agreements

The Struggle for Independence (pages 365–367)

Skimming

Skim the lesson by reading the text under each heading quickly to get a general idea of what it is about. Use one or two sentences to write that general idea in the spaces below. The first section has been completed.

Early Fighting > In 1835 fighting between Texans and Mexico broke out. The Texans seized the city of San Antonio but then did little to prepare for further fighting.

The Battle of the Alamo > _____
_____
_____

Texas Declares Its Independence > _____
_____
_____

The Battle of San Jacinto > _____
_____

Academic Vocabulary

Read the passage below. Put a checkmark in the space before the phrase that best explains what the academic vocabulary word **constitute,** *from this lesson, means in this sentence.*

The people of Texas do now <u>constitute</u> a free, sovereign, and independent republic.

_____ approve a plan of government

_____ make up

_____ write a document

 **Key Points**

 **Notes**

Choose a term you studied earlier from the list below to complete each sentence by writing the correct term in the space.

constitution (Chapter 7, Section 1)   petitioned (Chapter 5, Section 4)

republic (Chapter 7, Section 1)   violated (Chapter 5, Section 1)

1. The Texans claimed that the government of Mexico had

_____ their rights.

2. They declared that they were forming a new _____ .

3. A written _____ laid out the plan of government.

The Lone Star Republic *(pages 367–368)*

Drawing Conclusions

Read the lesson and then answer the questions to draw conclusions about what you read.

1. Why did Andrew Jackson not agree to bring Texas into the United States?

_____

_____

2. How had attitudes towards annexation changed by 1844?

_____

_____

3. What was the result of those changes?

_____

_____

Terms To Know

Define or describe the following term from this lesson.

annex ▷ _____

_____

Terms To Review

Use each of the following terms you studied earlier in a sentence.

Manifest Destiny
(Chapter 12, Section 1)

_____

_____

ratify
(Chapter 6, Section 4)

_____

_____

Section Wrap-up

Now that you have read the section, write the answers to the questions that were included in **Setting a Purpose for Reading** *at the beginning of the section.*

Why did problems arise between the Mexican government and the American settlers in Texas?

_____

_____

_____

_____

_____

How did Texas achieve independence and later become a state?

_____

_____

_____

_____

_____

Chapter 12, Section 3
War with Mexico

(pages 369–374)

Reason To Read

Setting a Purpose for Reading Think about these questions as you read:
- Why did Americans begin to settle in the Southwest?
- How did the United States acquire New Mexico and California?

Main Idea

As you read pages 369–374 in your textbook, complete this graphic organizer by describing the actions and achievements of each individual in the table.

	Actions taken
William Becknell	
Jedediah Smith	
John C. Frémont	

Sequencing Events

As you read, place the following events on the time line:
- **Treaty of Guadalupe Hidalgo ends the war with Mexico**
- **Congress declares war on Mexico**
- **Scott captures Veracruz and Mexico City**
- **U.S. and Mexico complete Gadsden Purchase**
- **U.S. annexes Texas**

◆1840   ◆1845   ◆1850   ◆1855

The New Mexico Territory (pages 369–370)

Reviewing

Review pages 369–370 and list two key facts about this topic.

The New Mexico Territory

_____

_____

_____

Terms To Know

Define or describe the following key term.

Santa Fe Trail

_____

_____

California's Spanish Culture (pages 370–371)

Drawing Conclusions

Read the lesson and then answer the questions to draw conclusions about what you read.

1. How strong was the Spanish effort to put missions in California? Why do you say that?

   _____

   _____

2. Why did Americans begin to talk about adding California to the nation?

   _____

   _____

Terms To Know

Write a sentence using each of the following key terms.

ranchos

_____

_____

rancheros >

_____

_____

Terms To Review

Read the sentence below. In the spaces that follow, explain the meaning of each **boldfaced** *term or academic vocabulary word you studied earlier.*

The Spanish set up several **missions** in California in the hopes of **converting** Native Americans to Catholicism.

mission
(Chapter 2, Section 3) >

_____

converting
(Chapter 2, Section 3) >

_____

War with Mexico *(pages 371–374)*

Sequencing

As you read, put the following events in the correct order by writing a number from 1 to 10 in the space to the left. Use the number 1 for the event that occurred first, 2 for the next event, and so on.

_____ **a.** United States annexes Texas.

_____ **b.** Bear Flag Republic declared in California.

_____ **c.** Polk sends Slidell to offer to buy California and New Mexico.

_____ **d.** Americans capture Veracruz.

_____ **e.** Americans capture Santa Fe.

_____ **f.** Mexican soldiers attack some of Taylor's forces in Texas.

_____ **g.** Americans gain control of California.

_____ **h.** Congress passes a declaration of war against Mexico.

_____ **i.** Mexican government surrenders.

_____ **j.** Americans capture Monterrey.

Terms To Know

Read the following sentences. Choose the correct term from this lesson to complete the sentence by circling the term.

1. The Mexicans who lived in California were called (Californios, rancheros).

2. After the war, Mexico agreed to (cede, secede) California and New Mexico to the United States in return for $15 million.

3. Soon after war broke out, Americans in California proclaimed the independent (Bear Flag Republic, Golden State Republic).

4. The land grant that ended the war with Mexico was called the (Manifest Destiny Acquisition, Mexican Cession).

5. The land purchase completed between Mexico and the United States in 1853 was called the (Gadsden Purchase, Southwest Purchase).

6. The Treaty of (Guadalupe Hidalgo, Mexico City) ended the war with Mexico.

 **Section Wrap-up**

Now that you have read the section, write the answers to the questions that were included in **Setting a Purpose for Reading** *at the beginning of the section.*

Why did Americans begin to settle in the Southwest?

_____

_____

_____

_____

_____

How did the United States acquire New Mexico and California?

_____

_____

_____

_____

_____

New Settlers in California and Utah

(pages 375–378)

Reason To Read

Setting a Purpose for Reading Think about these questions as you read:
- How did the hopes of getting rich draw thousands of people to California?
- How did the search for religious freedom lead to the settlement of Utah?

Main Idea

As you read pages 375–378 in your textbook, complete this graphic organizer by describing who these groups and individuals were and what their role was in the settlement of California and Utah.

	What was their role?
Forty-niners	
Mormons	
Brigham Young	

Sequencing Events

As you read, put the following events in the correct order by writing a number from 1 to 5 in the space to the left. Use the number 1 for the event that occurred first, 2 for the next event, and so on.

_____ **A.** Land Law passed to review land rights of Californios.

_____ **B.** Mormon migration to Utah begins.

_____ **C.** Thousands begin rushing to California to find their fortune.

_____ **D.** California applies for statehood.

_____ **E.** Utah becomes part of the United States.

California Gold Rush (pages 375–377)

Scanning

Scan the lesson by reading the heading and subheadings. Then write down three topics you think will be covered in this lesson. As you read, write down a fact about each topic.

Topic 1 > _____

Fact > _____

_____

_____

Topic 2 > _____

Fact > _____

_____

_____

Topic 3 > _____

Fact > _____

_____

_____

Terms To Know

Write a sentence that explains each of the terms listed below.

boomtowns > _____

_____

forty-niners > _____

_____

vigilantes > _____

Academic Vocabulary

Write the correct form of the academic vocabulary word from this lesson in the blank space to complete the sentence.

occur > Crimes like robbery and murder were a common _____ in the boomtowns of California.

A Religious Refuge in Utah (pages 377–378)

Summarizing

Write three things you learned about Mormon life.

_____

_____

_____

Terms To Know

Read the following sentences. Choose the correct term from this lesson to complete the sentence by circling the term.

1. The (forty-niners, Mormons) carried out the largest single migration in American history.

2. The Mormons called their community (Deseret, Mormonia).

Academic Vocabulary

Read the sentence below. Put a checkmark in the space before the word or phrase that best explains what the boldfaced academic vocabulary word from this lesson means in this lesson.

Utah was not easily **incorporated** into the United States.

____ added to the territory of

____ included in the government and society of

____ made a company

Now that you have read the section, write the answers to the questions that were included in Setting a Purpose for Reading *at the beginning of the section.*

How did the hopes of getting rich draw thousands of people to California?

_____

_____

_____

_____

_____

How did the search for religious freedom lead to the settlement of Utah?

_____

_____

_____

_____

_____

Chapter 13, Section 1
The North's Economy

(pages 386–390)

Reason To Read

Setting a Purpose for Reading Think about these questions as you read:
- How did advances in technology shape the economy of the North?
- How did new kinds of transportation and communication spur economic growth?

Main Idea

As you read pages 386–390 in your textbook, complete this graphic organizer by listing examples of advances in transportation and technology.

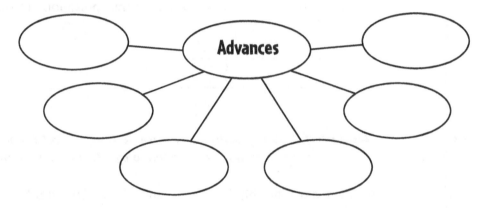

Sequencing Events

As you read, write the number of each event in the appropriate circle on the time line:

1. **Morse sends first telegraph message**
2. **Cooper builds first American steam locomotive**
3. **Fulton demonstrates reliable steamboat**
4. **McCormick patents reaper**

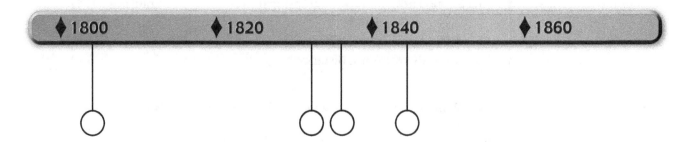

Technology and Industry (pages 386–389)

Previewing *As you read the subsection, answer the following questions.*

1. Look at the Read to Learn questions on page 386. What kinds of technological changes will you read about in this lesson?

   _____

2. Look at the picture on page 387. What kind of transportation is shown there?

   _____

   _____

3. Look at the map on page 388. What kind of transportation network is shown there?

   _____

   _____

Terms To Know *Read the following sentences. Choose the correct term from this lesson to complete the sentence by circling the term.*

1. (Clipper ships, Sailing ships) made ocean travel much faster by using sleek hulls and tall sails.

2. The new communication system used a special language called the (Morse code, Speed code).

Academic Vocabulary *Choose an academic vocabulary word from this lesson from the list below to complete each sentence by writing the correct term in the space. You may need to use a different form of the word.*

accommodate   transform   transmit

1. New inventions allowed people to _____ messages instantly over long distances.

2. Workers made canals wider and deeper so these waterways could

   _____ steamboats.

188   Chapter 13, Section 1

Agriculture (page 390)

Synthesizing

Read the information on agriculture in the North and then write three sentences explaining the key changes that took place in this time.

_____

_____

_____

_____

_____

_____

_____

Academic Vocabulary

In the space available, define the following academic vocabulary word.

labor ⟩

_____

_____

Section Wrap-up

Now that you have read the section, write the answers to the questions that were included in **Setting a Purpose for Reading** *at the beginning of the section.*

How did advances in technology shape the economy of the North?

_____

_____

How did new kinds of transportation and communication spur economic growth?

_____

_____

Chapter 13, Section 2
The North's People

(pages 391–395)

Reason To Read

Setting a Purpose for Reading Think about these questions as you read:
- How did working conditions in industries change?
- How did immigration affect American economic, political, and cultural life?

Main Idea

As you read pages 391–395 in your textbook, complete this graphic organizer by listing two reasons for the growth of cities.

Growth of cities

Sequencing Events

As you read, put the following events in the correct order by writing the number 1 through 5 in the space to the left. Use the number 1 for the event that occurred first, 2 for the next event, and so on.

_____ **A.** Female mill workers petition Massachusetts for 10-hour workday

_____ **B.** *Freedom's Journal,* African American newspaper, founded

_____ **C.** Democratic revolution in Germany fails, prompting more immigration

_____ **D.** Beginning of boom in Irish immigration

_____ **E.** Average factory workday reaches 11.4 hours

 **Key Points**

 **Notes**

Northern Factories (pages 391–393)

Inferring *Read the subsection and then answer the questions to make inferences about what you read.*

1. Why would factory owners want workers to produce more goods?

_____

_____

2. Why would women workers want to organize?

_____

_____

Terms To Know *Match the term from this lesson in the left column with the correct definition in the right column by writing the letter in the space to the left of the term.*

_____ **1.** discrimination

_____ **2.** prejudice

_____ **3.** strike

_____ **4.** trade union

a. factory owners' tool blocking workers from organizing

b. unfair schooling given to a particular group

c. organized group of unskilled workers with many different skills

d. workers' refusal to work in the hopes of winning better working conditions

e. unfair treatment of a group

f. organized group of skilled workers with the same skills

g. unfair attitudes toward a group not based on fact

Academic Vocabulary *Choose an academic vocabulary word from this lesson from the list below to complete each sentence by replacing the underlined word. Write the correct term in the space. You may have to use another form of the word.*

eliminate   series   shift   task

1. Changes in technology <u>moved</u> _____ manufacturing to factories.

2. In the new factories, machines did many <u>jobs</u> _____ instead of having workers do them.

3. New York <u>removed</u> _____ the requirement that white males own property to be able to vote, but still did not give the vote to free African Americans.

The Rise of Cities (pages 393–395)

Giving Examples

Read the following general statements. As you read the lesson, write down examples of each statement.

The cities that were centers of transportation grew larger.

Example
_____
_____
_____

Immigrants were no longer mainly from Britain, as before the early 1800s.

Example
_____
_____
_____

Immigrants faced prejudice and discrimination.

Example
_____
_____
_____

Terms To Know

Write a sentence using each of the following terms from this lesson.

famine
_____
_____

Know-Nothing Party
_____
_____

nativists

Read the following sentences. In the space below, write in your own words the meaning of the boldfaced academic vocabulary word from this lesson.

1. Most of the nation's factories were **located** in the growing cities of the North and Midwest.

_____

2. Many Irish immigrants did **manual** labor, such as working on railroads.

_____

Section Wrap-up

Now that you have read the section, write the answers to the questions that were included in Setting a Purpose for Reading *at the beginning of the section.*

How did working conditions in industries change?

_____

_____

How did immigration affect American economic, political, and cultural life?

_____

_____

Chapter 13, Section 3
Southern Cotton Kingdom
(pages 397–400)

Reason To Read

Setting a Purpose for Reading Think about these questions as you read:
- How did settlement expand in the South?
- Why did the economy of the South rely on agriculture?

Main Idea

As you read pages 397–400 in your textbook, complete this graphic organizer by giving reasons why cotton production grew in the South while industrial growth grew slower.

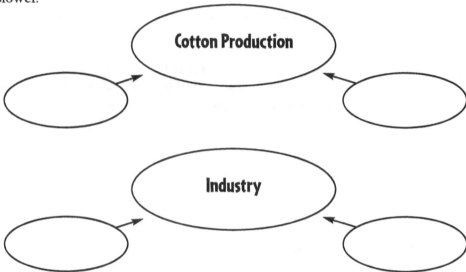

Sequencing Events

Match the date in the left column with the correct event in the right column by writing the letter in the space to the left of the date.

_____ **1.** 1793

_____ **2.** 1840s

_____ **3.** 1844

a. cotton first cultivated in Mississippi

b. Gregg opens textile factory in South Carolina

c. first railroad built in South

d. invention of cotton gin

e. Anderson takes over Tredegar Iron Works

Rise of the Cotton Kingdom *(pages 397–399)*

Monitoring Comprehension

Check how well you understood what you read in this lesson by answering the following questions.

1. Identify one geographic change that occurred in the South between 1790 and 1850.

_____

_____

2. Why did this change take place?

_____

_____

3. Which part of the South had a more varied economy?

_____

_____

Terms To Review

Read each sentence below. In the spaces that follow, explain the meaning of the boldface term or academic vocabulary word you studied earlier.

cotton gin
(Chapter 10, Section 1)

1. The cotton gin dramatically changed the economy of the South.

_____

_____

transport
(Chapter 4, Section 1)

2. The Upper South became a center for the transport of enslaved African Americans to the Deep South.

_____

_____

Industry in the South (pages 399–400)

Summarizing *As you read each subsection, write a one-sentence summary.*

Southern Factories > _____
_____
_____

Southern Transportation > _____
_____
_____

Academic Vocabulary *Circle the letter of the word or words that have the closest meaning to the underlined academic vocabulary word from this lesson.*

A Texas politician <u>summed</u> up the Southerners' belief that having industry was not important to the South's economy.

a. expressed forcefully   **b.** gave a brief version   **c.** spoke emotionally

Section Wrap-up *Now that you have read the section, write the answers to the questions that were included in* **Setting a Purpose for Reading** *at the beginning of the section.*

How did settlement expand in the South?

_____

_____

Why did the economy of the South rely on agriculture?

_____

_____

Chapter 13, Section 4
The South's People

(pages 401–407)

Reason To Read

Setting a Purpose for Reading Think about these questions as you read:
- What was life like on Southern plantations?
- How did enslaved workers maintain strong family and cultural ties?

Main Idea

As you read pages 401–407 in your textbook, complete this graphic organizer by describing the work that was done on Southern plantations.

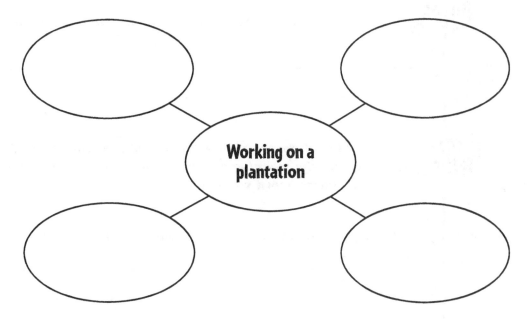

Sequencing Events

Read the following sentences. Choose the correct date from this lesson to complete the sentence by circling the date.

1. **Congress banned the slave trade in (1800, 1808), which meant no new slaves could be brought into the United States.**

2. **Nat Turner led a revolt of enslaved African Americans in (1820, 1831) that frightened white Southerners.**

3. **By (1850, 1860), Baltimore had more than 200,000 people and New Orleans had nearly 170,000.**

Small Farms (pages 401–402)

Visualizing

Read the material on small farms in the South and try to picture a scene of daily life from one of these farms. Describe what you see.

_____

_____

_____

_____

_____

Terms To Know

Define or describe the term yeomen *from this lesson.*

> **yeomen**

_____

_____

Terms To Review

Read each sentence below. In the spaces that follow, explain the meaning of the boldface term or academic vocabulary word you studied earlier.

> **estate**
> (Chapter 3, Section 3)

1. Some plantation owners were so wealthy they had vast estates.

_____

_____

> **tenant farmers**
> (Chapter 3, Section 4)

2. One group of Southern whites were the tenant farmers.

_____

_____

Plantations *(pages 402–403)*

Questioning

As you read each subsection, ask yourself: what is an important detail? Write one of those details about work on the plantation in the spaces below.

Work on the Plantation >

_____

_____

_____

Terms To Know

Read the following sentences. Choose the correct term from this lesson to complete the sentence by circling the term.

1. Planters often had to buy goods on (credit, debt) because they had to wait for their agents to sell their cotton before they received any cash.

2. The (overseer, supervisor) was the person who managed the work of the field hands.

3. Planters had many (fixed costs, variable costs) such as the expense of housing and feeding workers and maintaining equipment.

Academic Vocabulary

Read the following sentences. In the space below, write in your own words the meaning of the **boldfaced** *academic vocabulary word from this lesson.*

1. Only about 4 **percent** of all white Southerners owned large plantations with 20 or more slaves.

_____

2. Some enslaved African Americans worked on household chores. They were called **domestic** slaves.

_____

Life Under Slavery *(pages 403–406)*

Analyzing *Analyze the information in this lesson by answering the following questions.*

1. Why did African Americans develop extended families as a part of family life?

   _____

   _____

2. What role did Christianity play in the lives of enslaved African Americans?

   _____

   _____

Terms To Know *Define or describe the following key terms from this lesson.*

> **spiritual**

   _____

   _____

> **Underground Railroad**

   _____

   _____

Academic Vocabulary *Read the passage below. Put a checkmark in the space before the phrase that best explains what the academic vocabulary word constant, from this lesson, means in this passage.*

Enslaved people who were married had the <u>constant</u> worry that either the husband or wife might be sold to another plantation and separated from the rest of the family.

_____ fearful

_____ intense

_____ steady

City Life and Education (page 407–408)

Responding *As you read the lesson, respond to these questions.*

1. What important role did Southern cities play?

_____

_____

2. How would you describe the lives of free African Americans?

_____

_____

3. How did education change in the middle 1800s in the South?

_____

_____

4. What was the effect of the lack of strong public education in the South?

_____

_____

Terms To Review *In the space available, define the term* literacy, *which you studied earlier.*

literacy >

_____

_____

What was life like on Southern plantations?

_____

_____

How did enslaved workers maintain strong family and cultural ties?

_____

_____

Chapter 14, Section 1
Social Reform

(pages 412–415)

Reason To Read

Setting a Purpose for Reading Think about these questions as you read:

- How did religious and philosophical ideas inspire various reform movements?
- Why did educational reformers think all citizens should go to school?

Main Idea

As you read pages 412–415 in your textbook, complete this chart organizer by identifying these reformers' contributions.

	Contributions
Lyman Beecher	
Horace Mann	
Thomas Gallaudet	
Dorothea Dix	

Sequencing Events

As you read, write the number in the appropriate circle on the time line:

1. **First college for African Americans founded**
2. **Owen establishes New Harmony, Indiana**
3. **Lyon founds first women's college in America**

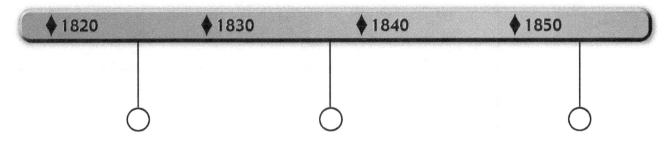

The Reforming Spirit (pages 412–413)

Outlining *Complete this outline as you read the lesson.*

I. The Reforming Spirit

    A. _____

        1. _____

        2. _____

    B. _____

        1. _____

        2. _____

        3. _____

II. The Religious Influence

    A. _____

        1. _____

        2. _____

    B. _____

        1. _____

        2. _____

III. War Against Alcohol

    A. _____

        1. _____

        2. _____

        3. _____

    B. _____

        1. _____

        2. _____

        3. _____

        4. _____

Terms To Know

Match the term from this lesson in the left column with the correct definition in the right column by writing the letter in the space to the left of the term.

_____ **1.** revival

_____ **2.** Second Great Awakening

_____ **3.** temperance

_____ **4.** temperance movement

_____ **5.** utopia

a. community based on vision of ideal society

b. deep religious feeling

c. campaign against alcohol use

d. religious camp meeting

e. group composed of reformers

f. wave of religious fervor

g. drinking little or no alcohol

h. fierce anger against reformers

Reforming Education (pages 413–415)

Summarizing

As you read pages 413–415, write a one-sentence summary for each of these topics.

Higher Education
_____
_____

People With Special Needs
_____
_____

Terms To Know

Define or describe the following term from this lesson.

normal school
_____
_____

Academic Vocabulary

Select the academic vocabulary word from this lesson that best completes the sentence. Write your answer in the space provided.

founded   focused   accepted

1. Some reformers _____ on improving the education of people with special needs.

Copyright © by The McGraw-Hill Companies, Inc.

Key Points | Notes

hearing   visually

2. The Perkins School provided education to students who were
_____ impaired.

Cultural Trends *(page 415)*

Synthesizing

Read the information on cultural trends and then write three sentences stating the main trends in the age of reform.

_____

_____

_____

_____

_____

_____

Terms To Know

Define or describe the following key terms from this lesson.

civil disobedience

_____

_____

transcendentalist

_____

_____

Section Wrap-up

Now that you have read the section, write the answers to the questions that were included in **Setting a Purpose for Reading** *at the beginning of the section.*

How did religious and philosophical ideas inspire various reform movements?

_____

_____

Why did educational reformers think all citizens should go to school?

_____

_____

Chapter 14, Section 2
The Abolitionists

(pages 418–424)

Reason To Read

Setting a Purpose for Reading Think about these questions as you read:
- How did some Americans work to eliminate slavery?
- Why did many Americans fear the end of slavery?

Main Idea

As you read pages 418–424 in your textbook, complete this graphic organizer by identifying five abolitionists and writing a sentence describing his or her role in the movement.

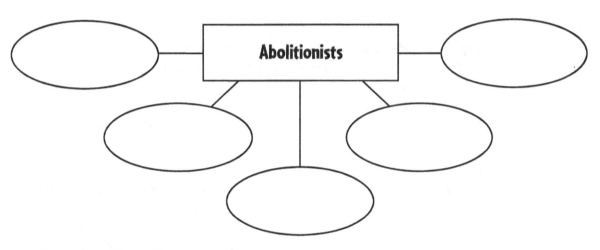

Sequencing Events

Read the following sentences. Choose the correct date from this lesson to complete the sentence by circling the date.

1. **White Virginians formed the American Colonization Society in (1816, 1836) to free enslaved people by buying their freedom and sending them abroad to start new lives.**

2. **The first African American newspaper, Freedom's Journal, was first published in (1822, 1827).**

3. **William Lloyd Garrison founded his newspaper *The Liberator* in (1831, 1851).**

4. **Angelina Grimké and Theodore Weld published the *influential* book *American Slavery As It Is* in (1833, 1839).**

5. **Frederick Douglass gained his freedom by escaping from slavery in (1833, 1838).**

Early Efforts to End Slavery (pages 418–419)

Questioning

As you read each subsection, ask yourself: what is an important detail? Write one of those details for each of these topics in the spaces below.

The Foundation of Abolitionism >
_____
_____
_____
_____

American Colonization Society >
_____
_____
_____
_____

Terms To Know

Read the following sentences. Choose the correct term from this lesson to complete the sentence by circling the term.

1. The people who fought to end slavery were called (abolitionists, emancipationists).

2. The (American Anti-slavery Society, American Colonization Society) was formed by a group of white Southerners.

Terms To Review

Write two words that are related to the term compromise, which you studied earlier.

compromise
(Chapter 7, Section 2) >
_____

The Movement Changes (pages 419–421)

Analyzing

Answer the following questions to explore how the abolitionist movement changed starting around 1830.

1. What did Garrison call for, and how was this different?

_____

_____

2. What was distinctive about Sarah and Angelina Grimké?

_____

_____

3. How did the roles of white and African American abolitionists compare?

_____

_____

Terms To Know

Define or describe abolitionist movement, *a term in this lesson.*

abolitionist movement ⟩ _____

_____

Academic Vocabulary

Circle the letter of the word or words that have the closest meaning to the underlined academic vocabulary word from this lesson.

1. The Grimké sisters <u>lectured</u> many audiences in their campaign against slavery.

   a. entertained   **b.** met   **c.** spoke to

2. Douglass said that, to the African American slave, the fourth of July <u>reveals</u> to him, more than all other days in the year, the gross injustice and cruelty to which he is the constant victim.

   a. highlights   **b.** intensifies   **c.** obscures

3. African Americans in the North were free. Still, laws <u>excluded</u> them from many rights.

    a. barred   **b.** guaranteed   **c.** helped

The Underground Railroad *(pages 422–424)*

Determining the Main Idea

Write down the main idea of this subsection and at least three details that support that idea.

Main Idea

_____

_____

_____

_____

_____

_____

_____

Terms To Know

Define or describe the following term from this lesson.

Underground Railroad

_____

_____

Academic Vocabulary

Read the passage below. Put a checkmark in the space before the phrase that best explains what the academic vocabulary word intense, *from this lesson, means in this passage.*

The abolitionist movement met with <u>intense</u> opposition, not only in the South but also in the North.

_____ forceful   _____ well-planned   _____ well-argued

Now that you have read the section, write the answers to the questions that were included in Setting a Purpose for Reading **at the beginning of the section.**

How did some Americans work to eliminate slavery?

_____

_____

Why did many Americans fear the end of slavery?

_____

_____

Chapter 14, Section 3
The Women's Movement
(pages 425–428)

Reason To Read

Setting a Purpose for Reading Think about these questions as you read:
- How were the antislavery and women's rights movements related?
- What progress did women make toward equality during the 1800s?

Main Idea

As you read pages 425–428 in your textbook, complete this graphic organizer by identifying the contributions these individuals made to women's rights.

	Contributions
Lucretia Mott	
Elizabeth Cady Stanton	
Susan B. Anthony	
Elizabeth Blackwell	

Sequencing Events

Match the date in the left column with the correct event in the right column by writing the letter in the space to the left of the date.

_____ **1.** 1848

_____ **2.** 1850

_____ **3.** 1866

_____ **4.** 1869

_____ **5.** 1920

a. women granted right to vote for first time but only in Wyoming Territory

b. first woman elected to Congress

c. Seneca Falls Convention

d. women granted right to vote for first time but only in New York State

e. first national women's rights convention

f. women granted right to vote nationwide

g. formation of Equal Rights Association

Women and Reform (pages 425–427)

Interpreting

Interpret the information you read about women reformers by answering the following questions.

1. How were Quaker women different from women in society at large?

   _____

   _____

2. Why did the people at the Seneca Falls Convention not support the idea of woman suffrage at first?

   _____

   _____

3. Who led the women's rights movement in the late 1800s?

   _____

Terms To Know

Read the following sentences. Choose the correct term from this lesson to complete the sentence by circling the term.

1. Anthony worked for (coeducation, free education) and equal pay for women.

2. Many reformers joined the (feminist, women's rights) movement of the 1800s.

Terms To Review

Use each of these terms, which you studied earlier, in a sentence that reflects the term's meaning.

discrimination
(Chapter 13, Section 2)

   _____

   _____

suffrage
(Chapter 11, Section 1)

   _____

   _____

Progress by American Women (pages 427–428)

Giving Examples

As you read the lesson, give examples of the general statements written below.

1. Women made some progress in education reform.

_____

_____

2. During the 1800s, some marriage and family laws were changed to be more fair to women.

_____

_____

3. A handful of women in the 1800s broke professional barriers.

_____

_____

Academic Vocabulary

Look up the academic vocabulary word **ministry**, *from this lesson, and define it in the space below.*

_____

_____

Section Wrap-up

Now that you have read the section, write the answers to the questions that were included in **Setting a Purpose for Reading** *at the beginning of the section.*

How were the antislavery and women's rights movements related?

_____

_____

What progress did women make toward equality during the 1800s?

_____

_____

Chapter 15, Section 1
Slavery and the West

(pages 436–439)

Reason To Read

Setting a Purpose for Reading Think about these questions as you read:
- How was the debate over slavery related to the admission of new states?
- What did the Compromise of 1850 accomplish?

Main Idea

As you read pages 436–439 in your textbook, complete this graphic organizer by describing how these compromises answered the question of admitting new states.

Admission of new states	
The Missouri Compromise	**The Compromise of 1850**

Sequencing Events

Read the following sentences. Choose the correct date from this lesson to complete the sentence by circling the date.

1. **The Fugitive Slave Act was passed in (1820, 1850), as part of the compromise Congress worked out that year.**
2. **Congress reopened the question of slavery when it passed the Kansas-Nebraska Act in (1852, 1854).**
3. **By January (1855, 1856), groups in Kansas had formed two rival governments, one free and one slave.**

The Missouri Compromise (pages 436–437)

Clarifying

As you read this lesson, answer the following questions to clarify the information about the Missouri Compromise.

1. Why was Missouri's request to be admitted as a state in 1819 a problem?

   _____

   _____

2. How did the Missouri Compromise settle that problem?

   _____

   _____

3. How did the Missouri Compromise try to resolve the issue of slavery in the territories in the future?

   _____

   _____

Terms To Know

Write a sentence in which you use the following key terms in a sentence.

Missouri Compromise

   _____

   _____

sectionalism

   _____

   _____

Academic Vocabulary

Read the sentence below. Explain in your own words what is meant by the academic vocabulary word volume *from this lesson.*

John Quincy Adams called the debate over Missouri's admission to the Union a "title-page to a great and tragic <u>volume</u>."

   _____

   _____

New Western Lands (pages 437–438)

Responding *As you read this lesson, respond to the following questions.*

1. Why did slavery become an important issue again in the 1840s?

_____

_____

2. What happened when California applied for statehood in 1849?

_____

_____

Terms To Know *Define or describe each of the following key terms.*

Free-Soil Party

_____

_____

fugitive

_____

_____

_____

Wilmot Proviso

_____

_____

Terms To Review *Choose a term from the list below to complete each sentence by replacing the underlined word. Write the correct term in the space. You may have to use a different form of the word.*

annex (Chapter 13, Section 2)   involve (Chapter 4, Section 1)

regulate (Chapter 3, Section 1)   secede (Chapter 9, Section 2)

1. Some Southerners backed a bill that would prevent Congress or

territorial governments from trying to _____ slavery.

2. Some Southerners began to argue that their states should

_____ from the Union.

3. In the late 1840s, the debate over slavery _____

areas that had once belonged to Mexico.

A New Compromise (pages 438–439)

Evaluating   *Read the lesson and then answer the questions to evaluate what you read.*

1. What did those opposed to slavery gain from Clay's compromise proposal?

_____

_____

2. What did those who favored slavery gain from Clay's compromise proposal?

_____

_____

Terms To Know   *Define or describe the following key terms.*

abstain >   _____

    _____

Compromise of 1850 >   _____

    _____

Terms To Review   *Read the sentence below. In the spaces that follow, explain the meaning of the boldface term or academic vocabulary word you studied earlier.*

plantation
(Chapter 2, Section 3) >   Webster believed that because of climate, the new territories in the West would not be useful for **plantation** agriculture.

_____

_____

Now that you have read the section, write the answers to the questions that were included in **Setting a Purpose for Reading** *at the beginning of the section.*

How was the debate over slavery related to the admission of new states?

_____

_____

What did the Compromise of 1850 accomplish?

_____

_____

Chapter 15, Section 2
A Nation Dividing
(pages 441–444)

Reason To Read

Setting a Purpose for Reading Think about these questions as you read:

- How did the Fugitive Slave Act and the Kansas-Nebraska Act further divide the North and South?
- How did popular sovereignty lead to violence?

Main Idea

As you read pages 441–444 in your textbook, complete this graphic organizer by describing how Southerners and Northerners reacted to the Kansas-Nebraska Act.

Kansas-Nebraska Act	
Southern reaction	**Northern reaction**

Sequencing Events

As you read, put the following events in the correct order by writing the number 1 through 4 in the space to the left. Use the number 1 for the event that occurred first, 2 for the next event, and so on.

_____ **A.** Franklin Pierce becomes president.

_____ **B.** Fugitive Slave Act is passed.

_____ **C.** *Uncle Tom's Cabin* is published.

_____ **D.** Elections take place in Kansas.

The Fugitive Slave Act (pages 441–442)

Connecting   *Answer the following questions to describe the Northern and Southern responses to the Fugitive Slave Act.*

1. Once the Act was passed, what did Southerners do?

_____

_____

2. How did Northerners react to those actions?

_____

_____

Terms To Know   *Define or describe the Fugitive Slave Act.*

Fugitive Slave Act > _____

_____

The Kansas-Nebraska Act (pages 442–443)

Analyzing   *As you read the lesson, identify the cause and two effects of the Kansas-Nebraska Act.*

Cause > _____

_____

Effect 1 > _____

_____

Effect 2 > _____

_____

Terms To Know

Define or describe the following key terms.

Kansas-Nebraska Act _____

_____

_____

popular sovereignty _____

_____

Conflict in Kansas *(pages 443–444)*

Outlining

Complete an outline of "Bleeding Kansas" you read the section.

I. "Bleeding Kansas"

    A. _____

        1. _____

        2. _____

    B. _____

Terms To Know

Use each of the following key terms from this lesson in a sentence.

border ruffians _____

_____

civil war _____

_____

Section Wrap-up

Now that you have read the section, write the answers to the questions that were included in Setting a Purpose for Reading *at the beginning of the section.*

How did the Fugitive Slave Act and the Kansas-Nebraska Act further divide the North and South?

_____

_____

How did popular sovereignty lead to violence?

_____

_____

Chapter 15, Section 3
Challenges to Slavery
(pages 445–448)

Reason To Read

Setting a Purpose for Reading Think about these questions as you read:
- Why was the Republican Party formed?
- How did the *Dred Scott* decision, the Lincoln-Douglas debates, and John Brown's raid affect Americans?

Main Idea

As you read pages 445–448 in your textbook, complete this graphic organizer by listing major events for each year.

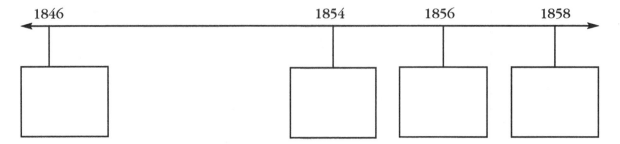

Sequencing Events

As you read, put the following events in the correct order by writing the number 1 through 4 in the space to the left. Use the number 1 for the event that occurred first, 2 for the next event, and so on.

_____ **A.** Lincoln and Douglas debate slavery.

_____ **B.** Supreme Court issues *Dred Scott* decision.

_____ **C.** John Brown carries out raid on Harpers Ferry.

_____ **D.** Northern Democrats suffer heavy losses in elections.

A New Political Party (pages 445–446)

Interpreting

Interpret the information you read about the Republican Party by answering the following questions.

1. What groups formed the Republican Party?

_____

_____

2. Why did the Republican Party have almost no support in the South?

_____

_____

3. What issues did the three parties support in the 1856 presidential election?

_____

_____

Terms To Know

Define or describe the following key term from this lesson.

Republican Party

_____

_____

The Dred Scott Decision (pages 446–448)

Monitoring Comprehension

Check how well you understood what you read in this lesson by answering the following questions.

1. Why did Dred Scott believe that he should be freed?

_____

_____

2. What did the Supreme Court rule in Dred Scott's case?

_____

_____

3. How did Northerners and Southerners respond to the decision?

_____

_____

4. What were the results of the Illinois election for senator in 1858?

_____

_____

5. What were the results of John Brown's raid?

_____

_____

Terms To Know

Match the term from this lesson in the left column with the correct definition in the right column by writing the letter in the space to the left of the term.

____ **1.** arsenal

____ **2.** Freeport Doctrine

____ **3.** martyr

a. person who dies for a cause

b. person who leads a revolt

c. place where weapons and ammunition are kept

d. Douglas's plan for handling slavery in territories

e. Lincoln's plan for handling slavery in territories

Academic Vocabulary

Read the passage below. Put a checkmark in the space before the phrase that best explains what the academic vocabulary word status, from this lesson, means in this passage.

The Supreme Court decided not only Dred Scott's **status**, but also the whole question of slavery in the territories.

____ condition as free or enslaved

____ level of society

____ occupation or job

Now that you have read the section, write the answers to the questions that were included in Setting a Purpose for Reading *at the beginning of the section.*

Why was the Republican Party formed?

_____

_____

How did the Dred Scott decision, the Lincoln-Douglas debates, and John Brown's raid affect Americans?

_____

_____

Chapter 15, Section 4
Secession and War

(pages 449–453)

Reason To Read

Setting a Purpose for Reading Think about these questions as you read:
- How did the 1860 election lead to the breakup of the Union?
- Why did secession lead to the Civil War?

Main Idea

As you read pages 449–453 in your textbook, complete this graphic organizer by listing the major events at each time.

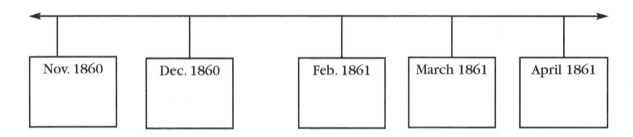

| Nov. 1860 | Dec. 1860 | Feb. 1861 | March 1861 | April 1861 |

Sequencing Events

As you read, put the following events in the correct order by writing the number 1 through 4 in the space to the left. Use the number 1 for the event that occurred first, 2 for the next event, and so on.

_____ **A.** Crittenden proposes constitutional amendments to end secession crisis.

_____ **B.** Fort Sumter attacked.

_____ **C.** Confederate States of America formed.

_____ **D.** South Carolina secedes from Union.

_____ **E.** Lincoln elected president.

The Election of 1860 *(pages 449–450)*

Analyzing   *Analyze the information on pages 449–450 by answering the following questions.*

1. What chance the Democrats have to win the 1860 election once they had both a Northern and Southern nominee? Why?

_____

_____

2. Why did Southerners fear a Republican victory?

_____

_____

3. Why is it accurate to say that the 1860 election was decided strictly on sectional grounds?

_____

_____

The South Secedes *(pages 451–452)*

Previewing   *Before reading the lesson, answer the following questions.*

1. Based on the main heading for this section, what do you think happened after the 1860 election?

_____

2. Look at the map on page 453. How many states seceded? Did they all do it at the same time, or in groups?

_____

_____

Terms To Know   *Define or describe the following key terms.*

Confederate States of America > _____

_____

secession _____

_____

Terms To Review

Match the term you studied earlier, in the left column, with the correct definition or description, in the right column, by writing the letter in the space to the left of the term.

____ **1.** amendment
(Chapter 7, Section 3)

____ **2.** contract
(Chapter 7, Section 3)

____ **3.** states' rights
(Chapter 8, Section 3)

____ **4.** theory
(Chapter 7, Section 3)

a. formal legal agreement
b. belief that the power of the national government exceeds that of the states
c. belief that the state power exceeds power of the national government
d. belief or idea
e. official change to a formal body of laws
f. basic part of a written constitution

Fort Sumter *(page 453)*

Determining the Main Idea

Write down the main idea of this lesson and at least three details that support that idea.

Main Idea _____

_____

_____

_____

_____

_____

Copyright © by The McGraw-Hill Companies, Inc.

Section Wrap-up

Now that you have read the section, write the answers to the questions that were included in Setting a Purpose for Reading *at the beginning of the section.*

How did the 1860 election lead to the breakup of the Union?

_____

_____

Why did secession lead to the Civil War?

_____

_____

Chapter 16, Section 1
The Two Sides

(pages 460-464)

Reason To Read

Setting a Purpose for Reading Think about these questions as you read:
- Why did the border states play an important part in the war?
- How did the North and South compare in terms of population, industry, resources, and war aims?

Main Idea

As you read pages 460-464 in your textbook, complete this graphic organizer by listing the strengths and weaknesses of the Union and Confederacy.

Union Strengths:	Confederacy Strengths:

Comparing the Union and the Confederacy

Union Weaknesses:	Confederacy Weaknesses:

Sequencing Events

As you read, write the significant event that took place on each of the following dates:

February 1861 _____

April 1861 _____

Summer 1861 _____

June 1863 _____

Choosing Sides (pages 460–462)

Reviewing

Reread "Choosing Sides" on pages 460–462 and list two key facts.

_____

_____

Terms To Know

Write a sentence that explains the meaning of border state in the spaces below.

border state

_____

_____

Academic Vocabulary

Write the correct form of the boldfaced *academic vocabulary word* from this section in the blank space to complete the sentence.

strategy
ADJECTIVE

With its _____ location, Missouri controlled parts of the Mississippi River.

Terms To Review

Write two words or phrases that are related to each of the terms you studied earlier.

isolate
(Chapter 1, Section 1)

_____

_____

secede
(Chapter 15, Section 1)

_____

_____

Comparing North and South (pages 462–463)

Connecting

Under each heading below, compare the North and the South by stating how they were similar and how they were different.

Material Resources

_____

_____

 **Key Points**

 **Notes**

Leadership ⟩ _____
_____
_____

War Aims ⟩ _____
_____

Terms To Know *Define or describe the following key terms from this lesson.*

blockade ⟩ _____
_____
_____

offensive ⟩ _____
_____

Academic Vocabulary *In the space available, write opposites of these academic vocabulary words.*

obvious ⟩ _____
_____

primary ⟩ _____
_____

American People at War (pages 463–464)

Inferring *Answer the question in the spaces provided to make an inference about the Civil War.*

Were the Confederates likely to have more soldiers in their armies than the Union? Why or why not?

Who Were the Soldiers? ⟩ _____
_____

234

Chapter 16, Section 1

Academic Vocabulary

Read the following sentence from the lesson. Then use the spaces below to explain the meaning of the two underlined academic vocabulary words used in this section.

The first spring of the war proved that Sherman's <u>prediction</u> was <u>accurate</u>.

> prediction

_____

_____

_____

> accurate

_____

_____

Section Wrap-up

Now that you have read the section, write the answers to the questions that were included in **Setting a Purpose for Reading** *at the beginning of the section.*

Why did the border states play an important part in the war?

_____

_____

How did the North and South compare in terms of population, industry, resources, and war aims?

_____

_____

Chapter 16, Section 2
Early Years of the War

(pages 466-472)

Reason To Read

Setting a Purpose for Reading Think about these questions as you read:
- What successes and failures did the North and the South have in the early years of the war?
- How did the North's naval blockade hurt the South?

Main Idea

As you read pages 466-472 in your textbook, complete this graphic organizer by describing the outcome of each of these battles.

Battle	Outcome
First Battle of Bull Run (Manassas)	
Monitor v. *Merrimack*	
Antietam	

Sequencing Events

As you read, place the following events on the time line:

- **Grant captures Fort Henry and Fort Donelson**
- **Battle of Antietam**
- **First Battle of Bull Run (Manassas)**
- **Battle of Shiloh**

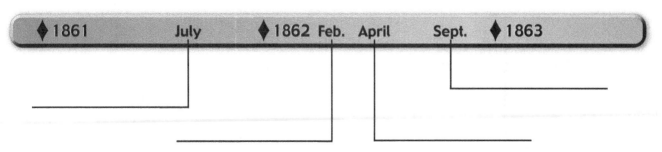

♦ 1861   July   ♦ 1862 Feb.   April   Sept.   ♦ 1863

First Battle of Bull Run *(pages 466–467)*

Analyzing

Answer the following questions to analyze the First Battle of Bull Run (Manassas).

1. Why did the Union troops retreat?

_____

_____

2. What effect did the battle have on people in the North?

_____

_____

Academic Vocabulary

*Read each sentence below. Put a checkmark in the space before the phrase that best explains what the **boldfaced** academic vocabulary word from this lesson means in this passage.*

outcome

1. Northerners were shocked by the **outcome** of the First Battle of Bull Run.

_____ defeat   _____ result   _____ retreat

pursue

2. The Confederate forces were too tired and disorganized to **pursue** the retreating Union soldiers at First Bull Run.

_____ go after   _____ fight further   _____ make suffer

War at Sea *(pages 467–468)*

Questioning

As you read each subsection, ask yourself: what is an important detail? Write one detail about the naval blockade in the spaces below.

_____

_____

_____

Terms To Know

Match the term in the left column with the correct definition in the right column by writing the letter in the space provided.

____ **1.** blockade runner

____ **2.** ironclad

____ **3.** Merrimack

____ **4.** Monitor

a. armored naval vessel

b. Union ironclad

c. Confederate ship that carried goods into and out of Southern ports

d. Confederate ironclad

e. Union tank

Academic Vocabulary

Choose a term from the list below to complete each sentence by replacing the underlined words. Write the correct term in the space. You might have to change the form of the word to fit the sentence.

abandon   enforce   export

1. Lincoln ordered the navy to <u>put into effect</u> _____ the blockade of Southern ports.

2. Union troops <u>left behind</u> _____ a ship, which the Confederates turned into the *Merrimack*.

War in the West (pages 468–469)

Scanning

Scan the lesson by reading each subsection quickly to get a general idea of what it is about. Use one or two sentences to write that general idea in the spaces below.

_____

_____

_____

_____

Terms To Know

Define or describe the following key terms from this lesson.

Battle of Shiloh >

_____
_____
_____

casualties >

_____
_____
_____

War in the East (pages 469–472)

Determining the Main Idea

Reread pages 469–472 and list two key facts about each of these events.

Union Defeat at Richmond >

1. _____
2. _____

Gloom in the North >

1. _____
2. _____

The Battle of Antietam >

1. _____
2. _____

Academic Vocabulary

Circle the letter of the word or words that have the closest meaning to the underlined academic vocabulary word from this lesson.

When faced with the <u>prospect</u> of battle, McClellan was cautious and worried that his troops were not ready.

a. outcome   **b.** possibility   **c.** view

"The slain lay in rows <u>precisely</u> as they had stood in their ranks a few minutes before."

a. exactly   **b.** opposite to   **c.** similar to

Now that you have read the section, write the answers to the questions that were included in **Setting a Purpose for Reading** *at the beginning of the section.*

What successes and failures did the North and the South have in the early years of the war?

_____

_____

How did the North's naval blockade hurt the South?

_____

_____

Chapter 16, Section 3
A Call for Freedom

(pages 473–477)

Reason To Read

Setting a Purpose for Reading Think about these questions as you read:
- Why did Lincoln issue the Emancipation Proclamation?
- What role did African Americans play in the Civil War?

Main Idea

As you read pages 473–477 in your textbook, complete this graphic organizer by describing what the Emancipation Proclamation and the Thirteenth Amendment to the Constitution were meant to accomplish.

	Goal
Emancipation Proclamation	
Thirteenth Amendment	

Sequencing Events

As you read, put the following events in the correct order by writing a number 1 to 4 in the space to the left. Use the number 1 for the event that occurred first, 2 for the next event, and so on.

_____ **A. Nearly half of the 54th Massachusetts regiment is wiped out**

_____ **B. Lincoln signs the Emancipation Proclamation**

_____ **C. African Americans are allowed to serve in the Union army**

_____ **D. Thirteenth Amendment is ratified**

Emancipation (pages 473–476)

1. Why did Lincoln hesitate to move against slavery?

_____

_____

2. What are the three reasons that Lincoln decided to end slavery?

_____

_____

3. After deciding to end slavery, why did Lincoln wait to announce his decision?

_____

_____

4. What effects did the Emancipation Proclamation have?

_____

_____

Terms To Know *Choose a term from this lesson from the list to complete each sentence by writing the term in the correct space.*

emancipate   Emancipation Proclamation
ratify   Thirteenth Amendment

1. The _____ had little actual impact on slavery, but it caused many changes to the war effort.

2. The _____ actually ended slavery throughout the United States.

3. In 1862, Lincoln decided to _____ the slaves.

Academic Vocabulary

Write two words that are related to each academic vocabulary word from this lesson.

attitude

_____
_____
_____

respond

_____
_____
_____

Terms To Review

Use each of these terms, which you studied earlier, in a sentence that reflects the term's meaning.

border states
(Chapter 16, Section 1)

_____
_____
_____

ratify
(Chapter 6, Section 4)

_____
_____
_____

African Americans in the War (pages 476–477)

Determining the Main Idea

Write down the main idea of this subsection and at least three details that support that idea.

Main Idea: _____

_____

1. _____

_____

2. _____

_____

3. _____

_____

Academic Vocabulary

In the space provided, write a definition of the following term.

civil rights  _____

_____

Section Wrap-up

Now that you have read the section, write the answers to the questions that were included in **Setting a Purpose for Reading** *at the beginning of the section.*

Why did Lincoln issue the Emancipation Proclamation?

_____

_____

What role did African Americans play in the Civil War?

_____

_____

Chapter 16, Section 4
Life During the Civil War
(pages 478–483)

Reason To Read

Setting a Purpose for Reading Think about these questions as you read:
- What was life like for the soldiers?
- What role did women play in the war?
- How did the war affect the economies of the North and South?

Main Idea

As you read pages 478–483 in your textbook, complete this graphic organizer by describing the roles of these individuals during the Civil War

	Role
Loretta Janeta Velázquez	
Dorothea Dix	
Clara Barton	

Sequencing Events

As you read, write the correct dates for each of these events:

_____ **Union Congress passes income tax**

_____ **Confederate Congress passes draft law**

_____ **Union passes draft law**

_____ **Angry mobs oppose the draft in New York City**

The Lives of Soldiers (pages 478–479)

Summarizing

Write a one-sentence summary of the subsection "The Reality of War."

> **The Reality of War**

_____

_____

Academic Vocabulary

Write two words or phrases that are related to the academic vocabulary word from this section.

> **medical**

_____

_____

Terms To Review

In the space available, define the following words you studied earlier.

> **casualties**
> (Chapter 16, Section 2)

_____

_____

> **desert**
> (Chapter 6, Section 2)

_____

_____

Women and the War (pages 479–481)

Synthesizing

Read the section on women and the war, and then write three sentences describing the contributions that women made to the war effort.

_____

_____

_____

_____

_____

Academic Vocabulary

Read the sentence below. Put a checkmark in the space before the word or words that best explain what the word distributed *means in this sentence.*

distributed ▷ Women on both sides worked to make bandages, ammunition, clothing, and medicine that could be <u>distributed</u> to the troops.

_____ handed out   _____ manufactured   _____ sold

Opposition to the War *(pages 481–482)*

Monitoring Comprehension

Check how well you have understood this subsection by answering the following questions.

1. Why did the governments of the North and South pass laws creating the draft?

   _____

   _____

2. How did people in the North and South respond to the draft?

   _____

   _____

Terms To Know

Choose a term from this lesson from the list to complete each sentence by writing the term in the correct space. You will not use all the terms.

bounty   draft   free speech
enlistment   habeas corpus

1. The South was the first to enact a _____ law, but the North later passed one also.

2. Lincoln and Davis both temporarily suspended _____ _____ , which allowed the government to jail opponents without a trial.

3. The drop-off in the number of volunteers led the North to pass a law giving a(n) _____ to any civilian who joined the army.

War and the Economy (pages 482–483)

Predicting

After reading the subsection, which section—North or South—do you think would have the better economy after the war? Why?

_____

_____

_____

Terms To Know

Define or describe the following terms.

greenbacks

_____

_____

_____

inflation

_____

_____

Academic Vocabulary

Choose an academic vocabulary word from this lesson from the list below to complete each sentence by replacing the underlined word. Write the correct term in the space.

impact   impose   income

1. The governments of the North and South both had to borrow money

   and <u>enact</u> _____ taxes to get the sums needed to pay
   for the war.

2. The Civil War had a deep <u>effect</u> _____ on the
   economies of the North and South.

Now that you have read the section, write the answers to the questions that were included in **Setting a Purpose for Reading** *at the beginning of the section.*

What was life like for the soldiers?

_____

_____

What role did women play in the war?

_____

_____

How did the war affect the economies of the North and South?

_____

_____

Chapter 16, Section 5
The Way to Victory

(pages 485-491)

Reason To Read

Setting a Purpose for Reading Think about these questions as you read:
- What battled turned the tide of the war in 1863?
- What events led the South to surrender in 1865?

Main Idea

As you read pages 485-491 in your textbook, complete this graphic organizer by describing the strategy Grant adopted to defeat the Confederacy.

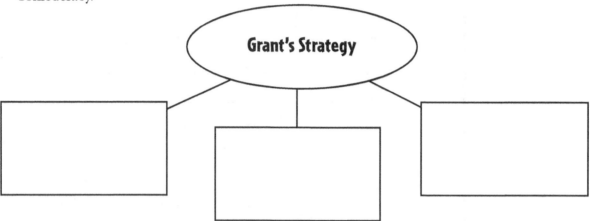

Grant's Strategy

Sequencing Events

As you read, place the following events on the time line:

- **Battle of Gettysburg**
- **Grant takes over Union command**
- **Lee surrenders to Grant**
- **Lee wins Battle of Fredericksburg**

Events of the Civil War

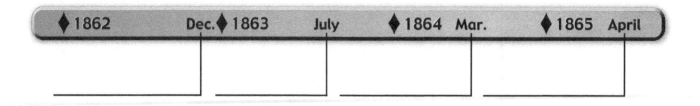

1862   Dec. ◆1863   July   ◆1864 Mar.   ◆1865 April

Southern Victories (pages 485–486)

Questioning

As you read the subsection "Fredericksburg and Chancellorsville," ask yourself: what is an important detail? Write one of those details in the spaces below.

_____

_____

Terms To Know

Identify the battle in which the Union army suffered heavy losses because it attacked Confederate forces that were <u>entrenched</u>. Then, in the space provided, explain what <u>entrenched</u> means.

_____

_____

The Tide of War Turns (pages 486–488)

Drawing Conclusions

Use the spaces provided to write a conclusion about the Union victory at Vicksburg.

_____

_____

Terms To Know

Match the term from this lesson in the left column with the correct definition in the right column by writing the letter in the space provided.

____ **1.** Gettysburg

____ **2.** Gettysburg Address

____ **3.** Pickett's Charge

____ **4.** Vicksburg

a. attack by about 14,000 Confederate soldiers

b. Confederate city on the Mississippi River

c. speech by Lincoln

d. Pennsylvania town that was the site of an important battle

e. Confederate defense of Richmond

Final Phases of War (pages 488–490)

Sequencing

As you read the subsection, put the following events in the correct order by writing a number from 1 to 6 in the space to the left. Use the number 1 for the event that occurred first, 2 for the next event, and so on.

_____ **A.** Sherman reaches Savannah.

_____ **B.** Lincoln wins reelection.

_____ **C.** Farragut captures Mobile Bay.

_____ **D.** Grant loses thousands at the Wilderness, Spotsylvania Courthouse, and Cold Harbor.

_____ **E.** Grant is bogged down at Petersburg.

_____ **F.** Sherman takes Atlanta.

Terms To Know

Define or describe the following key term from this lesson.

total war

_____

_____

Academic Vocabulary

Read the sentence below. Put a checkmark in the space before the word or words that best explain what the bold-faced *academic vocabulary word from this lesson means in this passage.

convinced

Sherman **convinced** Grant to allow him to carry out the "march to the sea."

_____ ordered   _____ persuaded   _____ urged

Victory for the North (pages 490–491)

Responding

Use the spaces provided to respond to the questions.

1. Why did Lee withdraw from Petersburg?

_____

_____

2. How did Grant treat Confederate soldiers when Lee surrendered?

_____

_____

Academic Vocabulary

In the space available, define the following academic vocabulary words from this lesson.

generation ⟩

_____

_____

_____

resident ⟩

_____

_____

Terms To Review

Read the sentence below. Put a checkmark in the space before the word or words that best explain the meaning of the boldfaced academic vocabulary word that you studied earlier.

federal
(Chapter 7, Section 3) ⟩

The <u>federal</u> government was strengthened and was now clearly more powerful than the states.

____ local   ____ municipal   ____ national

Section Wrap-up

Now that you have read the section, write the answers to the questions that were included in Setting a Purpose for Reading *at the beginning of the section.*

What battle turned the tide of the war in 1863?

_____

_____

What events led the South to surrender in 1865?

_____

_____

Chapter 17, Section 1
Reconstruction Plans

(pages 500–503)

Reason To Read

Setting a Purpose for Reading Think about these questions as you read:
- How did the Reconstruction plans of Lincoln and the Radical Republicans differ?
- What were President Johnson's Reconstruction plans?

Main Idea

As you read pages 500–503 in your textbook, complete this graphic organizer by describing each of the Reconstruction plans.

Plan	Description
Ten Percent Plan	
Wade-Davis Plan	
Restoration	

Sequencing Events

As you read, put the following events in the correct order by writing the number 1 through 5 in the space to the left. Use the number 1 for the event that occurred first, 2 for the next event, and so on.

_____ **A. Congress passes Wade-Davis Bill.**

_____ **B. Johnson announces his own Reconstruction plan.**

_____ **C. Lincoln assassinated.**

_____ **D. Lincoln announces Ten Percent Plan.**

_____ **E. Freedmen's Bureau formed.**

Reconstruction Debate *(pages 500–502)*

Questioning

As you read each subsection, ask yourself: what is an important detail? Write one of those details about the Freedmen's Bureau in the spaces below.

The
Freedmen's
Bureau

_____

_____

Terms To Know

Write a sentence that uses both of the terms in the following pairs of terms from this lesson.

Wade-Davis
Bill;
Reconstruction

_____

_____

Ten-Percent
Plan; amnesty

_____

_____

_____

radical;
Radical
Republicans

_____

_____

_____

freedmen;
Freedmen's
Bureau

_____

_____

Lincoln Assassinated! *(pages 502–503)*

Predicting

After you read the subsection, use the spaces below to answer the questions.

1. How do you think the Radical Republicans will view Johnson's plan? Why?

_____

_____

2. What do you think will happen as a result?

_____

_____

Terms To Know

Use the spaces below to describe the Thirteenth Amendment, a term in this lesson.

Thirteenth Amendment

_____

_____

Terms To Review

Read the passage below. In the spaces that follow, explain in your own words the meaning of the terms you studied earlier.

Johnson's plan required Southern state conventions to denounce <u>secession</u> and <u>ratify</u> the Thirteenth Amendment. To punish the wealthy slaveholders who had <u>dominated</u> the South before the war—and who he thought had tricked the Southern states into leaving the Union—he forced them to apply to him for a pardon.

secession
(Chapter 15, Section 4)

_____

_____

ratify
(Chapter 6, Section 4)

_____

_____

dominate
(Chapter 1, Section 3)

_____

_____

Now that you have read the section, write the answers to the questions that were included in **Setting a Purpose for Reading** *at the beginning of the section.*

How did the Reconstruction plans of Lincoln and the Radical Republicans differ?

_____

_____

What were President Johnson's Reconstruction plans?

_____

_____

Chapter 17 Section 2
Radicals in Control

(pages 504–508)

Reason To Read

Setting a Purpose for Reading Think about these questions as you read:
- What did some Southerners do to deprive freed people of their rights, and how did Congress respond?
- What were the main features of Radical Reconstruction?

Main Idea

As you read pages 504–508 in your textbook, complete this graphic organizer by providing information about impeachment.

Impeachment	
What is it?	
Who was impeached?	
Outcome of the trial?	

Sequencing Events

Read the following sentences. Choose the correct date from this lesson to complete the sentence by circling the date.

1. **Congress passed the first Civil Rights Act in (1865, 1866) to challenge the black codes passed in the South.**

2. **Congress passed the Fourteenth Amendment in 1866; it became official when it was ratified by Tennessee in (1868, 1878).**

3. **Congress passed the First Reconstruction Act in (1867, 1869).**

4. **Johnson was impeached in March (1867, 1868), but the Senate did not convict him.**

African Americans' Rights (pages 504–506)

Reviewing

Reread pages 504–506 and list a key fact about these topics.

> black codes ⟩ _____
> _____
> _____

> The Fourteenth Amendment ⟩ _____
> _____

Terms To Know

Read the following sentences. Choose the correct term from this lesson to complete the sentence by circling the term.

1. After the Civil War, new Southern state governments enacted (black codes, freedmen's codes) to limit the rights of African Americans.

2. Johnson vetoed the Freedmen's Bureau Act, but Congress voted to (override, uphold) that veto, making the Act a law.

3. The (Civil Rights Act of 1866, Freedmen's Bureau Act) gave full citizenship to African Americans.

4. Congress passed the (Fourteenth, Thirteenth) Amendment to make sure that African Americans were guaranteed their civil rights.

Academic Vocabulary

In the space available, define this academic vocabulary word from this lesson.

> exploit ⟩ _____
> _____

Radical Reconstruction (pages 506–508)

Identifying Cause and Effect

As you read the lesson, answer the following questions to identify the causes and effects of Radical Reconstruction.

Cause	Action	Effect
_____	Many white Southerners do not vote for constitutional conventions	_____
_____	Congress impeaches Johnson.	_____

Terms To Know

Match the term from this lesson in the left column with the correct definition in the right column by writing the letter in the space to the left of the term.

____ **1.** Fifteenth Amendment

____ **2.** First Reconstruction Act

____ **3.** impeach

____ **4.** Second Reconstruction Act

____ **5.** Tenure of Office Act

a. law that put Southern states under military rule
b. remove a president from office
c. constitutional change banning slavery
d. formally charge a president with wrongdoing
e. law that accepted newly formed Southern governments
f. constitutional change saying that African Americans were citizens
g. law that called for registration of new voters in the South
h. law barring presidents from firing top officials without Senate approval
i. constitutional change protecting African Americans' right to vote

Academic Vocabulary

Use each of the following academic vocabulary words in a sentence.

 confer

_____

_____

Key Points

Notes

register

Terms To Review

Write a definition of these words, which you studied earlier.

cabinet
(Chapter 8, Section 1)

guarantee
(Chapter 16, Section 4)

Section Wrap-up

Now that you have read the section, write the answers to the questions that were included in **Setting a Purpose for Reading** *at the beginning of the section.*

What did some Southerners do to deprive freed people of their rights, and how did Congress respond?

What were the main features of Radical Reconstruction?

Chapter 17 Section 3
The South During Reconstruction

(pages 509–512)

Reason To Read

Setting a Purpose for Reading Think about these questions as you read:
• What groups participated in Reconstruction in the South?
• How did Southern life change during Reconstruction?

Main Idea

As you read pages 509–512 in your textbook, complete this graphic organizer by listing the improvement in education that took place in the South during Reconstruction.

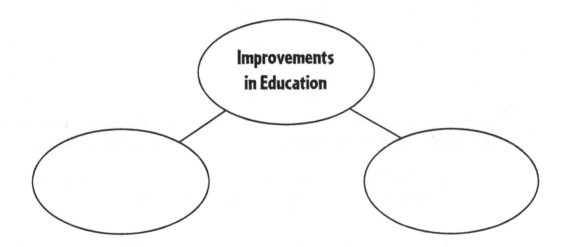

Sequencing Events

Read the following sentences. Choose the correct date from this lesson to complete the sentence by circling the date.

1. **Hiram Revels was elected to the Senate from Mississippi in (1868, 1870).**

2. **Congress passed the first of several laws aimed at breaking the power of the Ku Klux Klan in (1871, 1872).**

3. **In (1865, 1875), the Freedmen's Bank was established.**

New Groups Take Charge (pages 509–511)

Clarifying

As you read this lesson, answer the following questions to clarify the information about the South during Reconstruction.

1. What three groups formed the Republican Party in the Reconstruction South? What were they called?

   _____

   _____

2. What kind of representation did African Americans have in the new governments?

   _____

   _____

3. What did the Ku Klux Klan do?

   _____

   _____

Terms To Know

Read the following sentences. Choose the correct term from this lesson to complete the sentence by circling the term.

1. White Southerners who joined the Republicans were called (scalawags, scoundrels) by former Confederates.

2. Northern Republicans who came South during Reconstruction were given the name (carpetbaggers, invaders).

3. The (Knights of the South, Ku Klux Klan) used terror tactics to try to intimidate African Americans, especially near elections.

4. White Southerners accused the Republican state governments of (corruption, injustice), but those charges were mostly exaggerations.

Some Improvements *(pages 511–512)*

Outlining

Complete an outline that identifies improvements in education as you read the lesson.

Improvements in Education

A. _____

B. _____

C. _____

Terms To Know

Define or describe each of the following key terms from this lesson.

integrated

_____

_____

sharecropping

_____

_____

Section Wrap-up

Now that you have read the section, write the answers to the questions that were included in Setting a Purpose for Reading *at the beginning of the section.*

What groups participated in Reconstruction in the South?

_____

_____

How did Southern life change during Reconstruction?

_____

_____

Chapter 17 Section 4
Change in the South
(pages 513-520)

Reason To Read

Setting a Purpose for Reading Think about these questions as you read:
- What changes occurred in the South during the last years of Reconstruction?
- How were African Americans denied their rights?

Main Idea

As you read pages 513-520 in your textbook, complete this graphic organizer by listing the advantages and disadvantages of an agricultural economy.

Agricultural Economy	
Advantages	**Disadvantages**

Sequencing Events

As you read, write the number of the event in the appropriate circle on the time line:

1. **Poll taxes and literacy tests begin in Mississippi**
2. **Hayes wins presidency; Reconstruction ends**
3. **Supreme Court, in *Plessy* v. *Ferguson*, says segregation is constitutional**
4. **Congress passes Amnesty Act**

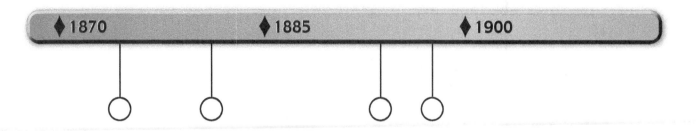

Reconstruction Declines (pages 513–515)

Interpreting

Interpret the information you read about the decline of Reconstruction by answering the following questions.

1. What factors led to the decline of Reconstruction?

_____

_____

2. What two issues caused Republicans to split from their party in 1872?

_____

_____

3. How did Democrats regain control of state governments in the South?

_____

_____

Terms To Know

Define or describe the following terms from this lesson.

Amnesty Act

_____

_____

reconciliation

_____

_____

Academic Vocabulary

Identify the academic vocabulary word from the list that best completes the sentence. Write your answer in the space provided.

principal   editor   professional

Horace Greeley, a newspaper _____ , ran for president in 1872.

The End of Reconstruction *(pages 515–517)*

Skimming

Skim the lesson by reading the text under each heading quickly to get a general idea of what it is about. Use one or two sentences to write that general idea in the spaces below.

The Election of 1876 >

_____

_____

_____

The Compromise of 1877 >

_____

_____

_____

_____

Terms To Know

Define or describe the following key term from this lesson.

commission >

_____

_____

Change in the South *(pages 517–518)*

Synthesizing

As you read the lesson, synthesize the information by answering the following questions.

1. How did the South change politically after the election of 1876?

_____

_____

2. How did the South change economically?

_____

_____

3. What happened in the rural South?

_____

_____

Terms To Know

Define or describe each of the following terms from this lesson.

> **Bessemer process**
> _____
> _____

> **cash crops**
> _____
> _____

> **Redeemers**
> _____
> _____

A Divided Society (pages 519–520)

Summarizing

As you read each subsection, write a one-sentence summary about each of these topics.

> **Jim Crow Laws**
> _____
> _____

> **Reconstruction's Impact**
> _____
> _____

Match the term from this lesson in the left column with the correct definition in the right column by writing the letter in the space to the left of the term.

_____ **1.** grandfather clauses

_____ **2.** Jim Crow laws

_____ **3.** literacy test

_____ **4.** lynching

_____ **5.** *Plessy* v. *Ferguson*

_____ **6.** poll tax

_____ **7.** segregation

a. law requiring voters to prove they could read

b. Supreme Court decision that allowed unequal facilities for African Americans and whites

c. policy of providing the same facilities for African Americans and whites

d. law allowing people to vote if ancestors had voted before Reconstruction

e. Supreme Court decision that struck down voting limits on African Americans

f. law that gave voting rights to females whose grandfathers had voted

g. having separate facilities for African Americans and whites

h. law that forced voters to pay money before voting

i. general name for laws that limited the rights of African Americans

j. killing by hanging

Now that you have read the section, write the answers to the questions that were included in **Setting a Purpose for Reading** *at the beginning of the section.*

What changes did the Redeemers and economic leaders play in the South?

_____

_____

How were African Americans denied their rights?

_____

_____

Chapter 18, Section 1
The Mining Booms

(pages 528–532)

Reason To Read

Setting a Purpose for Reading Think about these questions as you read:
- How did the rush to find gold and silver lead to the growth of new communities in the West?
- How did the development of the railroads affect the nation?

Main Idea

As you read pages 528–532 in your textbook, complete this graphic organizer by explaining why these places were significant to the mining boom.

	Significance
Pikes Peak	
Comstock Lode	
Promontory Point	

Sequencing Events

As you read, place the following events on the time line:
- **Transcontinental railroad completed**
- **Comstock Lode discovered**
- **Gold found on Pikes Peak**

◆1855   ◆1865   ◆1875

Mining Is Big Business (pages 528–529)

Skimming

Skim pages 528–529 by reading the text under each heading quickly to get a general idea of what it is about. Use one or two sentences to write that general idea in the spaces below.

Colorado Strike

_____

_____

_____

The Comstock Lode

_____

_____

_____

_____

Terms To Know

Read the following sentences. Choose the correct term from this lesson to complete the sentence by circling the term.

1. Miners hoped to find a rich deposit of minerals in rich streaks of ore called (lodes, veneers).

2. Miners dug out the (ore, vein) and then extracted the metal they wanted.

Academic Vocabulary

Read the following sentence. In the space below, write in your own words the meaning of the boldfaced *academic vocabulary word from this lesson.*

Expensive equipment was needed to **extract** the pure mineral from the surrounding rock.

extract

_____

_____

The Mining Frontier (pages 529–530)

Analyzing *As you read the lesson, give specific examples for each of the general statements.*

1. Boomtowns arose in the mining areas.

_____

_____

2. Later in the 1800s, mining operations focused on metals other than gold and silver.

_____

_____

Terms To Know *Choose a term from this lesson from the list below to complete each sentence by writing the term in the correct space. You will not use all the terms.*

boomtowns   citizen   cities

ghost towns   mining camps   vigilante

1. After mines were closed, people abandoned the thriving communities and left them as _____ .

2. Some people formed _____ groups, which dealt out justice without using courts.

3. When mining was being carried out at a high level, nearby communities grew and came to be called _____ .

Railroads Connect East and West (pages 530–532)

Evaluating *Read the lesson and then answer the questions to evaluate what you read.*

1. Why was transportation important to the mining communities?

_____

_____

Chapter 18, Section 1

2. How did the economy benefit from the coming of the railroad to the West?

_____

_____

Terms To Know

Define or describe the following key terms from this lesson.

subsidies

_____

_____

transcontinental

_____

_____

Academic Vocabulary

Read the following sentences. In the space below, write in your own words the meaning of the **boldfaced** academic vocabulary word from this lesson.

1. When the final work on the transcontinental railroad **occurred**, the news was telegraphed across the country.

_____

_____

2. The government **purchased** land or obtained it from Native Americans by treaties and gave some of that land to railroad companies.

_____

_____

3. Railroad lines needed a way to make it easy for everyone to follow their train **schedules**, so they created standard time zones across the country.

_____

_____

Chapter 18, Section 1

Now that you have read the section, write the answers to the questions that were included in **Setting a Purpose for Reading** *at the beginning of the section.*

How did the rush to find gold and silver lead to the growth of new communities in the West?

_____

_____

_____

How did the development of the railroads affect the nation?

_____

_____

_____

Chapter 18, Section 2
Ranchers and Farmers

(pages 534–539)

Reason To Read

Setting a Purpose for Reading Think about these questions as you read:
- How did the railroads help create a "Cattle Kingdom" in the Southwest?
- How did women contribute to the settling of the Great Plains?

Main Idea

As you read pages 534–539 in your textbook, complete this graphic organizer by listing the challenges settlers faced on the Great Plains.

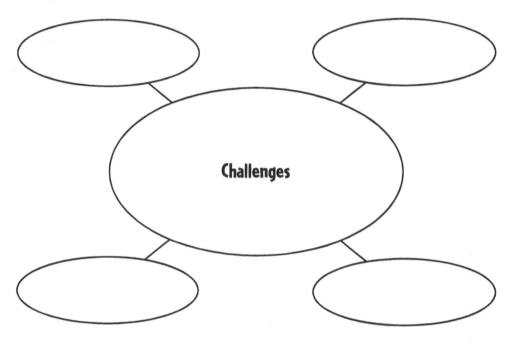

Challenges

Sequencing Events

As you read, write the year in which these events took place.

_____ **Oklahoma opens for settlement**

_____ **Missouri Pacific Railroad reaches Missouri**

_____ **Congress passes Homestead Act**

Cattle on the Plains (pages 534–535)

Identifying Cause and Effect

As you read the lesson, list the causes and effects of the first cattle drive.

Cause	Action	Effect
1. _____ _____ _____	**The First Cattle Drive**	1. _____ _____ _____
2. _____ _____ _____		2. _____ _____ _____
3. _____ _____ _____		3. _____ _____ _____

Terms To Know

Match the term from this lesson in the left column with the correct definition in the right column by writing the letter in the space to the left of the term.

_____ **1.** brand

_____ **2.** Chisholm Trail

_____ **3.** cow town

_____ **4.** Goodnight-Loving Trail

_____ **5.** Long Drive

_____ **6.** longhorn

_____ **7.** open range

a. destination for cattle drive

b. route from Texas through New Mexico to the north

c. herding of cattle 1,000 miles or more

d. symbol marking cattle trail

e. breed of cattle raised in Texas

f. route from Texas through Louisiana to the north

g. land not fenced or divided

h. route from Texas to Abilene

i. breed of cattle that could not survive drives

j. symbol placed on cattle's hide to show ownership

k. route that brought cattle from Texas to Montana

 **Key Points**

 **Notes**

Terms To Review

Use each of these terms, which you studied earlier, in a sentence that reflects the term's meaning.

decade
(Chapter 10, Section 2)

_____

_____

_____

locate
(Chapter 13, Section 2)

_____

_____

Life on the Trail (pages 535–536)

Visualizing

Read the lesson about life on the trail and try to picture what a cattle drive was like. Then write three sentences describing what you see.

_____

_____

_____

_____

_____

Terms To Know

Choose a term from this lesson from the list below to complete each sentence by writing the term in the correct space.

chaps   brand   lariat   stampede   vaqueros

1. Cowhands feared a _____, since thousands of animals would be running in a panic.

2. Hispanic ranch hands of the Spanish Southwest, called

_____ , developed many of the tools and techniques of herding cattle.

3. The rope, or _____ , was one of the cowhand's most important tools

4. Cowhands wore leather leggings called _____ to protect their legs from brush.

Academic Vocabulary

Read the sentence below. Put a checkmark in the space before the phrase that best explains what the academic vocabulary word derive, *from this lesson, means in this sentence.*

Much of the language used by ranchers even today <u>derives</u> from Spanish words used by Hispanic cowhands of the Southwest for centuries.

_____ has developed

_____ has ignored

_____ has been translated from

Farmers Settle the Plains *(pages 537–539)*

Determining the Main Idea

Write down the main idea of this lesson and at least three details that support that idea.

_____

_____

_____

_____

Terms To Know

Read the following sentences. Choose the correct term from this lesson to complete the sentence by circling the term.

1. By passing the (Homestead Act, Plains Act), Congress encouraged people to settle on the Plains.

2. A family could gain land by (homesteading, squatting).

3. African Americans who moved from the South to Kansas were called ("Exodusters," Free Soilers).

 Notes

4. Farmers on the Plains used (barbed wire, hurricane) fences because they had no wood.

5. Farmers on the Plains had to develop a new technique called (dry farming, sod farming).

6. Because farmers had to break through the thick grass on the Plains, they were called (grass busters, sodbusters).

7. The people who took part in the Oklahoma land rush of 1889 were called (boomers, okies).

8. Some people had settled on the Oklahoma land before the official opening, gaining the name (cheaters, sooners).

Academic Vocabulary

Read the following sentences. In the space below, write in your own words the meaning of the **boldfaced** *academic vocabulary word from this lesson.*

1. Several **factors** influenced thousands of people to settle on the Plains.

_____

2. After settlers **filed** a claim to land, they could settle on it.

_____

 Section Wrap-up

Now that you have read the section, write the answers to the questions that were included in **Setting a Purpose for Reading** *at the beginning of the section.*

How did the railroads help create a "Cattle Kingdom" in the Southwest?

_____

_____

How did women contribute to the settling of the Great Plains?

_____

_____

Native American Struggles

(pages 542–547)

Reason To Read

Setting a Purpose for Reading Think about these questions as you read:
- Why did the government force Native Americans to move to reservations?
- How did conflict between Native Americans and whites grow?

Main Idea

As you read pages 542–547 in your textbook, complete this graphic organizer by describing how Western settlement affected Native Americans

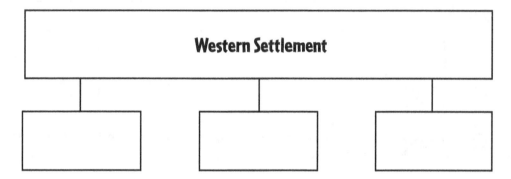

Sequencing Events

Read the following sentences. Choose the correct date from this lesson to complete the sentence by circling the date.

1. In (1870, 1872), hunters began targeting buffalo to sell the hides in the East.

2. Native Americans attacked whites in the Fetterman Massacre in (1864, 1866).

3. White volunteers killed hundreds of Cheyenne at Sand Creek in (1864, 1866).

4. Custer and his troops were wiped out after he ordered an attack on a larger Native American force on June 25, (1870, 1876).

5. The Dawes Act changed Native American policy in (1887, 1890).

6. A confrontation turned into fierce fighting at Wounded Knee in (1887, 1890).

Following the Buffalo (pages 542–543)

Analyzing

Spanish explorers introduced horses to Native Americans. Analyze how the lives of the Plains peoples in North America might have been changed by having horses.

_____

_____

_____

Terms To Know

Define or describe the following key term.

nomadic

_____

_____

Conflict (pages 543–547)

Clarifying

Answer the following questions to clarify the information in this lesson.

1. What happened when the government first began pushing its policy of putting Native Americans on reservations?

_____

_____

2. Which group suffered in the Fetterman Massacre? Which group suffered in the attack at Sand Creek?

_____

_____

3. What led to the fighting in the Black Hills?

_____

_____

4. How did government policy toward Native Americans change in 1887?

_____

_____

5. What happened to the Sioux in 1890?

_____

_____

Terms To Know

Read the following sentences. Choose the correct term from this lesson to complete the sentence by circling the term.

1. In the 1860s, the government began to push hard on its policy of placing Native Americans on special tracts of land called (preserves, reservations).

2. In 1866, a Native American attack on fewer than 100 soldiers resulted in an army defeat called the (Fetterman Massacre, Sand Creek Massacre).

3. In 1887, the (Dawes Act, Indian Removal Act) changed policy toward Native Americans in an effort to lead them to adopt white culture.

4. The government's attempt to stop the (Ghost Dance, Sun Dance) ritual ended in tragedy in 1890.

Academic Vocabulary

Write two words that are related to the academic vocabulary word site *from this lesson.*

site >

_____

_____

Now that you have read the section, write the answers to the questions that were included in **Setting a Purpose for Reading** *at the beginning of the section.*

Why did the government force Native Americans to move to reservations?

_____

_____

How did conflict between Native Americans and whites grow?

_____

_____

Chapter 18, Section 4
Farmers in Protest

(pages 548–551)

Reason To Read

Setting a Purpose for Reading Think about these questions as you read:
- Why did farmers face hard times in the late 1800s?
- How did farmers try to solve their problems?

Main Idea

As you read pages 548–551 in your textbook, complete this graphic organizer by identifying the problems farmers faced in the late 1800s.

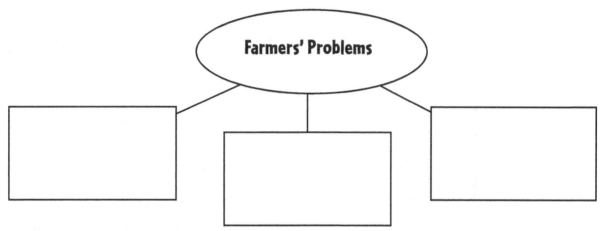

Sequencing Events

As you read, put the following events in the correct order by writing a number from 1 to 4 in the space to the left. Use the number 1 for the event that occurred first, 2 for the next event, and so on.

_____ **A.** Farmers' Alliances formed in West and South

_____ **B.** Populist Party formed

_____ **C.** Grange issues a declaration of purpose

_____ **D.** Populist Party nominates Bryan for president

 **Key Points**

 **Notes**

The Farmers Organize *(pages 548–549)*

Monitoring Comprehension — *Check how well you understood what you read in this lesson by answering the following questions.*

1. What financial problems did farmers have?

_____

_____

2. What factors did they blame for those problems?

_____

_____

3. How did the National Grange try to help farmers both individually and as a group?

_____

_____

4. How did the Alliances plan to help farmers financially?

_____

_____

Terms To Know — *Choose a term from this lesson from the list below to complete each sentence by writing the term in the correct space. You will not use all the terms.*

associations   cooperatives   Farmers' Alliances   National Grange

1. The_____ helped break up the loneliness of rural life by staging social gatherings.

2. Regional differences and personality conflicts kept the

_____ from being very influential.

3. Some farmers joined in _____ , where they bought produce from each other.

Terms To Review

Use each of the following terms, which you studied earlier, in a sentence that reflects the meaning of the term.

federal
(Chapter 16, Section 5)

_____
_____
_____

repeal
(Chapter 5, Section 1)

_____
_____
_____

A Party of the People *(pages 550–551)*

Summarizing

Write a one-sentence summary on each of the following topics.

The Populist Party

_____
_____
_____

The Election of 1896

_____
_____

Terms To Know

Define or describe the following key terms from this lesson.

free silver

_____
_____
_____

populism

_____
_____
_____

Populist Party

_____
_____
_____

Terms To Review

Use each of these terms, which you studied earlier, in a sentence that reflects the term's meaning.

debtor
(Chapter 3, Section 4)

_____

_____

_____

inflation
(Chapter 6, Section 2)

_____

_____

Section Wrap-up

Now that you have read the section, write the answers to the questions that were included in **Setting a Purpose for Reading** *at the beginning of the section.*

Why did farmers face hard times in the late 1800s?

_____

_____

How did farmers try to solve their problems?

_____

_____

Chapter 19, Section 1
Railroads Lead the Way

(pages 556–559)

Reason To Read

Setting a Purpose for Reading Think about these questions as you read:
• How did the railroad barons make huge fortunes?
• How did the national railroad system change the American economy?

Main Idea

As you read pages 556–559 in your textbook, complete this graphic organizer.
Describe how a national railroad system contributed to the growth of industry.

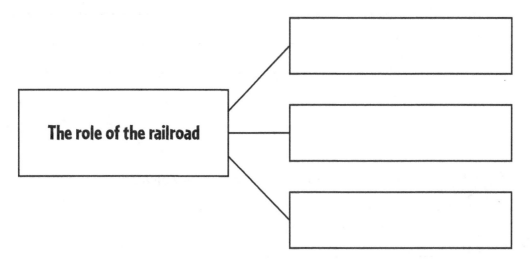

The role of the railroad

Sequencing Events

As you read, put the following events in the correct order by writing a number
from 1 to 3 in the space to the left. Use the number 1 for the event that
occurred first, 2 for the next event, and so on.

_____ **A. Railroads adopt standard gauge**

_____ **B. Nation has almost 250,000 total miles of track**

_____ **C. First transcontinental railroad completed**

Railroad Expansion (pages 556–557)

Outlining

Complete this outline as you read pages 556–557. The first part has been done for you.

I. The Spread of Railroads

    A. Measures of growth

        1. 1869—transcontinental railroad; 1890s—5 lines

        2. 1860—30,000 miles of track; 1900—250,000 miles

    B. Trend toward consolidation

II. Railroad Barons

    A. _____

        1. _____

        2. _____

        3. _____

    B. _____

Terms To Know

Define or describe the following key terms.

consolidation >

_____

_____

railroad barons >

_____

_____

Railroads Stimulate the Economy (pages 557–559)

Analyzing

Analyze the information in this lesson by answering the following questions.

1. What industries grew partly as a result of the construction of railroads and their spread?

_____

_____

2. What was the advantage of adopting a standard gauge?

_____

_____

Terms To Know

Read the following sentences. Choose the correct term from this lesson to complete the sentence by circling the term.

1. By adopting (regular, standard) gauges, railroads cut the time and cost of moving goods.

2. Large railroads offered (Pullman cars, rebates) to their biggest customers, cutting their costs for shipping.

3. By forming (cooperatives, pools), the railroad companies fixed prices in a region.

Academic Vocabulary

In the space available, define the following academic vocabulary words from this lesson.

refine

_____

_____

unify

_____

_____

Section Wrap-up

Now that you have read the section, write the answers to the questions that were included in **Setting a Purpose for Reading** _at the beginning of the section._

How did the railroad barons make huge fortunes?

_____

_____

How did the national railroad system change the American economy?

_____

_____

Chapter 19, Section 2
Inventions

(pages 561-566)

Reason To Read

Setting a Purpose for Reading Think about these questions as you read:
- What changes in transportation and communication transformed America?
- How did labor-saving inventions, such as the vacuum cleaner, affect life?

Main Idea

As you read pages 561-566 in your textbook, complete this graphic organizer by listing each person's invention.

	Invention
Samuel Morse	
Alexander Bell	
Thomas Edison	

Sequencing Events

As you read, place the following events on the time line:
- **Bell invents the telephone**
- **Field lays telegraph cable across Atlantic Ocean**
- **Westinghouse invents electrical transformer**
- **Thurman develops vacuum cleaner**
- **Burroughs invents adding machine, Kodak invents camera**
- **Edison invents workable lightbulb**

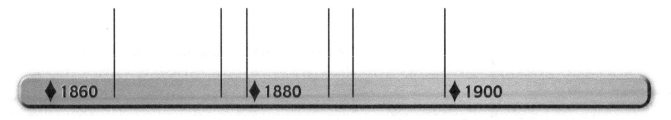

1860   1880   1900

Communication Changes (pages 561–563)

Clarifying

Write at least three details that support the main idea below.

Main Idea ▶ During the 1800s, many new inventions dramatically changed communications.

_____

_____

_____

_____

The Genius of Invention (pages 563–564)

Sequencing

As you read, put the following inventions in the correct order by writing a number from 1 to 5 in the space to the left. Use the number 1 for the event that occurred first, 2 for the next event, and so on.

_____ **a.** Transformer

_____ **b.** Typewriter

_____ **c.** Vacuum cleaner

_____ **d.** Lightbulb

_____ **e.** Box camera

Academic Vocabulary

Explain how the academic vocabulary words device *and* mechanism, *both found in this lesson, are similar.*

_____

_____

A Changing Society (pages 564–566)

Reviewing

Reread each subsection and list two key facts from each.

Henry Ford's Automobiles

_____

_____

_____

Selling Goods

_____

_____

_____

Terms To Know

Write one or more sentences connecting the following key terms from this lesson: **assembly line, mass production,** *and* **Model T.**

_____

_____

_____

_____

Academic Vocabulary

Write two words that are related to the academic vocabulary word from this lesson.

assign

_____

_____

 *Now that you have read the section, write the answers to the questions that were included in* Setting a Purpose for Reading *at the beginning of the section.*

What changes in transportation and communication transformed America?

_____

_____

How did labor-saving inventions, such as the vacuum cleaner, affect life?

_____

_____

Chapter 19, Section 3
An Age of Big Business
(pages 567–571)

Reason To Read

Setting a Purpose for Reading Think about these questions as you read:
- How did new discoveries and inventions help industries grow?
- Why did the development of large corporations bring both benefits and problems?

Main Idea

As you read pages 567–571 in your textbook, complete this graphic organizer by explaining the significance of each of these concepts to business in the late 1800s.

	Significance
Shareholders	
Stock exchanges	
Mergers	

Sequencing Events

As you read, write the correct dates for each of these events:

_____ **Drake drills oil well in Titusville, Pennsylvania**

_____ **Rockefeller organizes Standard Oil of Ohio**

_____ **Rockefeller forms an oil trust**

_____ **Congress passes Sherman Antitrust Act**

_____ **Morgan and others form U.S. Steel**

Foundations for Growth (pages 567–568)

Questioning

As you read pages 567–568, write an important detail about each of these topics.

Factors of Production

_____

_____

Raising Capital

_____

_____

Growth of Corporations

_____

_____

Terms To Know

Match the term from this lesson in the left column with the correct definition in the right column by writing the letter in the space to the left of the term.

_____ **1.** capital

_____ **2.** corporation

_____ **3.** dividend

_____ **4.** factors of production

_____ **5.** land

_____ **6.** labor

_____ **7.** shareholder

_____ **8.** stock

_____ **9.** stock exchange

a. partial owner of a company

b. partner

c. all the human effort needed to make goods

d. place where livestock is traded

e. workers organized in unions

f. all the buildings, machinery, and tools used to make goods

g. type of business that can raise large amounts of money

h. all the natural resources needed to make goods

i. three categories of resources needed to make goods

j. cash paid to a business's owners out of profits the business earned

k. place where shares in corporations are traded

l. paper that represents part ownership in a company

m. one of two or more people who share in founding a company

n. working together

The Oil Business *(pages 569–570)*

Summarizing

As you read each subsection, write a one-sentence summary about each of these topics.

Rise of the Oil Business ⟩ _____

_____

John D. Rockefeller ⟩ _____

_____

_____

The Standard Oil Trust ⟩ _____

_____

Terms To Know

Match the term from this lesson in the left column with the correct definition in the right column by writing the letter in the space to the left of the term.

____ **1.** horizontal integration

____ **2.** monopoly

____ **3.** trust

a. group of companies managed by the same board of directors

b. a plant that processes a raw material

c. control of a company by a single set of owners

d. combining competing firms into one corporation

e. almost total control of an industry by a single producer

Academic Vocabulary

Define or describe partner, *an academic vocabulary word in this lesson.*

_____

_____

Terms To Review

Read the sentence below. In the spaces that follow, explain the meaning of the boldfaced term you studied earlier.

Rockefeller persuaded the railroads to give him a **rebate** on his shipping costs.

rebate
(Chapter 19, Section 1)

_____

_____

The Steel Business *(pages 570–571)*

Scanning

Scan "The Steel Business" by reading the headings. Then write down three topics you think will be covered in "The Steel Business."

_____

_____

_____

_____

_____

_____

Terms To Know

Read the following sentences. Choose the correct term from this lesson to complete the sentence by circling the term.

1. Carnegie used (horizontal, vertical) integration, acquiring his suppliers, to build his steel company.

2. Many corporate leaders grew interested in (philanthropy, philosophy) and gave millions of dollars to cultural and educational organizations.

3. New state laws encouraged corporations to carry out (the Bessemer process, mergers) and grow larger.

4. The Sherman (Antitrust, Anti-Corporate) Act aimed to block corporations from doing business in ways that would hurt competition.

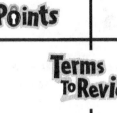 **Key Points**

 **Notes**

Terms To Review

Read the sentence below. In the spaces that follow, explain the meaning of the boldfaced term you studied earlier.

Carnegie bought ships that carried iron **ore** to cut the cost of getting that important raw material.

ore
(Chapter 18, Section 1)

_____

_____

Section Wrap-up

Now that you have read the section, write the answers to the questions that were included in Setting a Purpose for Reading *at the beginning of the section.*

How did new discoveries and inventions help industries grow?

_____

_____

Why did the development of large corporations bring both benefits and problems?

_____

_____

Chapter 19, Section 4
Industrial Workers

(pages 573–575)

Reason To Read

Setting a Purpose for Reading Think about these questions as you read:
- Why did workers demand changes in their working conditions and wages?
- How did the membership of the Knights of Labor differ from that of the American Federation of Labor (AFL)?

Main Idea

As you read pages 573–575 in your textbook, complete this graphic organizer by listing actions that labor unions took to improve working conditions.

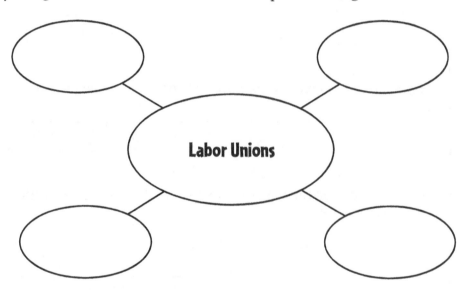

Labor Unions

Sequencing Events

As you read, place the following events on the time line:
- Haymarket Riot occurs in Chicago
- Triangle Shirtwaist Company fire kills almost 150
- Knights of Labor established
- Pullman strike begins

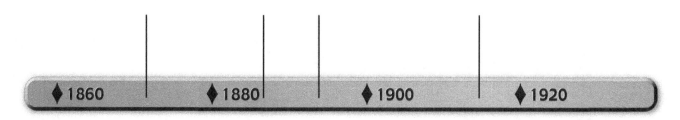

◆ 1860   ◆ 1880   ◆ 1900   ◆ 1920

Key Points

Working Conditions (pages 572–573)

Interpreting

Interpret the information you read about working conditions in the late 1800s by answering the following questions.

1. How hard did factory workers work?

   _____

   _____

2. How safe were working conditions?

   _____

   _____

   _____

   _____

3. How were women workers treated compared to men workers?

   _____

   _____

4. Why did child labor laws not fix the problems associated with children working?

   _____

   _____

Terms To Review

In the space available, define the following word you studied earlier.

mass production
(Chapter 19, Section 2)

_____

_____

Labor Unions Form (pages 573–574)

Responding   *As you study the lesson, respond to the following questions.*

1. What groups did the Knights of Labor accept that other unions did not?

_____

_____

2. What aims did the AFL have?

_____

_____

3. What was the result of the Triangle Shirtwaist Company fire?

_____

_____

Clarifying   *Imagine that you are an industrial worker in the late 1800s. List the advantages and disadvantages of joining a union.*

_____

_____

Terms To Know   *Read the following sentences. Choose the correct term from this lesson to complete the sentence by circling the term.*

1. One of the earliest labor movements, which gained more than 700,000 members, was the (Knights of Labor, Laborers' Collective).

2. The (American Federation of Labor, Congress of Laborers) was formed when several national trade unions joined together.

3. A fire in the factory of the (Triangle Shirtwaist Company, Triborough Textile Company) led to the deaths of nearly 150 workers.

4. Some unions fought for the right of (collective bargaining, collective ownership).

5. (Technical unions, Trade unions) were formed by everyone who worked in a particular craft.

6. The International Ladies' (Garment Workers, Textile Workers) Union tried to get safer conditions for its workers.

The Unions Act *(page 575)*

Synthesizing *Read the section on major strikes and then write two or three sentences summarizing it.*

_____

_____

_____

Terms To Know *Choose a term from this lesson from the list below to complete each sentence by writing the term in the correct space.*

| Haymarket Riot | Homestead Strike | injunctions |
| Pullman Strike | strikebreakers | corporations |

1. The _____ ended when federal troops were sent to stop the workers.

2. Violence in the _____ resulted in the deaths of several police officers and cost unions public support.

3. The government sometimes got _____ to block workers from striking.

4. Some companies used _____ to replace striking workers.

5. The _____ produced violence that the Pennsylvania state militia ended.

Terms To Review

Use each of the following terms you studied earlier in a sentence.

depression
(Chapter 7, Section 2)

_____

_____

militia
(Chapter 4, Section 3)

_____

_____

Section Wrap-up

Now that you have read the section, write the answers to the questions that were included in Setting a Purpose for Reading *at the beginning of the section.*

Why did workers demand changes in their working conditions and wages?

_____

_____

How did the membership of the Knights of Labor differ from that of the AFL?

_____

_____

_____

Chapter 20, Section 1
The New Immigrants

(pages 582–587)

Reason To Read

Setting a Purpose for Reading Think about these questions as you read:
- What opportunities and difficulties did immigrants find in the United States?
- How did the arrival of new immigrants change American society?

Main Idea

As you read pages 582–587 in your textbook, complete this graphic organizer by writing the reasons immigrants came to America

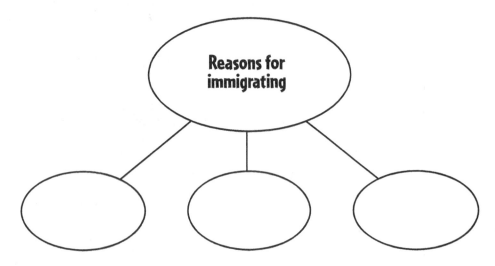

Sequencing Events

As you read, write the correct dates for each of these events:

_____ U.S. and Japan reach "gentleman's agreement" limiting Japanese immigration

_____ Statue of Liberty first appears in New York Harbor

_____ Ellis Island becomes station for processing immigrants

_____ Congress passes Chinese Exclusion Act

_____ Congress passes Immigration Act

A Flood of Immigrants (pages 582–583)

Comparing and Contrasting

After reading the lesson, answer the following questions to make some comparisons about the immigration of the late 1800s.

1. How did the "new" immigrants compare to the "old" immigrants?

_____

_____

2. What problems in Europe were "push" factors that led people to emigrate? What features of American life were "pull" factors that attracted them to the United States?

_____

_____

Terms To Know

Read the following sentences. Choose the correct term from this lesson to complete the sentence by circling the term.

1. In the late 1800s and early 1900s, millions of people (emigrated, assimilated) from Europe for the United States.

2. Some (ethnic groups, enslaved groups) suffered persecution in their homelands, persuading them to leave for a new life.

Terms To Review

In the space available, define the following word you studied earlier.

discrimination
(Chapter 13, Section 2)

_____

_____

The Journey to America (page 584)

Drawing Conclusions

Read the lesson and then answer the questions to draw conclusions about what you read.

1. Why was the journey of immigrants to America difficult?

_____

_____

2. Why were immigrants taken through Ellis Island or Angel Island?

_____

_____

3. What information was taken about the immigrants?

_____

_____

Terms To Know

Define or describe each of the following key terms from this lesson.

Statue of Liberty >

_____

_____

steerage >

_____

_____

The Immigrant Experience (pages 584–586)

Responding

As you read the lesson, give examples for the following topics.

Where Immigrants Worked >

_____

_____

> **Difficulties
> Adjusting**

> **Forming
> Communities**

**Terms
To Know**
Write a sentence that explains the meaning of assimilate, *a
term from this lesson.*

> **assimilate**

**Academic
Vocabulary**
*Read the sentence below. Put a checkmark in the space
before the word or phrase that best explains what the
boldfaced academic vocabulary word from this lesson
means in this sentence.*

Language **highlighted** the differences among immigrant grandparents,
parents, and children.

_____ heightened   _____ revealed   _____ shined a light on

Nativist Movement (pages 586–587)

**Monitoring
Comprehension**
*Check how well you understood what you read in this
lesson by answering the following questions.*

1. What fears did native-born American workers have about immigrants?

_____

_____

2. How did the government respond to the fears of immigration?

_____

_____

3. What group spoke out in support of immigrants?

_____

_____

Terms To Know

Using the spaces below, define or describe each of the following key terms form this lesson.

Chinese Exclusion Act

_____

_____

Immigration Act of 1917

_____

_____

nativist

_____

_____

Academic Vocabulary

Read the sentence below. Put a checkmark in the space before the word or phrase that best explains what the boldfaced academic vocabulary word, from this lesson means in this sentence.

The effects of immigration were most **visible** in the cities.

_____ easily seen   _____ obscured from view   _____ unclear

Section Wrap-up

Now that you have read the section, write the answers to the questions that were included in Setting a Purpose for Reading *at the beginning of the section.*

What opportunities and difficulties did immigrants find in the United States?

_____

_____

How did the arrival of new immigrants change American society?

_____

_____

Chapter 20, Section 2
Moving to the City

(pages 590–595)

Reason To Read

Setting a Purpose for Reading Think about these questions as you read:
- How did American cities grow and change?
- What problems did cities face and how did people try to solve them?

Main Idea

As you read pages 590–595 in your textbook, complete this graphic organizer by listing three serious problems facing American cities in the late 1800s.

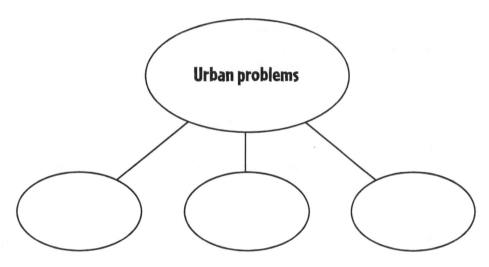

Urban problems

Sequencing Events

As you read, place the following events on the time line:

- **Woolworth Building completed in New York**
- **Brooklyn Bridge opens**
- **Chicago's World's Fair begins**
- **New York opens first section of its subway**

♦ 1880   ♦ 1900   ♦ 1920

Growth of Cities (pages 590–592)

Determining the Main Idea

Write down the main idea of this lesson and at least three details that support that idea.

Main Idea ▷

_____

_____

_____

_____

_____

_____

Terms To Know

Choose a term from this lesson from the list below to complete each sentence by writing the term in the correct space. You will not use all the terms.

Gilded Age   slums   suburbs

tenements   Wealthy Age

1. Many people in the growing middle class lived comfortably in

   _____ just outside the cities.

2. Immigrants crowded into _____ , or apartment buildings.

3. Two writers, looking at the lifestyles of the few fabulously wealthy and the poverty of the many poor, called the late 1800s the

   _____ .

4. The city's poor lived in run-down neighborhoods called

   _____ .

Academic Vocabulary

Define or describe the following academic vocabulary words from this lesson.

migrate ▷

_____

_____

Key Points	Notes

professional >

Cities in Crisis (pages 592–593)

Inferring

Read the lesson and then answer the questions to make inferences about what you read.

1. How good do you think fire protection was in cities of the late 1800s and early 1900s? Why?

_____

_____

2. How safe would you say cities were? Why?

_____

_____

3. How do you think immigrants responded to the settlement houses? Why?

_____

_____

Terms To Know

Read the following sentences. Choose the correct term from this lesson to complete the sentence by circling the term.

1. Religious groups set up the (YMCA and YWCA, NBA and WNBA) to provide recreational opportunities for city children.

2. (Halfway houses, Settlement houses) like (Addams House, Hull House) provided teaching and help to immigrant families in the cities.

The Changing City *(pages 593–595)*

Outlining   *Complete this outline as you read the section.*

I. Building Up—Not Out

    A. _____

        1. _____

        2. _____

    B. _____

II. New Designs

    A. _____

    B. _____

III. New Forms of Transportation

    A. _____

    B. _____

IV. Building Bridges

    A. _____

    B. _____

    C. _____

Terms To Know   *Match the term from this lesson in the left column with the correct description in the right column by writing the letter in the space to the left of the term.*

_____ **1.** Brooklyn Bridge

_____ **2.** Eads Bridge

_____ **3.** skyscraper

_____ **4.** Woolworth Building

    a. high-rising building

    b. office building in New York City

    c. crosses Missouri River

    d. crosses Mississippi River

    e. connects Brooklyn and Manhattan

    f. connects Brooklyn and Long Island

    g. crowded apartment building

Academic Vocabulary

Circle the letter of the word or phrase that has the closest meaning to the underlined academic vocabulary word from this lesson.

1. Architect Louis Sullivan and his <u>colleagues</u> changed the face of America's cities with the new buildings they designed.

   a. fellow architects   **b.** friends   **c.** rivals

2. The buildings that American architects designed <u>adapted</u> the appearance of traditional European buildings to create a whole new look.

   a. copied   **b.** departed from   **c.** used, but with changes

3. The result of the architects' work was to create a special American <u>style</u>.

   a. design   **b** manner of speaking   **c** way of dressing

Now that you have read the section, write the answers to the questions that were included in **Setting a Purpose for Reading** *at the beginning of the section.*

How did American cities grow and change?

_____

_____

What problems did cities face and how did people try to solve them?

_____

_____

Chapter 20, Section 3
A Changing Culture
(pages 597–602)

Reason To Read

Setting a Purpose for Reading Think about these questions as you read:
- How did education become more widely available?
- How did Americans spend their leisure time?

Main Idea

As you read pages 597–602 in your textbook, complete this graphic organizer
by describing the achievements of the persons listed.

	Achievements
John Dewey	
George Washington Carver	
Mary Cassatt	
Scott Joplin	

Sequencing Events

Read the following sentences. Choose the correct date from this section
to complete the sentence by circling the date.

1. By (1904, 1914), most states required children to attend school.
2. The Morrill Act of (1862, 1882) gave states large amounts of
   land that could be sold to raise money for education.
3. Booker T. Washington opened the Tuskegee Institute in (1871,
   1881) to train teachers for African Americans.
4. In (1880, 1881) Andrew Carnegie donated millions of dollars to
   found libraries.
5. Joseph Pulitzer bought the New York *World* in (1883, 1888) and
   began to change journalism.

Expanding Education (pages 597–600)

Clarifying

As you read this lesson, answer the following questions to clarify the information about education in the late 1800s and early 1900s.

1. How many children attended school in this period?

_____

_____

2. How did a new idea aim to change education?

_____

_____

Terms To Know

Define or describe the following key terms.

Morrill Act

_____

_____

land-grant colleges

_____

_____

Tuskegee Institute

_____

_____

Academic Vocabulary

In the space available, define the following academic vocabulary word from this lesson.

institute

_____

_____

Key Points

Notes

A Nation of Readers (pages 600–601)

Skimming

Skim the lesson by reading the text under each heading quickly to get a general idea of what it is about. Use one or two sentences to write that general idea in the spaces below.

Public Libraries

_____

_____

_____

Spreading the News

_____

_____

_____

Changes in Literature

_____

_____

_____

Terms To Know

Match the term from this lesson in the left column with the correct definition in the right column by writing the letter in the space to the left of the term.

_____ **1.** realism

_____ **2.** regionalism

_____ **3.** yellow journalism

a. writing that focused on a particular area of the country

b. writing that focused on political news

c. writing that covered news in sensational ways

d. writing that aimed to portray people's actual lives

e. writing that tried to explore new areas of life

Art, Music, and Leisure (pages 601–602)

Outlining

Complete this outline as you read the lesson.

I. American Artists

   A. _____

   B. _____

II. Music in America

   A. _____

   B. _____

   C. _____

III. Leisure Time

A. _____

    1. _____

    2. _____

    3. _____

B. _____

C. _____

    1. _____

    2. _____

Terms To Know

Read the following sentences. Choose the correct term from this lesson to complete the sentence by circling the term.

1. A new music style called (blues, jazz) arose that combined elements of work songs, gospel music, spirituals, and African rhythms.

2. Another music style, (ragtime, rock and roll), used complex rhythms and became the dominant force in music in the early 1900s.

3. (Participatory, Spectator) sports like baseball and football became popular in this period.

4. (Yellow journalism, Vaudeville) offered many different kinds of entertainment, such as dancing, singing, and comedy.

Section Wrap-up

Now that you have read the section, write the answers to the questions that were included in Setting a Purpose for Reading *at the beginning of the section.*

How did education become more widely available?

_____

_____

How did Americans spend their leisure time?

_____

_____

Chapter 21, Section 1
The Progressive Movement

(pages 610-614)

Reason To Read

Setting a Purpose for Reading Think about these questions as you read:
- How did journalists help shape the reform movement?
- How did cities, states, and Congress answer the call for reform of the government?

Main Idea

As you read pages 610-614 in your textbook, complete this graphic organizer by listing two or more reforms for each category.

Reforms		
Government	**Business**	**Voting**

Sequencing Events

As you read, write the correct dates for each of these events:

_____ **Tidal wave destroys Galveston, leading to adoption of new form of city government**

_____ **Congress passes Pendleton Act, creating Civil Service Commission**

_____ **Seventeenth Amendment ratified**

_____ **Tom Johnson brings reform to Cleveland, Ohio**

_____ **Garfield assassinated by unsuccessful office seeker**

Fighting Corruption (pages 610–612)

Clarifying

As you read this lesson, answer the following questions to clarify the information about the progressive movement.

1. How did political machines work in the cities?

_____

_____

2. What steps were made to fight this corruption?

_____

_____

3. How did the way federal government jobs were filled change?

_____

_____

Terms To Know

Match the term from this lesson in the left column with the correct definition in the right column by writing the letter in the space to the left of the term.

_____ **1.** civil service

_____ **2.** Civil Service Commission

_____ **3.** kickback

_____ **4.** patronage

_____ **5.** Pendleton Act

_____ **6.** political boss

_____ **7.** political machine

a. name for civilians who work alongside the armed forces

b. law that changed the way jobs were filled in the federal government

c. name given to the granting of jobs to friends under the spoils system

d. name for all nonelected government workers

e. the group of corrupt officials who run city government

f. law that outlawed corruption in city politics

g. money which came from charging too much for a government contract and is given by a business to a government official

h. group that set up exams for federal jobs

i. representative of the political machine in a city

Controlling Business (page 612)

Synthesizing

Read the lesson and then write three sentences summarizing the actions taken to regulate businesses.

_____

_____

_____

_____

_____

Terms To Know

Choose a term from this lesson from the list below to complete each sentence by writing the term in the correct space. You will not use all the terms.

Interstate Commerce Act   Interstate Commerce Commission

monopoly   oligopoly

Sherman Antitrust Act   Sherman Commerce Commission

1. The _____ was used mostly against unions and not businesses until the early 1900s.

2. The _____ was given the role of overseeing the railroad industry.

3. The railroad industry was a(n) _____ with just a few firms controlling the industry.

4. Congress passed the _____ to lessen the power of railroads.

Terms To Review

In the space available, define or describe the following terms you studied earlier.

tariff
(Chapter 8, Section 1)

_____

_____

trust
(Chapter 19, Section 3)

_____
_____

The New Reformers (page 613)

Monitoring Comprehension

Check how well you understood what you read in this lesson by answering the following questions.

1. What did socialists believe?

_____
_____

2. What did progressives want to do?

_____
_____

3. What issues did the muckrakers write about?

_____
_____

Terms To Know

Define or describe the following key terms from this lesson.

Meat Inspection Act

_____
_____

muckrakers

_____
_____

Pure Food and Drug Act

_____
_____

Academic Vocabulary

Read the following sentences. In the space below, write in your own words the meaning of the boldfaced academic vocabulary word from this lesson.

1. One group of reformers wanted the government to own major industries, running them on **behalf** of all the people.

_____

2. Progressives brought great **energy** to the push for reform..

_____

3. Some journalists wrote about the corruption **underlying** city governments.

_____

Expanding Democracy (pages 613–614)

Complete this outline on state and national reforms as you read the lesson. Part of the outline has been done for you.

I. State Reforms

    A. LaFollette in Wisconsin

        1. _____

        2. _____

    B. Oregon System

        1. _____

        2. _____

        3. _____

II. National Reforms

    A. _____

Terms To Know

Choose a term from this lesson from the list below to complete each sentence by writing the term in the correct space.

initiative	Oregon	primary	recall
referendum	Seventeenth	Thirteenth	Wisconsin

1. Several election reforms spread from one state to others under the

name the _____ System.

2. Many states began to use the _____ as the method
for choosing candidates for political office instead of allowing bosses
to make the decisions.

3. Using a(n) _____ , a state's citizens could place a
measure on the ballot for all voters to approve or reject.

4. Another reform, called a(n) _____ , allowed voters to
remove elected officials from office before their terms ended.

5. With a(n) _____ , legislators submitted laws to the
voters, who had the final say on whether the were adopted.

6. Congress approved the direct election of senators by passing the

_____ Amendment.

Section Wrap-up

*Now that you have read the section, write the answers to
the questions that were included in* **Setting a Purpose for
Reading** *at the beginning of the section.*

How did journalists help shape the reform movement?

_____

_____

How did cities, states, and Congress answer the call for reform of the
government?

_____

_____

Chapter 21, Section 2
Women and Progressives

(pages 615–619)

Reason To Read

Setting a Purpose for Reading Think about these questions as you read:
- How did the role of American women change during the Progressive Era?
- How did women fight for the right to vote?

Main Idea

As you read pages 615–619 in your textbook, complete this graphic organizer by describing the role of each individual.

Individual	Role in Progressive Movement
Mary Church Terrell	
Susan B. Anthony	
Frances Willard	

Sequencing Events

Match the date in the left column with the correct events in the right column by writing the letter in the space to the left of the date.

_____ **1.** 1890

_____ **2.** 1894

_____ **3.** 1896

_____ **4.** 1903

_____ **5.** 1916

a. Anti-Saloon League is formed.

b. Women's Trade Union League is formed.

c. Wyoming Territory gives women right to vote.

d. National American Woman Suffrage Association is formed.

e. Utah becomes first state to give women right to vote.

f. National Association of Colored Women is established.

g. National Woman's Party is founded.

h. Congress gives women right to vote nationwide.

Women's Roles Change (pages 615–616)

Analyzing   *Analyze the information in this lesson by answering the following questions.*

1. How did women's clubs change in this period?

_____

_____

2. What activities did the National Association of Colored Women engage in?

_____

_____

The Fight for Suffrage (pages 616–618)

Questioning   *As you read "The Fight for Suffrage", ask yourself: what is an important detail about each of the listed topics? Write one of those details in the spaces below.*

The Drive for Suffrage >

_____

_____

Opposition to Woman Suffrage >

_____

_____

Continuing the Fight >

_____

_____

Women Vote Nationally >

_____

_____

 # Key Points

 # Notes

Terms To Know

Read the following sentences. Choose the correct term from this lesson to complete the sentence by circling the term.

1. The (American Woman Suffrage Association, National Woman Suffrage Association) aimed to win suffrage by getting a constitutional amendment passed.

2. Some men and even some women opposed the (sufferers, suffragists) and their drive to get the vote for women.

3. The (Nineteenth, Seventeenth) Amendment gave women the right to vote.

Women and Social Reform (pages 618–619)

Summarizing

As you read pages 618–619, write a short description of the Prohibition Amendment.

_____

_____

_____

Terms To Know

Define or describe the following key term from this lesson.

Anti-Saloon League

_____

_____

Section Wrap-up

Now that you have read the section, write the answers to the questions that were included in **Setting a Purpose for Reading** *at the beginning of the section.*

How did the role of American women change during the Progressive Era?

_____

_____

How did women fight for the right to vote?

_____

_____

Chapter 21, Section 3
Progressive Presidents
(pages 620–624)

Reason To Read

Setting a Purpose for Reading Think about these questions as you read:
- How did President Theodore Roosevelt take on big business?
- Why did the progressives form their own political party?

Main Idea

As you read pages 620–624 in your textbook, complete this graphic organizer by explaining why each of these acts of legislation is important.

Legislation	Importance
Sixteenth Amendment	
Pure Food and Drug Act	
Federal Reserve Act	

Sequencing Events

As you read, put the following events in the correct order by writing the number 1 through 5 in the space to the left. Use the number 1 for the event that occurred first, 2 for the next event, and so on.

_____ **A. Roosevelt forms U.S. Forest Service.**

_____ **B. Roosevelt runs for president on Bull Moose Party ticket.**

_____ **C. Roosevelt takes action to end coal strike.**

_____ **D. Roosevelt becomes president.**

Key Points

Notes

Theodore Roosevelt (pages 620–622)

Academic Vocabulary

Read the passage below. Put a checkmark in the space before the phrase that best explains what the academic vocabulary word considerable, *from this lesson, means in this sentence.*

Roosevelt's "square deal" meant there would be a <u>considerable</u> amount of government regulation of business.

_____ less than before   _____ more than before   _____ large

William Howard Taft (pages 622–624)

Drawing Conclusions

Review the subsection and then answer the questions to draw conclusions about what you read.

1. How did Taft's policies compare to Roosevelt's?

_____

_____

2. What effect did Roosevelt's campaign have on the election of 1912?

_____

_____

Terms To Know

Define or describe the following terms from this lesson.

Bull Moose Party >

_____

_____

Sixteenth Amendment >

_____

_____

 **Key Points**

 **Notes**

Read the following sentences. In the space below, write in your own words the meaning of the boldfaced academic vocabulary word from this lesson.

1. The new income tax **generated** money for the government.

_____

_____

2. The amendment that created the income tax did not **specify** how incomes should be taxed. Congress had to pass another law creating rules for taxation.

_____

_____

3. That gain in **revenue** allowed the progressives to lower the tariff.

_____

_____

4. Taft angered Roosevelt by **modifying** some of his conservation policies.

_____

_____

Section Wrap-up

Now that you have read the section, write the answers to the questions that were included in Setting a Purpose for Reading *at the beginning of the section.*

How did President Theodore Roosevelt take on big business?

_____

_____

Why did the progressives form their own political party?

_____

_____

Chapter 21, Section 4
Excluded from Reform

(pages 628–633)

Reason To Read

Setting a Purpose for Reading Think about these questions as you read:
- Why did progressive reforms not include all Americans?
- How did minorities work to move toward greater equality?

Main Idea

As you read pages 628–633 in your textbook, complete this graphic organizer by describing each person's accomplishments.

Individual	Accomplishments
Booker T. Washington	
Ida Wells	
W.E.B. Du Bois	
Carlos Montezuma	

Sequencing Events

As you read, place the following events on the time line:
- **Racial riot erupts in Springfield, Illinois**
- **The anti-Catholic American Protective Association is founded**
- **California bars Japanese immigrants from buying land**
- **Alianza Hispano Americo is formed in Tucson**

◆1880   ◆1900   ◆1920

Prejudice and Discrimination *(pages 628–631)*

Terms To Know

Define or describe the following key term from this lesson.

Gentlemen's Agreement

_____

_____

Academic Vocabulary

Use each of the following vocabulary words from this lesson in a sentence.

bias

_____

_____

_____

ethnic

_____

_____

Terms To Review

In the space available, define or describe the term which you studied earlier.

discrimination
(Chapter 13, Section 2)

_____

_____

Struggle for Equal Opportunity *(pages 631–633)*

Interpreting

Answer the following questions to interpret the information in this lesson.

Why did African Americans, Hispanics, and Native Americans form groups of their own?

_____

_____

_____

Terms To Know

Read the following sentences. Choose the correct term from this lesson to complete the sentence by circling the term.

1. Some Mexican Americans tried to improve conditions in the (barrios, ghettos) where they lived.

2. They formed groups called (associations, *mutualistas*) to work for better lives.

3. Native Americans formed the Society of (American Indians, the Indian Peoples) to try to work for better treatment.

4. African Americans tried to promote economic growth in the black community through the (National Association for the Advancement of Colored People, National Negro Business League).

Section Wrap-up

Now that you have read the section, write the answers to the questions that were included in* Setting a Purpose for Reading *at the beginning of the section.

Why did progressive reforms not include all Americans?

_____

_____

How did minorities work to move toward greater equality?

_____

_____

Chapter 22, Section 1
Expanding Horizons
(pages 638–641)

Reason To Read

Setting a Purpose for Reading Think about these questions as you read:
- What factors contributed to the growth of American imperialism?
- How did the United States expand its economic and political influence in the late 1800s?

Main Idea

As you read pages 638–641 in your textbook, complete this graphic organizer by explaining how the United States made its presence felt in each country or region.

	U.S. role
Japan	
Latin America	
Russia	

Sequencing Events

As you read, place the following events on the time line:
- **Seward buys Alaska.**
- **U.S. holds Pan-American Conference.**
- **Congress approves construction of first steel-hulled warships.**
- **Perry reaches Japan.**

◆1850   ◆1870   ◆1890

American Foreign Policy (pages 638–639)

Analyzing   *Read pages 638–639 and then answer these questions.*

1. How did the end of the frontier affect Americans' view of the world?

_____

_____

2. What was the significance of Perry's voyage?

_____

_____

Terms To Know   *Define or describe the following key terms from this lesson.*

expansionism >
_____

_____

isolationism >
_____

_____

An Age of Imperialism (pages 639–641)

Determining the Main Idea   *Write down the main idea of this lesson and at least three details that support that idea.*

Main Idea >
_____

_____

_____

_____

_____

_____

_____

Terms To Know

Use these key terms from the lesson in a sentence.

imperialism

_____

_____

_____

Pan-American Union

_____

_____

Terms To Review

In the space available, define the following terms or academic vocabulary words you studied earlier.

canal
(Chapter 10, Section 2)

_____

_____

_____

dominate
(Chapter 1, Section 3)

_____

_____

region
(Chapter 1, Section 3)

_____

_____

vision
(Chapter 8, Section 1)

_____

_____

Section Wrap-up

Now that you have read the section, write the answers to the questions that were included in Setting a Purpose for Reading *at the beginning of the section.*

What factors contributed to the growth of American imperialism?

_____

_____

How did the United States expand its economic and political influence in the late 1800s?

_____

_____

Chapter 22, Section 2
Imperialism in the Pacific

(pages 644–648)

Reason To Read

Setting a Purpose for Reading Think about these questions as you read:
- How did the United States gain control of Hawaii and Samoa?
- How did competition for influence in China and the Pacific region lead to new foreign policies?

Main Idea

As you read pages 644–648 in your textbook, complete this graphic organizer by filling in the time line with important events in Hawaii's history.

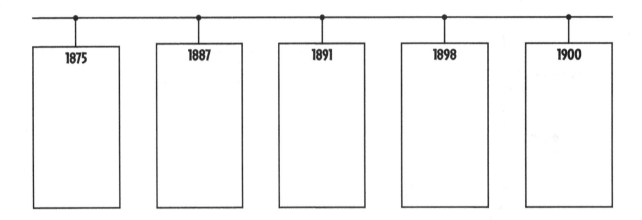

| 1875 | 1887 | 1891 | 1898 | 1900 |

Sequencing Events

As you read, write the year in which each of these events took place:

_____ U.S. gains special trading rights in Samoa

_____ U.S. obtains part of Samoa

_____ Boxer Rebellion in China

_____ Roosevelt helps win peace ending Russo–Japanese War

Hawaii (pages 644–646)

Skimming   *Skim the lesson by reading the text under each heading quickly to get a general idea of what it is about. Use one or two sentences to write that general idea in the spaces below.*

First Contact with Hawaii >

_____
_____

Missionaries and Sugar Growers >

_____
_____
_____

American Planters' Revolt >

_____
_____
_____

Annexation >

_____
_____
_____

The Islands of Samoa >

_____
_____

Terms To Know   *Read the following sentences. Choose the correct term from this lesson to complete the sentence by circling the term.*

1. Hawaiian sugar planters overthrew Hawaii's queen and took control, creating a new (permanent, provisional) government.

2. The planters of Hawaii pushed for the (annexation, purchase) of the islands by the United States.

China and the Open Door (page 647)

Responding   *As you read the lesson, respond to the following questions.*

1. How did the imperialist powers treat China?

_____
_____

2. What did the United States propose doing there?

_____

_____

3. Why did other countries accept John Hay's suggestion?

_____

_____

Terms To Know

Define or describe the following terms from this lesson.

spheres of influence

_____

_____

_____

Open Door Policy

_____

_____

Terms To Review

Use each of these terms, which you studied earlier, in a sentence that expresses the meaning of the term.

exploit
(Chapter 17, Section 2)

_____

_____

_____

maintain
(Chapter 5, Section 2)

_____

_____

Japan (page 648)

Summarizing

As you read the material under each heading, write a one-sentence summary.

War with Russia

_____

_____

Treaty of
Portsmouth > _____

_____

**Terms
To Know** *Define or describe the following key terms from this
lesson.*

Russo-
Japanese War > _____

_____

Treaty of
Portsmouth > _____

_____

_____

"Great White
Fleet" > _____

_____

Section Wrap-up *Now that you have read the section, write the answers to
the questions that were included in* Setting a Purpose for
Reading *at the beginning of the section.*

How did the United States gain control of Hawaii and Samoa?

_____

_____

How did competition for influence in China and the Pacific region lead to
new foreign policies?

_____

_____

_____

Chapter 22, Section 3
Spanish-American War
(pages 649–654)

Reason To Read

Setting a Purpose for Reading Think about these questions as you read:
• Why did the Spanish-American War begin?
• How did the United States's role in global affairs grow after the war?

Main Idea

As you read pages 649–654 in your textbook, complete this graphic organizer by listing two reasons the United States went to war over Cuba.

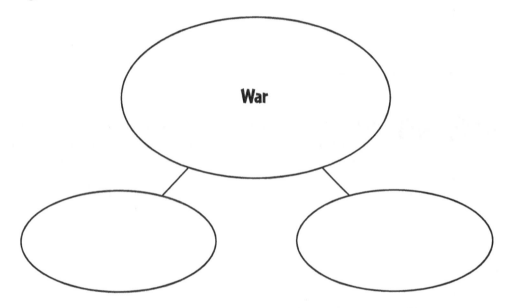

War

Sequencing Events

As you read, write the correct dates for each of these events from 1898:

_____ *Maine* **explodes**

_____ **Congress recognizes Cuban independence**

_____ **Congress declares war on Spain**

_____ **Dewey defeats Spanish fleet in Manila Bay**

_____ **Battle of San Juan Hill occurs in Cuba**

_____ **Spain signs armistice**

The Cuban Rebellion (pages 649–652)

Scanning

Scan the lesson by reading the headings and looking at the map on page 651. Then write down three topics you think will be covered in this lesson.

_____

_____

_____

Terms To Know

Read the following sentences. Choose the correct term from this lesson to complete the sentence by circling the term.

1. Newspapers used sensational reporting—a style called (lying journalism, yellow journalism)—to try to convince Americans to go to war against Spain.

2. When a battleship blew up in Havana Harbor, the slogan "Remember the (*Alamo, Maine*)" became popular.

3. Theodore Roosevelt led a group of volunteers called the (Bull Moose, Rough Riders) to Cuba.

4. The charge up (San Juan Hill, Santiago Hill) ended in the defeat of the Spanish troops.

5. Spain quickly agreed to an (appeasement, armistice).

Academic Vocabulary

Read the sentence below. Put a checkmark in the space before the word or phrase that best explains what the academic vocabulary word **trigger,** *from this lesson, means in this sentence.*

The events in Cuba triggered the Spanish-American War.

_____ prevented _____ shot off _____ started

 **Key Points**

 **Notes**

Terms To Review

In the space available, define the following words you studied earlier.

debate
(Chapter 5, Section 4)

_____

_____

enforce
(Chapter 4, Section 2)

_____

_____

intense
(Chapter 10, Section 3)

_____

_____

Acquisitions *(pages 652–654)*

Terms To Know

Choose a term from this lesson from the list below to complete each sentence by writing the term in the correct space. You will not use all the terms.

anti-imperialists   Foraker Act   imperialists

Jones Act   Platt Amendment   protectorate

territory

1. The United States agreed to Cuban independence, but through the

   _____ forced Cubans to give the U.S.
   certain rights on the island.

2. Before Cuba's status was settled, it was a(n) _____
   of the United States.

3. The _____ set up a new government for
   Puerto Rico.

4. _____ argued that the people of the
   Philippines should be allowed to have their independence as well.

Academic Vocabulary

Use the academic vocabulary word clause *in a sentence.*

clause

_____

_____

Section Wrap-up

Now that you have read the section, write the answers to the questions that were included in Setting a Purpose for Reading *at the beginning of the section.*

Why did the Spanish-American War begin?

_____

_____

How did the United States's role in global affairs grow after the war?

_____

_____

Chapter 22, Section 4
Latin American Policies

(pages 656–661)

Reason To Read

Setting a Purpose for Reading Think about these questions as you read:
- What shaped the policies the United States followed in Latin America?
- Where and how did the United States intervene in Latin America?

Main Idea

As you read pages 656–661 in your textbook, complete this graphic organizer by describing these policies.

	Description
Roosevelt Corollary	
Dollar Diplomacy	
Moral Diplomacy	

Sequencing Events

Match the date in the left column with the correct event in the right column by writing the letter in the space to the left of the date.

_____ **1.** 1879

_____ **2.** 1903

_____ **3.** 1906

_____ **4.** 1914

a. U.S. recognizes Panama's independence, signs treaty for canal

b. Panama canal opens to ships

c. French acquire right to build canal at Panama

d. U.S. starts working on canal

e. French abandon efforts to build canal

f. medical improvements reduce death toll from disease in Panama

 Key Points

 Notes

Panama (pages 656–658)

Monitoring Comprehension

Check how well you understood what you read in this section by answering the following questions.

1. Why did the United States want to sign a treaty with Colombia to gain the right to build a canal in Panama? What happened to that treaty?

_____

_____

2. What role did the United States play in Panama's independence?

_____

_____

3. What major problem was an obstacle to building the Panama Canal?

_____

_____

4. What effect did the canal have?

_____

_____

Terms To Know

Define or describe the key term from this lesson below.

isthmus

_____

_____

 **Key Points**

 **Notes**

Terms To Review

Choose a term you studied earlier from the list below to complete each sentence by replacing the underlined word. Write the correct term in the space.

access (Chapter 2, Section 1)   acquire (Chapter 5, Section 4)

instruct (Chapter 5, Section 4)   reject (Chapter 2, Section 4)

site (Chapter 18, Section 3)   undertaking (Chapter 10, Section 2)

1. Many thought that Panama was the perfect <u>location</u> _____ for a canal.

2. Once the French company failed in its effort to build a canal in

Panama, the United States hoped to <u>obtain</u> _____ the right to do the project.

3. Colombia's senate <u>turned down</u> _____ the treaty with the United States, seeming to end American chances to build the canal.

4. Once the United States had a treaty with Panama, it still faced the

difficult <u>task</u> _____ of building the canal.

5. Gorgas <u>told</u> _____ his workers how to rid Panama of mosquitoes.

Policing the Western Hemisphere *(pages 658–660)*

Interpreting

As you read the lesson, give examples of the general statements written below.

1. Events in Latin America confirmed Roosevelt's fear of disorder.

_____

_____

2. The United States applied the Roosevelt Corollary soon after it was announced.

_____

_____

3. Taft hoped to use economic rather than military power in his foreign policy.

_____

_____

Terms To Know

Define or describe the following key terms from this lesson.

anarchy

_____

_____

Roosevelt Corollary

_____

_____

dollar diplomacy

_____

_____

Academic Vocabulary

Read each sentence below. Put a checkmark in the space before the word or words that best explains what the boldfaced academic vocabulary word from this lesson means in the sentence.

1. Roosevelt often **quoted** a proverb that said, "Speak softly and carry a big stick."

_____ complained about   _____ misstated   _____ referred to

2. Taft hoped to **substitute** economic influence for military influence.

_____ overcome   _____ replace   _____ undermine

Relations with Mexico *(pages 660–661)*

Inferring

Read the lesson and then answer the questions to make inferences about what you read.

1. Would American business leaders have supported Madero? Why or why not?

_____

_____

2. Why would Wilson support Carranza even though Carranza did not support democratic ideals?

_____

_____

3. What fact makes it clear that Mexicans supported Pancho Villa?

_____

_____

Terms To Review

Use each of these terms, which you studied earlier, in a sentence that expresses the meaning of the term.

principle
(Chapter 5, Section 4)

_____

_____

reveal
(Chapter 14, Section 2)

_____

_____

Section Wrap-up

Now that you have read the section, write the answers to the questions that were included in **Setting a Purpose for Reading** *at the beginning of the section.*

What shaped the policies the United States followed in Latin America?

_____

_____

_____

Where and how did the United States intervene in Latin America?

_____

_____

_____

Chapter 23, Section 1
War in Europe

(pages 666–670)

Reason To Read

Setting a Purpose for Reading Think about these questions as you read:
- What factors led to World War I?
- How did the early fighting progress in Europe?

Main Idea

As you read pages 666–670 in your textbook, complete this graphic organizer by identifying four cases of World War I

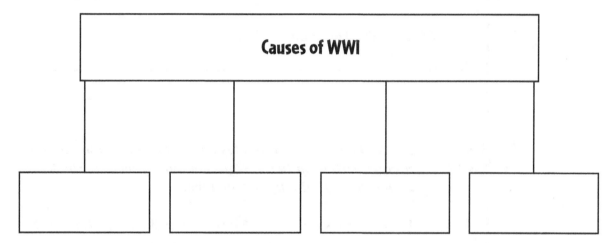

Sequencing Events

As you read, put the following events in the correct order by writing the numbers 1 through 6 in the spaces to the left. Use the number 1 for the event that occurred first, 2 for the next event, and so on.

_____ **A.** Austria-Hungary declares war on Serbia

_____ **B.** Britain declares war on Germany

_____ **C.** Ottoman Empire joins Central Powers

_____ **D.** Germany invades Belgium

_____ **E.** Archduke Franz Ferdinand assassinated

_____ **F.** Germany declares war on Russia

Troubles in Europe (pages 666–667)

Analyzing Analyze the information in this lesson by answering the following questions.

1. How did nationalism contribute to the tensions building in Europe?

   _____

   _____

2. Why was there a military buildup in Europe in the early 1900s?

   _____

   _____

3. What was the danger built into the alliance system?

   _____

   _____

Terms To Know Match the term from this lesson in the left column with the correct definition in the right column by writing the letter in the space to the left of the term.

____ **1.** alliance system

____ **2.** balance of power

____ **3.** entente

____ **4.** militarism

____ **5.** Triple Alliance

____ **6.** Triple Entente

a. focusing on building up armed forces

b. agreement that linked Germany, Austria-Hungary, and Italy

c. agreement between Germany, Britain, and France

d. agreement that joined Britain, France, and Russia

e. an understanding among nations

f. rule of a country by the armed forces

g. international system in which no country has more power than others

h. peace treaty

i. structure of defense agreements among nations

Terms To Review

Use each of these terms, which you studied earlier, in a sentence that expresses the meaning of the term.

ethnic group
(Chapter 20, Section 1)

_____

_____

nationalism
(Chapter 9, Section 3)

_____

_____

_____

unify
(Chapter 19, Section 1)

_____

_____

Crisis in the Balkans *(pages 667–668)*

Previewing *As you read the section, answer the following questions.*

1. Look at the map on page 668. Which countries formed the Central Powers? Which made up the Allies?

_____

_____

2. About how quickly was much of Europe plunged into war?

_____

_____

Terms To Review

Read the below. Put a checkmark in the space before the word or phrase that best explains the meaning of each term or academic vocabulary word that you studied earlier.

Germany's invasion of Belgium violated that country's neutrality. Britain had guaranteed to protect Belgium, so it declared war on Germany.

violate
(Chapter 5, Section 1)

_____ fight for   _____ ignore   _____ solemnly promise

neutrality
(Chapter 8, Section 2)

_____ having a democratic government

_____ lack of armed forces

_____ taking no sides

A World War Begins (pages 668–670)

Outlining *Complete this outline as you read the lesson.*

I. The Two Sides

    A. The Allied Powers included Great Britain, France, and Russia.

    B. The Central Powers included Germany, Austria-Hungary, and the Ottoman Empire.

II. Fighting on the Western Front

    A. _____

        1. _____

        2. _____

        3. _____

    B. _____

        1. _____

        2. _____

III. Deadly Technology

    A. _____

    B. _____

    C. _____

    D. _____

IV. On the Seas

    A. _____

    B. _____

Chapter 23, Section 1

Terms To Know

Choose a term from this lesson from the list below to complete each sentence by writing the term in the correct space.

Allied Powers	battleships	Central Powers	Marne
Somme	trenches	U-boats	Verdun

1. The Germans' most effective naval weapon was the ships called

_____ .

2. The _____ included Britain, France, and Russia.

3. Italy left the _____ to join the other side.

4. In France, fighting settled into a pattern of fighting from

_____ that led to high casualties.

5. The French saved Paris by winning the Battle of the

_____ .

6. Huge battles like the German offensive at _____ and

the British and French attack at the _____ ended with
very heavy casualties for very little gain of ground.

Academic Vocabulary

Read the sentence below. Put a checkmark in the space before the phrase that best explains what the academic vocabulary word dimension, *from this lesson, means in this sentence.*

The use of airplanes in World War I added a whole new dimension to warfare.

dimension

_____ element   _____ shape   _____ size

Now that you have read the section, write the answers to the questions that were included in Setting a Purpose for Reading *at the beginning of the section.*

What factors led to World War I?

_____

_____

How did the early fighting progress in Europe?

_____

_____

Copyright © by The McGraw-Hill Companies, Inc.

Chapter 23, Section 2
America's Road to War

(pages 671–676)

Reason To Read

Setting a Purpose for Reading Think about these questions as you read:
- How did Americans respond to the war in Europe?
- What led to American involvement in the war?

Main Idea

As you read pages 671–676 in your textbook, complete this graphic organizer by listing two reasons the United States found it difficult to maintain neutrality.

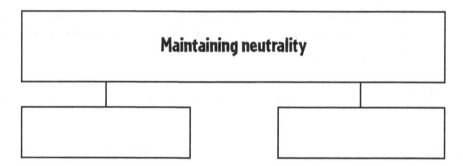

Maintaining neutrality

Sequencing Events

As you read, place the following events on the time line:
- **Wilson asks Congress for declaration of war**
- ***Lusitania* sunk, killing about 1,000 people**
- **Zimmermann telegram published**
- **Germany resumes submarine warfare**

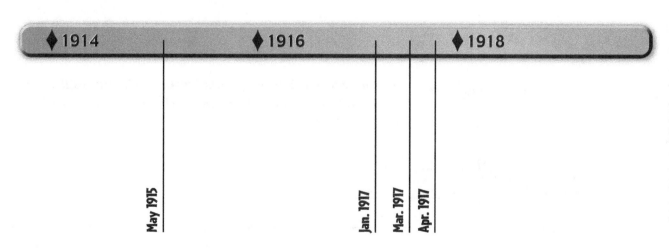

1914   1916   1918

May 1915   Jan. 1917   Mar. 1917   Apr. 1917

Copyright © by The McGraw-Hill Companies, Inc.

 **Key Points**

 **Notes**

American Neutrality *(pages 671–674)*

Determining the Main Idea

Write down the main idea of the lesson as you read pages 671–674.

_____

_____

_____

Academic Vocabulary

Read the sentence below. Put a checkmark in the space before the phrase that best explains what the academic vocabulary word compensate, *from this lesson, means in this sentence.*

After attacking the *Sussex*, Germany feared that the United States would enter the war, so it promised to compensate the Americans injured when the ship was hit.

_____ give money to   _____ pay honor to   _____ treat medically

Terms To Review

In the space available, define the following words you studied earlier.

blockade
(Chapter 6, Section 3)

_____

_____

propaganda
(Chapter 5, Section 2)

_____

_____

The End of Neutrality *(pages 674–676)*

Questioning

As you read each part of this lesson, ask yourself: What is an important detail? Write one of those details in the spaces below.

Strengthening the Military

_____

_____

_____

On the Brink of War >

_____
_____
_____
_____

Revolution in Russia >

_____
_____
_____
_____

America Enters the War >

_____
_____
_____
_____

Terms To Know

Read the following sentences. Choose the correct term from this lesson to complete the sentence by circling the term.

1. The German message called the (Kaiser Wilhelm, Zimmermann) telegraph outraged many Americans.

2. Rebels in Russia overthrew the ruler, replacing (autocracy, democracy) with more popular rule.

3. In passing the (Draft, Selective Service) Act, Congress created a system for enlisting American men into the army.

Academic Vocabulary

Write two words related to the academic vocabulary word from this lesson.

reverse >

_____
_____

Read each sentence below. In the spaces that follow, explain the meaning of the boldfaced term or academic vocabulary word you studied earlier.

publication
(Chapter 2, Section 1)

1. The <u>publication</u> of a German telegram to Mexico offering to help that country regain Arizona, New Mexico, and Texas outraged many Americans.

_____

_____

draft
(Chapter 16, Section 4)

2. Congress created a <u>draft</u> to fill the army with troops.

_____

_____

register
(Chapter 17, Section 2)

3. Millions of Americans <u>registered</u> for the draft.

_____

_____

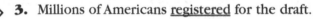

Now that you have read the section, write the answers to the questions that were included in Setting a Purpose for Reading *at the beginning of the lesson.*

How did Americans respond to the war in Europe?

_____

_____

What led to American involvement in the war?

_____

_____

Chapter 23, Section 3
Americans Join the Allies

(pages 677–681)

Reason To Read

Setting a Purpose for Reading Think about these questions as you read:
- What was happening in Europe when the United States entered the war?
- What role did American troops play in the fighting?

Main Idea

As you read pages 677–681 in your textbook, complete this graphic organizer by identifying the events that took place on these dates.

Nov. 1917	June 1918	Oct. 4, 1918	Nov. 11, 1918

Sequencing Events

As you read, write the correct dates for each of these events:

_____ **Germany launches offensive on Western Front**

_____ **First American troops reach Europe**

_____ **Democratic government established in Russia**

Copyright © by The McGraw-Hill Companies, Inc.

Supplying the Allies (pages 677–680)

Reviewing

Reread each part of this lesson and list two key facts.

> Giving Supplies

_____

_____

> Russian Withdrawal

_____

_____

> New German Offensive

_____

_____

> American Troops in the War

_____

_____

Terms To Know

Define or describe the following key terms.

> American Expeditionary Force

_____

_____

> Bolsheviks

_____

_____

> convoys

_____

_____

The End of the War (pages 680–681)

Clarifying

As you read this lesson, answer the following questions to clarify the information about the war's end.

1. What led the Germans to request an end to the fighting?

_____

_____

2. What happened to Germany's government?

_____

_____

Terms To Know

Define or describe each of the following terms from this lesson.

armistice 〉

_____

_____

kaiser 〉

_____

_____

Terms To Review

Use each of these terms, which you studied earlier, in a sentence that reflects the meaning of the term.

consent
(Chapter 5, Section 1) 〉

_____

_____

republic
(Chapter 7, Section 1) 〉

_____

_____

Section Wrap-up

Now that you have read the section, write the answers to the questions that were included in **Setting a Purpose for Reading** *at the beginning of the section.*

What was happening in Europe when the United States entered the war?

_____

_____

What role did American troops play in the fighting?

_____

_____

Chapter 23, Section 4
The War at Home

(pages 683–686)

Reason To Read

Setting a Purpose for Reading Think about these questions as you read:
- What steps did the United States take to organize and prepare for World War I?
- How did the war affect Americans?

Main Idea

As you read pages 683–686 in your textbook, complete this graphic organizer by describing the goals of these agencies.

Agency	Goals
Food Administration	
War Industries Board	
Committee on Public Information	

Sequencing Events

Read the following sentences. Choose the correct date from this section to complete the sentence by circling the date.

1. **The government created the National War Labor Board in (April, August) 1918.**
2. **Congress passed the Espionage Act in (1916, 1917).**
3. **In (1917, 1918), Congress passed the Sabotage Act.**

Mobilizing the Nation (pages 683–685)

Identifying Cause and Effect

As you read the lesson, answer the following questions to identify the causes and effects of the war on the home front.

Cause	Action	Effect
Need to mobilize workers and industry	_____ _____ _____	_____ _____ _____
_____ _____ _____	Jobs are available, but immigration is down.	_____ _____ _____
Need to supply food for army and for Allies	_____ _____ _____	_____ _____ _____
Antiwar feeling remains strong even after U.S. enters the war	_____ _____ _____	_____ _____

Terms To Know

Match the term from this lesson in the left column with the correct definition in the right column by writing the letter in the space to the left of the term.

_____ **1.** Committee on Public Information

_____ **2.** Food Administration

_____ **3.** Liberty Bonds

_____ **4.** mobilization

_____ **5.** National War Labor Board

_____ **6.** rationing

_____ **7.** War Industries Board

a. limiting people's use of goods

b. tried to make sure workers and businesses cooperated with war effort

c. supervised nation's industrial production

d. built support for the war through propaganda

e. prevented factories from increasing production

f. encouraged farmers to grow more and people to eat less

g. censored news accounts about the war

h. blocked workers from striking

i. called on farmers to grow less so food would not reach enemy soldiers

j. technique for financing the war

k. gathering of resources and preparation for war

Academic Vocabulary

In the space available, define the following academic vocabulary words from this lesson.

bond > _____
_____

job > _____
_____

Chapter 23, Section 4

Terms To Review

Choose a term you studied earlier from the list below to complete each sentence by writing the correct term in the space.

emigrate (Chapter 20, Section 1)   export (Chapter 2, Section 3)

impose (Chapter 16, Section 4)   migrate (Chapter 20, Section 2)

1. The government _____ higher taxes on wealthy Americans and corporations to help pay for the war.

2. Many _____ to the United States during the war to get a job.

3. As production went up, American companies _____ more goods.

Americans and the War *(pages 685–686)*

Inferring

Read the lesson and then answer the questions to make inferences about what you read.

1. Why did African Americans migrate to the North? What did they find when they did?

_____

_____

2. What complaint did socialists have against the war?

_____

_____

3. Would it have been difficult to be a German American during World War I? Why?

_____

_____

Terms To Know

Complete each sentence by circling the correct term or phrase.

1. Some people opposed the war because they were (pacifists, socialists) and did not believe that fighting was just.

2. Those who (dissented, withdrew) from the war were treated with suspicion.

3. The movement of large numbers of African Americans to Northern cities to find work is called the (Great Exodus, Great Migration).

4. The (Alien and Sedition Acts, Sabotage and Sedition Acts) made it a crime to speak or write against the war.

5. The (Enemy Aliens Act, Espionage Act) gave a broader definition to the crime of spying.

6. (Pacifists, Socialists) objected to the profits that businesses could make from the war.

7. Under some new laws, many people could be accused of (espionage and sabotage, propaganda and lying).

Now that you have read the section, write the answers to the questions that were included in **Setting a Purpose for Reading** *at the beginning of the section.*

What steps did the United States take to organize and prepare for World War I?

_____

_____

How did the war affect Americans?

_____

_____

Chapter 23, Section 5
Searching for Peace
(pages 688–691)

Reason To Read

Setting a Purpose for Reading Think about these questions as you read:
• What principles did Woodrow Wilson propose as the basis for peace?
• Why did many Americans oppose the Treaty of Versailles?

Main Idea

As you read pages 688–691 in your textbook, complete this graphic organizer by identifying these individuals and the role each played in the postwar era.

Individual	Identity and Role
Woodrow Wilson	
David Lloyd George	
Henry Cabot Lodge	

Sequencing Events

Match the date in the left column with the correct event in the right column by writing the letter in the space provided.

_____ **1. January 1919**

_____ **2. June 1919**

_____ **3. September 1919**

_____ **4. March 1920**

a. Treaty of Versailles signed

b. Senate begins debating treaty

c. Wilson collapses in midst of campaign to raise support for treaty

d. Versailles conference begins

e. Senate rejects treaty

After the War (pages 688–689)

Evaluating   *Read the lesson and then answer the questions to evaluate what you read.*

1. What were conditions like in Europe when the war ended?

_____

_____

2. What kind of peace was Wilson seeking?

_____

_____

3. What problems were there in Wilson's ideas?

_____

_____

Terms To Know   *Define or describe the following key terms.*

Fourteen Points >

_____

_____

League of Nations >

_____

_____

national self-determination >

_____

_____

The Peace Conference (pages 689–690)

Comparing and Contrasting

Compare and contrast the information in this lesson by answering the following questions.

1. How did the attitudes of European leaders toward Wilson's plans differ from those of their people?

_____

_____

2. What did Clemenceau and Lloyd George think should be done with Germany?

_____

_____

3. How did the final terms of the treaty compare to Wilson's original ideas?

_____

_____

Terms To Know

Define or describe each of the following terms from this lesson.

reparations ▷

_____

_____

Treaty of Versailles ▷

_____

_____

Opposition at Home (pages 690–691)

Synthesizing

Read the lesson on the debate over the treaty of Versailles. Then write the information in your own words in a few sentences.

_____

_____

_____

_____

_____

Terms To Review

Choose a term you studied earlier from the list below to complete each sentence by writing the correct term in the space.

ratify (Chapter 6, Section 4)   rebate (Chapter 19, Section 1)

reject (Chapter 2, Section 4)

1. For the United States to be part of the Treaty of Versailles, the Senate

   had to _____ the treaty.

2. In the end, the Senate _____ the treaty and U.S. involvement in the League of Nations.

Section Wrap-up

Now that you have read the section, write the answers to the questions that were included in Setting a Purpose for Reading *at the beginning of the section.*

What principles did Woodrow Wilson propose as the basis for peace?

_____

_____

Why did many Americans oppose the Treaty of Versailles?

_____

_____

_____

Chapter 24, Section 1
Time of Turmoil

(pages 700–703)

Reason To Read

Setting a Purpose for Reading Think about these questions as you read:
- What factors contributed to prejudice toward foreigners?
- How did the labor and racial unrest of the 1920s affect the nation?

Main Idea

As you read pages 700–703 in your textbook, complete this graphic organizer by answering the question for each blank.

	What was it?
The Red Scare	
Sacco-Vanzetti trial	
UNIA	

Sequencing Events

As you read, place the following events on the time line:
- **Thousands arrested in Palmer raids**
- **Bolsheviks seize control of Russian government**
- **Trial of Sacco and Vanzetti**
- **Steel strike, Boston police strike**

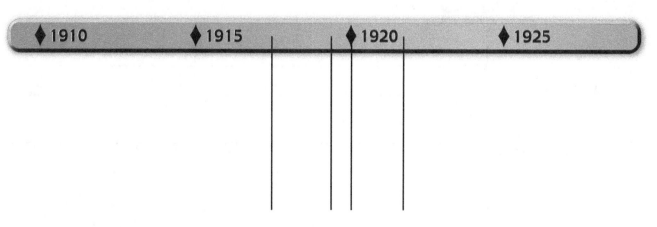

 **Notes**

Fear of Radicalism *(pages 700–702)*

Drawing Conclusions

Read the lesson and then answer the questions to draw conclusions about what you read.

1. What concerns troubled Americans at the beginning of the 1920s?

_____

_____

2. What did the Sacco and Vanzetti case reveal?

_____

_____

Terms To Know

Read the following sentences. Choose the correct term from this lesson to complete the sentence by circling the term.

1. The Senate's rejection of the Treaty of (Paris, Versailles) was one signal that Americans were tired of world responsibility in the 1920s.

2. (Anarchists, Socialists) wanted no government at all.

3. The government arrested many people it considered suspicious and had a few hundred (deported, exported).

4. The arrests came in the midst of a period called the (Communist Crackdown, Red Scare).

Terms To Review

In the space available, define the following words you studied earlier.

capitalism
(Chapter 10, Section 1)

_____

_____

commission
(Chapter 8, Section 3)

_____

_____

Key Points

Notes

Labor Unrest *(pages 702–703)*

Summarizing

Read the lesson on labor unrest and then write three or more sentences summarizing the information.

_____

_____

_____

_____

_____

Terms To Review

Use each of the following terms, which you studied earlier, in a sentence that reflects the meaning of the term.

decline
(Chapter 2, Section 1)

_____

_____

occur
(Chapter 12, Section 4)

_____

_____

Racial Unrest *(page 703)*

Skimming

Skim the lesson by reading the text under each heading quickly to get a general idea of what it is about. Use one or two sentences to write that general idea in the space below.

_____

_____

_____

_____

_____

Now that you have read the section, write the answers to the questions that were included in Setting a Purpose for Reading *at the beginning of the section.*

What factors contributed to prejudice toward foreigners?

_____

_____

How did the labor and racial unrest of the 1920s affect the nation?

_____

_____

Chapter 24, Section 2
Desire for Normalcy

(pages 704–707)

Reason To Read

Setting a Purpose for Reading Think about these questions as you read:
- What problems faced the Harding presidency?
- What policies did Presidents Harding and Coolidge follow in business and foreign affairs?

Main Idea

As you read pages 704–707 in your textbook, complete this graphic organizer by describing the policies the Harding and Coolidge administrations followed.

Administration policies	
Domestic affairs	Foreign affairs

Sequencing Events

As you read, put the following events in the correct order by writing the numbers 1 through 4 in the spaces to the left. Use the number 1 for the event that occurred first, 2 for the next event, and so on.

_____ **A.** Harding dies; Coolidge becomes president

_____ **B.** Coolidge elected president

_____ **C.** Harding elected president

_____ **D.** Kellogg-Briand Pact signed

_____ **E.** Fall leases oil lands in return for payments

The Harding Presidency *(pages 704–707)*

Interpreting

Interpret the information you read about Harding and Coolidge by answering the following questions.

1. Why were Harding and Coolidge given the Republican nominations for president and vice president in 1920?

_____

_____

2. How did Coolidge contrast with Harding?

_____

_____

3. What pro-business policies did Coolidge pursue?

_____

_____

Terms To Know

Choose a term from this lesson from the list below to complete each sentence by writing the term in the correct space. You will not use all the answers.

California Gusher	grant	Kitchen Cabinet
lease	Ohio Gang	Teapot Dome

1. Harding's close friends, called the _____ , were involved in several corruption scandals.

2. Harding's secretary of the interior made a secret deal to _____ land filled with oil to an oil company in return for a payment.

3. This scandal was named the _____ after one of the well sites.

Academic Vocabulary

Read the following sentence. In the space below, write in your own words the meaning of the boldfaced *academic vocabulary word from this lesson.*

If the federal government should go out of existence, the common run of the people would not **detect** the difference for a considerable length of time.

_____

Foreign Policy (page 707)

Questioning

As you read each part of the lesson, ask yourself: What is an important detail? Write one of those details in the spaces below.

A New Mood

_____
_____
_____

Promoting Peace

_____
_____
_____

A More Friendly Neighbor

_____
_____
_____

Terms To Review

Choose a term you studied earlier from the list below to complete each sentence by writing the correct term in the space.

expansionism (Chapter 22, Section 1)   intervene (Chapter 4, Section 1)

isolationism (Chapter 22, Section 1)   involve (Chapter 4, Section 4)

1. Most Americans did not want to be _____ in world affairs.

2. They wanted the government to return to _____ .

3. The Republican presidents chose not to _____ in Latin America, taking a different approach to relations with countries there.

Section Wrap-up

Now that you have read the section, write the answers to the questions that were included in Setting a Purpose for Reading *at the beginning of the section.*

What problems faced the Harding presidency?

_____

_____

What policies did Presidents Harding and Coollidge follow in business and foreign affairs?

_____

_____

Chapter 24, Section 3
A Booming Economy

(pages 709–712)

Reason To Read

Setting a Purpose for Reading Think about these questions as you read:
- How did the prosperity of the 1920s affect the nation and the American people?
- What impact did the automobile have on American life?

Main Idea

As you read pages 709–712 in your textbook, complete this graphic organizer by describing how these ideas affected the American economy

	Effect on economy
Scientific management	
Assembly line	
Installment buying	

Sequencing Events

As you read, place the following events on the time line:
- **Electricity reaches 70 percent of factories**
- **Price of Model T drops under $300**
- **Nation's GNP reaches $70 billion**
- **Ford releases Model A**

♦1920   ♦1925   ♦1930

Growth in the 1920s (pages 709–711)

Reviewing Reread each part of the lesson and list two key facts about each.

Economic Growth >
_____
_____

Scientific Management >
_____
_____

Worker Relations >
_____
_____

Consumer Economy >
_____
_____

Terms To Know Match the term from this lesson in the left column with the correct definition in the right column by writing the letter in the space to the left of the term.

_____ **1.** gross national product

_____ **2.** installment buying

_____ **3.** productivity

_____ **4.** recession

_____ **5.** scientific management

_____ **6.** welfare capitalism

a. business philosophy based on caring for workers' welfare

b. system based on focusing on precisely crafting products to emphasize quality

c. partnership between business and unions to ensure workers' welfare

d. the amount of work each worker could do

e. using credit to purchase expensive goods in steps

f. measure of the country's economic output

g. economic slowdown

h. buying goods only after they have been delivered or installed

i. measure of a country's foreign trade

j. system based on hiring experts to study how goods could be made more quickly

The Automobile Age (pages 711–712)

Monitoring Comprehension

Check how well you understood what you read in this lesson by answering the following questions.

1. How important was the automobile to the country in the 1920s?

_____

_____

2. How did Ford benefit by paying his workers a high wage?

_____

_____

3. What effect did the growing popularity of cars have on other industries?

_____

_____

4. What groups had problems in the 1920s?

_____

_____

Terms To Know

Use the space below to explain the differences between the Model T and the Model A, two terms discussed in this lesson.

_____

_____

_____

Academic Vocabulary

Read the sentence below. Put a checkmark in the space before the phrase that best explains what the academic vocabulary word potential, *from this lesson, means in this sentence.*

By paying his workers more than they would typically earn, Henry Ford turned them into potential customers for his cars.

_____ eager _____ obvious _____ possible

Section Wrap-up

Now that you have read the section, write the answers to the questions that were included in Setting a Purpose for Reading *at the beginning of the section.*

How did the prosperity of the 1920s affect the nation and the American people?

_____

_____

What impact did the automobile have on American life?

_____

_____

Chapter 24, Section 4
The Roaring Twenties

(pages 713–719)

Reason To Read

Setting a Purpose for Reading Think about these questions as you read:
- How did lifestyles in America change in the 1920s?
- What cultural clashes occurred in the United States in the 1920s?

Main Idea

As you read pages 713–719 in your textbook, complete this graphic organizer by describing the accomplishments of these individuals.

	Accomplishments
Charles Lindbergh	
Bessie Smith	
Langston Hughes	
Ernest Hemingway	

Sequencing Events

As you read, write the year in which these events took place.

_____ **Lindbergh flies across Atlantic**

_____ **Prohibition repealed**

_____ **Scopes trial**

_____ **First commercial radio broadcast**

_____ **Hoover elected president**

_____ **First Miss America Pageant held**

_____ **Congress passes National Origins Act**

New Directions (pages 713–714)

Reviewing

Review the lesson and list two key facts about each of the following.

Lindbergh

_____

_____

_____

_____

Changes for Women

_____

_____

_____

Terms To Know

Write a sentence that explains the term from this lesson below.

flapper

_____

_____

Academic Vocabulary

Read the sentence below. Put a checkmark in the space before the word or phrase that best explains what the academic vocabulary word image, *from this lesson, means in this sentence.*

The image of the flapper dominated talk about women in the 1920s.

_____ illustration   _____ look   _____ public perception

Entertainment (pages 714–715)

Questioning

As you read each part of the lesson, ask yourself: What is an important detail? Write one of those details in the spaces below.

The Movies and Radio

_____

_____

Sports and Fads	_____
	_____

Terms To Know

Define or describe the following key term from this lesson.

Mass Media	_____
	_____

The Jazz Age (pages 715–716)

Outlining

Complete this outline as you read the section. Some of the outline is already completed.

I. The Rise of Jazz

   A. Significance and features of jazz

      1. _____

      2. _____

   B. _____

   C. _____

II. Harlem Renaissance

   A. _____

   B. _____

III. A Lost Generation of Writers

   A. _____

   B. Writers

      1. Hemingway

      2. _____

      3. _____

      4. _____

Terms To Know

Read the following sentences. Choose the correct term from this lesson to complete the sentence by circling the term.

1. The 1920s are often called the (Flapper Age, Jazz Age).

2. Jazz was a new form of music marked by dynamic rhythms and (impressionism, improvisation).

3. African American writers enjoyed a flowering of culture called the (Harlem Golden Age, Harlem Renaissance).

4. Some writers moved abroad, becoming (exiles, expatriates).

Academic Vocabulary

*Read the sentence below. Put a checkmark in the space before the phrase that best explains what the academic vocabulary word **unique**, from this lesson, means in this sentence.*

Jazz helped create a unique African American recording industry.

_____ important   _____ sole   _____ ordinary

Prohibition (pages 716–717)

Synthesizing

Read the lesson on Prohibition and then write three sentences synthesizing the information.

_____

_____

_____

_____

_____

Terms To Know

Match the term from this lesson in the left column with the correct definition in the right column by writing the letter in the space to the left of the term.

_____ **1.** bootlegging

_____ **2.** Eighteenth Amendment

_____ **3.** Volstead Act

_____ **4.** Twenty-first Amendment

a. change to Constitution that ended ban on alcohol sales

b. illegally made alcohol

c. change to Constitution that put ban on alcohol sales

d. law that made sale of alcohol legal again

e. making and selling illegal alcohol

f. law that enforced the ban on alcohol

Academic Vocabulary

Read the sentence below. Put a checkmark in the space before the phrase that best explains what the academic vocabulary word aspect, *from this lesson, means in this sentence.*

The clash of cultures during the 1920s affected many _aspects_ of American life.

_____ elements   _____ industries   _____ qualities

Terms To Review

Use each of these terms, which you studied earlier, in a sentence that reflects the meaning of the term.

Prohibition
(Chapter 21, Section 2)

_____

_____

repeal
(Chapter 5, Section 1)

_____

_____

temperance movement
(Chapter 14, Section 1)

_____

_____

Nativism (pages 717–718)

Copyright © by The McGraw-Hill Companies, Inc.

Scanning

Quickly scan over the material in this lesson. Then write down two topics you think will be covered in this lesson. As you read, write down a fact about each topic.

Topic 1 > _____

Fact > _____
_____
_____

Topic 2 > _____

Fact > _____
_____
_____

Terms To Know

Match the term from this lesson in the left column with the correct definition in the right column by writing the letter in the space to the left of the term.

____ **1.** Emergency Quota Act

____ **2.** National Origins Act

____ **3.** nativism

____ **4.** quota system

a. law that further reduced the number of immigrants allowed from different countries

b. law that limited the number of immigrants allowed from different countries

c. law that banned immigrants from certain countries

d. belief that Native Americans needed to renew their culture

e. arrangement of unlimited immigration

f. belief in the superiority of native-born Americans

g. arrangement of limits on immigration from different countries

Terms To Review

Match the term you studied earlier in the left column with the correct definition or description in the right column by writing the letter in the space to the left of the term.

____ **1.** exclude
(Chapter 14, Section 2)

____ **2.** Ku Klux Klan
(Chapter 17, Section 3)

____ **3.** revise
(Chapter 11, Section 2)

a. change or alter

b. group that was limited to the South in the 1920s

c. organization that supports nativist causes

d. prevent from entering

e. send abroad

The Scopes Trial (pages 718–719)

Analyzing

Analyze the information in this lesson by answering the following questions.

1. What issue did the debate over evolution highlight?

_____

_____

2. Why did the Scopes trial draw such attention?

_____

_____

3. What happened to fundamentalism after the Scopes trial?

_____

_____

Terms To Know

Define or describe the following terms from this lesson.

evolution
_____
_____

Scopes trial
_____
_____

The Election of 1928 (page 719)

Inferring

Read the lesson and then answer the questions to make inferences about what you read.

1. How did Coolidge surprise people in 1927?

   _____

   _____

2. Why did Hoover seem well-qualified for president?

   _____

   _____

Terms To Review

Match the term you studied earlier in the left column with the correct definition or description in the right column by writing the letter in the space to the left of the term.

_____ **1.** symbol
(Chapter 1, Section 2)

_____ **2.** target
(Chapter 3, Section 2)

a. object of something

b. sign of something

c. a narrow passageway

Section Wrap-up

Now that you have read the section, write the answers to the questions that were included in **Setting a Purpose for Reading** *at the beginning of the section.*

How did lifestyles in America change in the 1920s?

_____

_____

What cultural clashes occurred in the United States in the 1920s?

_____

_____

Chapter 25, Section 1
The Great Depression
(pages 724–728)

Reason To Read

Setting a Purpose for Reading Think about these questions as you read:
- What caused the stock market crash?
- How did the Great Depression plunge many Americans into poverty?
- How did Hoover react to the Great Depression?

Main Idea

As you read pages 724–728 in your textbook, complete this graphic organizer by explaining how the Great Depression affected each of these groups.

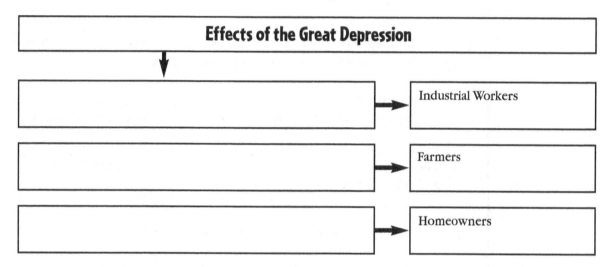

Effects of the Great Depression

	Industrial Workers
	Farmers
	Homeowners

Sequencing Events

As you read, place the following events on the time line:
- **The Great Depression worsens**
- **Herbert Hoover is elected president**
- **Bonus Army marches**
- **Stock market crashes**

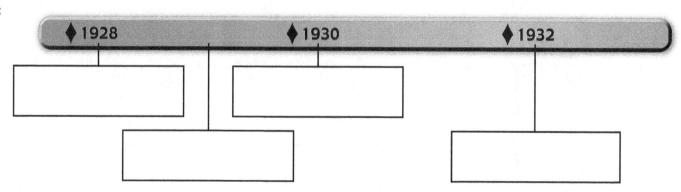

1928   1930   1932

Key Points

Notes

The Stock Market (pages 724–725)

Analyzing

Analyze the information in this section by answering the following questions.

1. How did many investors get the money needed to buy stocks in the

1920s? _____

_____

2. Why did the stock market crash?

_____

_____

Terms To Know

Choose a term from this section to complete each sentence by writing the term in the correct space.

1. Many investors bought stocks _____ , paying only a part of the price and borrowing the money for the rest.

2. The _____ is the system for buying and selling shares of corporations.

3. The day the stock market crashed came to be known as

_____

The Great Depression (pages 725–727)

Monitoring Comprehension

Check how well you have understood what you have read so far by describing four causes of the Great Depression.

Cause ⟩ _____

_____

Cause ⟩ _____

_____

Cause >

Cause >

Terms To Know

Define or describe the following key terms from this section.

default >

Great Depression >

Hoovervilles >

Academic Vocabulary

Circle the letter of the words that have the closest meaning to the underlined academic vocabulary word from this section.

credit >

1. Farmers and consumers both faced a <u>credit</u> crisis in the years leading up to the Depression.

   a. borrowed money

   b. ounterfeit money

   c. saved money

2. The Depression was marked by a sharp drop in the country's economic <u>output</u>.

   a. income from taxes

   b. stock market value

   c. total value of goods and services produced

Terms To Review

Using the part of speech specified, write the correct form of the boldfaced academic vocabulary word from this lesson in the blank space to complete the sentence.

construct
(Chapter 20, Section 2)
NOUN

1. The _____ industry suffered even before the Depression started.

economy
(Chapter 19, Section 1)
ADJECTIVE

2. The Depression was a severe _____ crisis.

income
(Chapter 21, Section 3)
NOUN

3. People's _____ dropped when they were laid off work.

Hoover and the Crisis *(pages 727–728)*

Clarifying

Clarify the information in this lesson by answering the following questions.

1. How did Hoover respond to the Depression at first?

_____

_____

2. How did Hoover's actions change?

_____

_____

Terms To Know

Explain the significance of each of the following key terms from this lesson.

Bonus Army

_____

_____

public works

_____

_____

 Key Points

 Notes

Reconstruction
Finance
Corporation

_____
_____
_____

relief

_____
_____

Academic Vocabulary

Read each sentence below. Use the space below the sentence to explain what the boldfaced *academic vocabulary word from this lesson means in this passage.*

1. In 1931 Hoover authorized the government to give money for public works **projects** such as highways, parks, and libraries.

_____

_____

2. At first, Hoover thought the Depression had to be solved by the **voluntary** work of private organizations.

_____

_____

Terms To Review

Use this term, which you studied earlier, in a sentence that reflects its meaning.

aid
(Chapter 18, Section 1)

_____
_____

What caused the stock market crash?

_____

_____

How did the Great Depression plunge many Americans into poverty?

_____

_____

How did Hoover react to the Great Depression?

_____

_____

Chapter 25, Section 2
Roosevelt's New Deal

(pages 729–734)

Reason To Read

Setting a Purpose for Reading Think about these questions as you read:
- How did Roosevelt try to restore the confidence of the American people?
- What programs were created in FDR's first 100 days?

Main Idea

As you read pages 729–734 in your textbook, complete this graphic organizer by identifying each of the listed items.

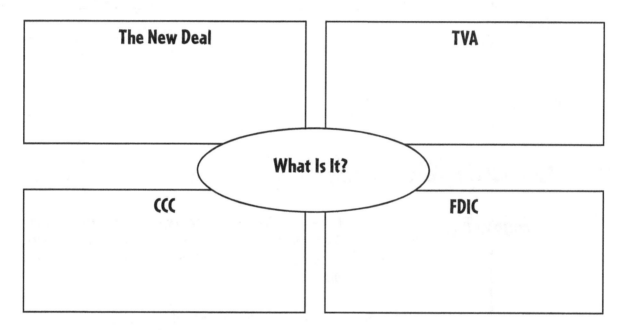

The New Deal		TVA
	What Is It?	
CCC		**FDIC**

Sequencing Events

As you read, write the correct dates for each of these events:

_____ **Franklin Roosevelt is elected president**

_____ **Programs during the Hundred Days improve the economy**

_____ **Securities and Exchange Commission is created**

Franklin D. Roosevelt *(pages 729–731)*

Questioning

As you read this subsection, ask yourself: what is an important detail about the Brain Trust? Write one of those details in the spaces below.

_____

_____

Academic Vocabulary

In the space available, define the following academic vocabulary words from this lesson.

> **persistent**

_____

_____

> **recovery**

_____

_____

FDR Takes Charge *(pages 731–732)*

Sequencing

As you read, put the following events in the correct order by writing the number 1 through 5 in the space to the left. Use the number 1 for the event that occurred first, 2 for the next event, and so on.

_____ **a.** Emergency Banking Relief Act passed

_____ **b.** Hundred Days completed

_____ **c.** Depression worsens, causing bank crisis

_____ **d.** Roosevelt elected

_____ **e.** Roosevelt gives first fireside chat

Terms To Know

Read the following sentences. Choose the correct term from this lesson to complete the sentence by circling the term.

1. After becoming president, Roosevelt used (fireside chats, press conferences) to talk informally to Americans about important matters.

2. Roosevelt called a special session of Congress that passed many laws aimed at improving the economy. This period is called the (Hundred Days, Second New Deal).

Academic Vocabulary

Circle the letter of the word or words that have the closest meaning to the underlined academic vocabulary word from this lesson.

collapsing

1. As more and more people withdrew their money from banks, the banking system was <u>collapsing</u>.

   a. falling apart   **b.** losing loan business   **c.** reducing hours

assured

2. Roosevelt's <u>assured</u> people by saying that the reopened banks were safe.

   a. angered   **b.** convinced   **c.** fooled

The New Deal Takes Shape *(pages 733–734)*

Synthesizing

Read the lesson on the early New Deal and write three sentences describing Roosevelt's programs.

1. _____

   _____

2. _____

   _____

3. _____

   _____

 Notes

Terms To Know

Match the term from this lesson in the left column with the correct definition in the right column by writing the letter in the space to the left of the term.

_____ **1.** Agricultural Adjustment Act (AAA)

_____ **2.** Civilian Conservation Corps (CCC)

_____ **3.** Federal Deposit Insurance Corporation (FDIC)

_____ **4.** Federal Emergency Relief Administration (FERA)

_____ **5.** National Recovery Administration (NRA)

_____ **6.** National Industrial Recovery Act

_____ **7.** New Deal

_____ **8.** Public Works Administration (PWA)

_____ **9.** Securities and Exchange Commission (SEC)

_____ **10.** subsidies

_____ **11.** Tennessee Valley Authority (TVA)

_____ **12.** work relief

a. program to protect people's money placed in banks

b. agency formed to hire workers to build roads, bridges, and buildings

c. agency formed to give money to states to help needy people

d. agency formed to control flooding and bring electricity to rural areas

e. law aimed at solving the banking crisis

f. grants of money paid by the government

g. agency formed to give young men work improving parks and building levees

h. law aimed at having businesses regulate themselves

i. agency formed to oversee the sale of stocks and bonds

j. agency formed to make payments to unemployed farmers

k. programs to give needy people government jobs

l. law aimed at helping farmers

m. agency formed to encourage businesses to pay a minimum wage and stop hiring children

n. name given to all Roosevelt's programs to end the Depression

Academic Vocabulary

Choose an academic vocabulary word from this lesson from the list to complete each sentence by replacing the underlined word. Write the correct term in the space. You might have to change the form of some of the words.

create   promote   priority

1. Roosevelt gave <u>importance</u> _____ to finding ways to make new jobs.

Chapter 25, Section 2

2. One New Deal law aimed at <u>encouraging</u> _____ businesses to stop hiring child workers so they would hire adults instead.

3. Many New Deal laws <u>established</u> _____ new agencies in the government to oversee new actions. to make new jobs.

Section Wrap-up

Now that you have read the section, write the answers to the questions that were included in Setting a Purpose for Reading *at the beginning of the section.*

How did Roosevelt try to restore the confidence of the American people?

_____

_____

What programs were created in FDR's first 100 days?

_____

_____

Chapter 25, Section 3
Life During the Depression

(pages 735–739)

Reason To Read

Setting a Purpose for Reading Think about these questions as you read:
- How did the Depression affect minority groups?
- What radical political movements gained influence?

Main Idea

As you read pages 735–739 in your textbook, complete this graphic organizer by describing how different groups of people coped with difficult times.

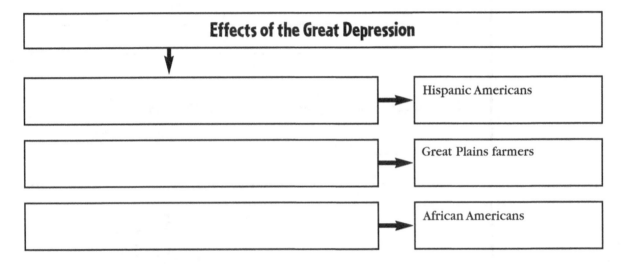

Effects of the Great Depression	
	Hispanic Americans
	Great Plains farmers
	African Americans

Sequencing Events

As you read, place the following events on the time line:
- *Gone With the Wind* **film is released**
- **Hattie Caraway is elected first woman senator**
- **Indian Reorganization Act is passed**

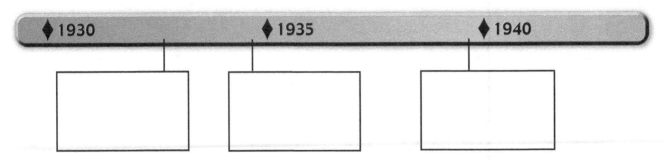

Hard Times in America (pages 735–736)

Reviewing

Reread each subsection and list two key facts.

Impact of the Depression

_____

_____

_____

Women Go to Work

_____

_____

_____

The Dust Bowl (pages 736–737)

Analyzing

Using the spaces below, explain what caused the Dust Bowl.

_____

_____

_____

_____

Terms To Know

Define or describe the following terms.

Dust Bowl

_____

_____

_____

migrant workers

_____

_____

_____

The Plight of Minorities (pages 737–738)

Outlining

Complete this outline as you read pages 737–738.

I. African Americans

A. _____

B. _____

II. Native Americans

A. _____

B. _____

III. Hispanic Americans

A. _____

B. _____

Terms To Know

Using the spaces provided, explain what the Indian Reorganization Act did.

_____

_____

_____

Academic Vocabulary

In the space available, define the following academic vocabulary words from this lesson.

decade

_____

_____

Radical Political Movements (pages 738–739)

Responding

After reading the subsection, answer the following questions.

1. How did socialists and communists view the Depression?

_____

_____

2. In what countries did fascism rise?

_____

_____

 Key Points

 Notes

Terms To Know

Choose a term from this lesson from the list below to complete each sentence by writing the term in the correct space.

American Civil War fascists   radicals

socialists   Spanish Civil War

1. A group of fascists tried to take over the government in one country, leading to the _____ .

2. Some _____ —people with extreme political views—gained support during the Depression.

3. _____ believed that the individual should be subordinate to the government and support government by dictators.

Academic Vocabulary

Read each sentence below. Put a checkmark in the space before the word or words that best explains what the bold-faced academic vocabulary word from this lesson means in this passage.

advocate

1. The severe economic problems of the Depression caused some people to **advocate** immediate changes to the economic system.

____ argue for ____ reject ____ revolt to achieve

philosophies

2. Economic problems led more and more people to accept extreme political **philosophies**.

____ governments ____ parties ____ ways of thinking

Entertainment and the Arts (page 739)

Connecting

Give two examples of each of these trends in the arts and entertainment during the Great Depression.

light or romantic entertainment

_____

_____

_____

Key Points

> social criticism

> topic

> trend

Notes

_____
_____
_____
_____

Academic Vocabulary

Write two words that are related to each academic vocabulary word from this lesson.

_____
_____

_____
_____

Section Wrap-up

Now that you have read the section, write the answers to the questions that were included in **Setting a Purpose for Reading** *at the beginning of the section.*

How did the Depression affect minority groups?

_____
_____

What radical political movements gained influence?

_____
_____

Chapter 25, Section 4
Effects of the New Deal

(pages 742–746)

Reason To Read

Setting a Purpose for Reading Think about these questions as you read:
- Why did people criticize Roosevelt and the New Deal?
- How did the Second New Deal create new economic and social roles for government?

Main Idea

As you read pages 742–746 in your textbook, complete this graphic organizer by describing the aims of the programs and laws listed.

Program	Aim
Works Progress Administration	
Social Security Act	
Fair Labor Standards Act	

Sequencing Events

As you read, place the following events on the time line:

Match the date in the left column with the correct achievement in the right column by writing the letter in the space to the left of the place.

_____ **1. 1935**

_____ **2. 1936**

_____ **3. 1937**

a. FDR begins First New Deal

b. FDR launches Second New Deal

c. Liberty League formed

d. Sit-down strike in Flint, Michigan

e. Long develops "Share Our Wealth" plan

f. Roosevelt reelected to third term

New Deal Opponents *(pages 742–743)*

Determining the Main Idea

Write down the main idea of this subsection and at least three details that support that idea.

Main Idea: _____

_____

1. _____

_____

2. _____

_____

3. _____

_____

Terms To Know

Write a sentence that explains the meaning of pension in the spaces below.

pension >

_____

_____

The Second New Deal *(pages 743–744)*

Questioning

As you read each subsection, ask yourself: what is an important detail? Write one of those details in the spaces below.

Need for Change >

_____

_____

Creating Jobs >

_____

_____

 **Key Points**

 **Notes**

Help for Those in Need >

Terms To Know *Explain the significance of each of the following terms from this lesson.*

Second New Deal >

Social Security Act >

---

unemployment insurance >

Academic Vocabulary *Circle the letter of the word or words that have the closest meaning to the underlined academic vocabulary word from this lesson.*

fund >

1. Roosevelt used the Revenue Act to help <u>fund</u> the programs of the Second New Deal.

   a. defeat   **b.** finance   **c.** gain support for

welfare >

2. Laws that created the social security system and unemployment insurance involved the American government in providing for people's <u>welfare</u> for the first time.

   a. education   **b.** health care   **c.** overall well-being

The Labor Movement (pages 744–745)

Scanning

Scan the subsection and then use the spaces below to write one or two sentences stating the general idea expressed in it.

_____

_____

_____

Terms To Know

Explain the significance of each of the following terms from this lesson.

Congress of Industrial Organizations

_____

_____

Fair Labor Standards Act (FLSA)

_____

_____

National Labor Relations Act

_____

_____

Academic Vocabulary

*Read each sentence below. Put a checkmark in the space before the phrase that best explains what the **boldfaced** academic vocabulary word from this lesson means in this passage.*

minimum

1. One New Deal law created a **minimum** wage for all workers.

____ average amount   ____ greatest amount   ____ least amount

technique

2. Auto workers in Flint, Michigan, used a new **technique** by sitting down on the job until their union was recognized.

____ form of boycott   ____ method   ____ protest

The Supreme Court (pages 745–746)

Evaluating *As you read, evaluate the information in this lesson by answering the following questions.*

1. By January 1936, why might Roosevelt have seen the Supreme Court as a problem?

   _____

   _____

   _____

2. What happened in the 1936 presidential election?

   _____

   _____

   _____

3. After that election, what did Roosevelt want to do with the Supreme Court?

   _____

   _____

   _____

4. What was the effect of that move?

   _____

   _____

   _____

Academic Vocabulary

In the space available, write three examples of a political issue, *an academic vocabulary word from this lesson.*

_____

_____

_____

Now that you have read the section, write the answers to the questions that were included in Setting a Purpose for Reading *at the beginning of the section.*

Why did people criticize Roosevelt and the New Deal?

_____

_____

How did the Second New Deal create new economic and social roles for government?

_____

_____

Chapter 26, Section 1
Road to War

(pages 752–755)

Reason To Read

Setting a Purpose for Reading Think about these questions as you read:
- Why did dictators come to power around the world?
- What actions led to the outbreak of World War II?

Main Idea

As you read pages 752–755 in your textbook, complete this graphic organizer by listing three dictators and the countries they ruled in the 1920s and 1930s.

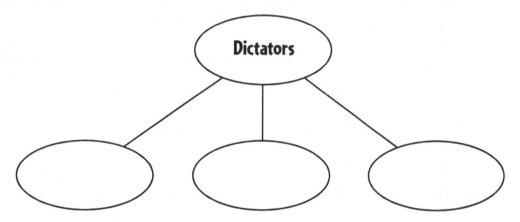

Sequencing Events

From the list, choose the event that completes the time line and write the event on the space provided.

- **Hitler sends troops into Rhineland**
- **Munich Conference gives Hitler the Sudetenland**
- **Hitler becomes chancellor of Germany**

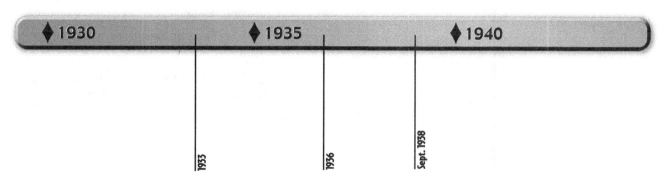

The Rise of Dictators *(pages 752–755)*

Comparing and Contrasting

Answer the following questions to compare and contrast political developments in Germany and Japan.

What problems brought new leaders to power in Germany and Japan? What plans did those new leaders have affecting their neighbors?

_____

_____

_____

Terms To Know

Match the term from this lesson in the left column with the correct definition in the right column by writing the letter in the space to the left of the term.

_____ **1.** anti-Semitism

_____ **2.** dictator

_____ **3.** fascism

_____ **4.** Fascist Party

_____ **5.** Nazi Party

_____ **6.** Neutrality Acts

_____ **7.** totalitarian

a. referring to a country in which one party rules and the leader suppresses all opposition and controls all aspects of people's lives

b. political group that came to control Germany

c. political philosophy that insisted on state ownership of all property and rule by the workers

d. rule by an unelected tyrant

e. political group that came to control Japan

f. prejudice against people from another country

g. U.S. laws calling for trade only with neutral nations

h. leader who controls a nation by force

i. U.S. laws banning the sale of weapons during a war

j. political group that came to control Italy

k. political philosophy combining extreme nationalism and racism

l. hatred of the Jews

Terms To Review

Choose a term or academic vocabulary word you studied earlier from the list below to complete each sentence by writing the correct word in the space.

annex (Chapter 11, Section 1)   enforce (Chapter 4, Section 2)

established (Chapter 2, Section 4)   exploiting (Chapter 17, Section 2)

occupy (Chapter 5, Section 2)

1. Hitler and other dictators rose to power by _____ the fears, anger, and resentment of people in their countries.

2. Once he gained power, Hitler _____ a dictatorship, taking control of all areas of people's lives.

3. Italy moved to _____ Ethiopia, formally claiming that it was part of Italy.

4. The League of Nations condemned Italy's action, but had no power to

_____ its opposition.

Germany on the March *(page 755)*

Sequencing

As you read, put the following events in the correct order by writing the numbers 1 through 6 in the spaces to the left. Use the number 1 for the event that occurred first, 2 for the next event, and so on.

_____ **a.** Hitler takes Austria.

_____ **b.** Hitler and Stalin sign a non-aggression pact.

_____ **c.** Hitler announces Germany's right to take the Sudetenland.

_____ **d.** Chamberlain meets with Hitler in Munich.

_____ **e.** Hitler annexes Czechoslovakia.

_____ **f.** Hitler sends troops into the Rhineland.

Notes

Terms To Know

Define or describe the following terms from this lesson.

appeasement

_____

_____

Munich Conference

_____

_____

Soviet-German Non-Aggression Pact

_____

_____

Section Wrap-up

Now that you have read the section, write the answers to the questions that were included in Setting a Purpose for Reading *at the beginning of the section.*

Why did dictators come to power around the world?

_____

_____

What actions led to the outbreak of World War II?

_____

_____

Chapter 26, Section 2
War Begins

(pages 758–763)

Reason To Read

Setting a Purpose for Reading Think about these questions as you read:
- Which European nations fell to Germany in 1939 and 1940?
- How did the United States respond to the war in Europe?

Main Idea

As you read pages 758–763 in your textbook, complete this graphic organizer by explaining the importance of each event.

	Importance
The Battle of Britain	
Signing the Atlantic Charter	
Attack on Pearl Harbor	

Sequencing Events

As you read, place the following events on the time line:
- **Battle of Britain begins**
- **Japan attacks Pearl Harbor**
- **FDR and Churchill issue Atlantic Charter**
- **Hitler invades Poland, launching World War II**

♦1939   ♦1940   ♦1941   ♦1942

Sept. 1939   Aug. 1940   Aug. 1941   Dec. 1941

War in Europe *(pages 758–760)*

Identifying Cause and Effect

As you read the lesson, complete the chart to identify the causes and effects of the early years of World War II.

Cause	Action	Effect
_____ _____ _____	Germany conquers Poland.	_____ _____ _____
_____ _____ _____	_____ _____ _____	British ships rescue stranded troops.
_____ _____ _____	_____ _____ _____	Hitler launches invasion of Soviet Union.

Terms To Know

Read the following sentences. Choose the correct term from this lesson to complete the sentence by circling the term.

1. The Germans and their allies were called the (Axis, Central) Powers.

2. Britain, France, and their allies were called the (Allies, Associates).

3. Hitler's strategy of lightning war had the name (blitzkrieg, Nazi storm).

4. Germany's air attack on Britain was given the name the Battle of (Britain, the Skies).

America and the War (pages 760–761)

Questioning

As you read the lesson, ask yourself: What is an important detail? Write one of those details about the presidential election of 1940 in the space below.

The 1940
Election

> _____
> _____
> _____
> _____
> _____

Terms To Know

Define or describe the following key terms from this lesson.

America First
Committee

> _____
> _____

Lend-Lease Act

> _____
> _____

Atlantic
Charter

> _____
> _____

disarmament

> _____
> _____

Terms To Review

Choose a term you studied earlier from the list below to complete each sentence by writing the correct term in the space.

convoy (Chapter 23, Section 3)   draft (Chapter 16, Section 4)
subsidy (Chapter 25, Section 2)

1. The Selective Service and Training Act put in place the country's first

   peacetime _____ .

2. Roosevelt ordered American ships to escort a _____
   of ships carrying supplies to Britain.

The Japanese Threat (pages 762–763)

Terms To Review

Choose an academic vocabulary word you studied earlier from the list below to complete each sentence by writing the correct term in the space.

acquire   obtain   default   responded

1. Japan needed to _____ from other countries natural resources such as oil and rubber that it lacked.

2. To fill that need, its leaders decided to _____ resource-rich areas in Asia.

3. The United States _____ to Japan's aggressive acts by denying it trade and taking other actions.

Section Wrap-up

Now that you have read the section, write the answers to the questions that were included in **Setting a Purpose for Reading** *at the beginning of the section.*

Which European nations fell to Germany in 1939 and 1940?

_____

_____

How did the United States respond to the war in Europe?

_____

_____

420

Chapter 26, Section 2

Chapter 26, Section 3
On the Home Front
(pages 764–768)

Reason To Read

Setting a Purpose for Reading Think about these questions as you read:
• What steps did the United States take to prepare for fighting the war?
• How did the war affect Americans?

Main Idea

As you read pages 764–768 in your textbook, complete this graphic organizer by identifying three ways Americans on the home front helped the war effort.

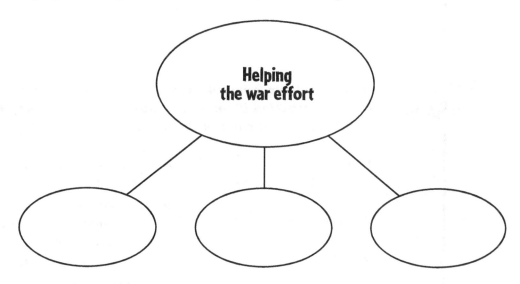

Helping
the war effort

Sequencing Events

As you read, write the correct dates for each of these events:

_____ **A. Philip Randolph demands end to discrimination in war industries**

_____ **Congress passes Revenue Act to fund the war**

_____ **Supreme Court upholds order placing Japanese Americans in internment camps**

America Prepares (pages 764–765)

Inferring *Read the lesson and then answer the questions to make inferences about what you read.*

1. How did women serving in the armed forces help the war effort if they were not involved in combat?

_____

_____

2. How does government spending show that the United States was more involved in World War II than it had been in World War I?

_____

_____

Terms To Know *Match the term from this lesson in the left column with the correct definition in the right column by writing the letter in the space to the left of the term.*

_____ **1.** Office of
    Price Administration

_____ **2.** Revenue Act of 1942

_____ **3.** WACs

_____ **4.** War Production Board

_____ **5.** WAVES

a. name for women who served in the navy

b. law that set terms of bonds the United States would sell to fund the war

c. name for women who served in the air force

d. government agency that worked to prevent inflation

e. government agency that worked to increase farm production

f. name for women who served in the army

g. law that increased taxes to help pay for the war

h. government agency that worked to boost industrial output

Copyright © by The McGraw-Hill Companies, Inc.

Wartime America (pages 765–766)

Reviewing — *Review this lesson and list two key facts under each topic.*

Making Sacrifices
_____
_____
_____
_____

Helping the War Effort
_____
_____
_____
_____

Terms To Know — *Read the following sentences. Choose the correct term from this lesson to complete the sentence by circling the term.*

1. The government set up an Office of War (Information, Propaganda) to promote patriotism and keep people united behind the war effort.

2. Many consumer goods were (boycotted, rationed), making them available in only limited supplies.

3. Some people joined (civil defense, homeland defense) groups to help protect the country from any possible attacks.

Academic Vocabulary — *Read each sentence below. Put a checkmark in the space before the word or words that best explains the meaning of the boldfaced vocabulary word.*

1. The government managed to keep prices more or less **stable** during the war.

_____ at about the same level

_____ falling

_____ rising slowly

2. Many **items** were not available to consumers because they were needed for the war effort.

_____ autos   _____ goods   _____ services

Women and Minorities *(pages 766–768)*

Responding *As you read the lesson, respond to the following questions.*

1. What was the effect of so many women working in war industries?

    _____

2. How did the roles that African Americans played in the armed forces change during the war?

    _____

3. What roles did Native Americans and Hispanic Americans play during the war?

    _____

4. What happened to Japanese Americans during the war?

    _____

    _____

Terms To Know *Use each of the following terms or phrases in a sentence.*

bracero _____

_____

internment camp _____

_____

Nisei _____

_____

Tuskegee Airmen _____

_____

Terms To Review

Choose a term you studied earlier from the list below to complete each sentence by writing the correct term in the space.

abandon (Chapter 4, Section 4) assigned (Chapter 19, Section 2)
expatriate (Chapter 24, Section 4)

1. Japanese Americans on the West Coast were forced to

   _____ their homes with very little preparations.

2. African American soldiers were at first not _____ to
   integrated units.

Section Wrap-up

Now that you have read the section, write the answers to the questions that were included in **Setting a Purpose for Reading** *at the beginning of the section.*

What steps did the United States take to prepare for fighting the war?

_____

_____

How did the war affect Americans?

_____

_____

Chapter 26, Section 4
War in Europe and Africa

(pages 770-776)

Reason To Read

Setting a Purpose for Reading Think about these questions as you read:
- What important battles took place in North Africa, Italy, and the Soviet Union between 1942 and 1944?
- What factors contributed to the Allied victory in Europe?

Main Idea

As you read pages 770-776 in your textbook, complete this graphic organizer by identifying important events during the war.

1942   **1943**   **1944**   **1945**
            Nov.   May   June

Sequencing Events

As you read, put the following events in the correct order by writing the numbers 1 through 8 in the spaces to the left. Use the number 1 for the event that occurred first, 2 for the next event, and so on.

_____ **A. British turn back Germans at El Alamein**

_____ **B. Allies land at Normandy**

_____ **C. Germans reach outskirts of Moscow**

_____ **D. V-E Day**

_____ **E. Germans pushed out of North Africa**

_____ **F. Sicily invaded**

_____ **G. Germany invades Soviet Union**

_____ **H. Germans forced to surrender at Stalingrad**

North African Campaign (pages 770–773)

Summarizing — *As you read each part of the lesson, write a one-sentence summary.*

Fighting in North Africa >
_____
_____

The Invasion of Italy >
_____
_____
_____

Air War Over Germany >
_____
_____

Academic Vocabulary — *Read the sentence below. Put a checkmark in the space before the phrase that best explains what the academic vocabulary word* conclude, *from this lesson, means in this sentence.*

Churchill thought it would be too difficult to invade Europe in 1942, and Roosevelt concluded that he was right.

_____ admitted   _____ decided   _____ ended

The Tide Turns in Europe (pages 773–775)

Terms To Know — *Read the following sentences. Choose the correct term from this lesson to complete the sentence by circling the term.*

1. Russians were forced to eat horses, cats, and dogs when food ran out during the (blockade, siege) of one of their cities.

2. The Allies planned an invasion of France that was called Operation (Overload, Overlord).

3. The invasion took place on June 6, 1944, a date that was code-named (D-Day, I-Day).

4. In December 1944, the Germans counterattacked, producing the fierce fight called the Battle of (Christmas, the Bulge).

5. When the Germans surrendered in May 1945, the Allies declared (V-E Day, V-G Day) to celebrate their victory.

Terms To Review

Read the sentence below. Put a checkmark in the space before the phrase that best explains the meaning of the boldfaced academic vocabulary word you studied earlier.

casualty
(Chapter 16, Section2)

The Germans suffered heavy casualties in their counterattack of late 1944, which was their last strong attack.

_____ difficult defeats to strategy

_____ equipment destroyed

_____ soldiers killed, wounded, captured, or missing

The Holocaust (pages 775–776)

Determining the Main Idea

Write down the main idea of this lesson and at least three details that support that idea.

_____

_____

_____

_____

Terms To Know

Match the term from this lesson in the left column with the correct definition in the right column by writing the letter in the space to the left of the term.

_____ **1.** concentration camp

_____ **2.** death camp

_____ **3.** genocide

_____ **4.** Holocaust

a. name given to Nazi attempts to kill all Jews under their control

b. prison camp for civilians

c. camps where prisoners of war were held

d. wiping out an entire group of people

e. camps where Nazis killed thousands of people

f. forcing people out of their homes

Now that you have read the section, write the answers to the questions that were included in Setting a Purpose for Reading *at the beginning of the section.*

What important battles took place in North Africa, Italy, and the Soviet Union between 1942 and 1944?

_____

_____

What factors contributed to the Allied victory in Europe?

_____

_____

Chapter 26, Section 5
War in the Pacific
(pages 777-780)

Reason To Read

Setting a Purpose for Reading Think about these questions as you read:
- How did the United States plan to gain control of the Pacific region?
- What role did the atomic bomb play in ending the war?

Main Idea

As you read pages 777-780 in your textbook, complete this graphic organizer by explaining the importance of each subject.

	Importance
Island hopping	
Manhattan Project	
V-J Day	

Sequencing Events

As you read, identify the year in which each of these battles took place. Write the year in the space provided.

_____ **Battle of Midway**

_____ **Allied victory at Leyte Gulf**

_____ **Allies capture Okinawa**

_____ **Surrender at Bataan**

_____ **Battle of Iwo Jima**

_____ **Allied victory at Guadalcanal**

_____ **Battle of the Coral Sea**

The Pacific Front (pages 777–779)

Clarifying

Write one or two sentences to describe the strategy of island hopping.

island
hopping >

_____

_____

Terms To Know

Match the term from this lesson in the left column with the correct definition in the right column by writing the letter in the space to the left of the term.

_____ **1.** Bataan Death March

_____ **2.** Battle of Leyte Gulf

_____ **3.** Battle of Midway

_____ **4.** Battle of the Coral Sea

_____ **5.** island hopping

_____ **6.** kamikaze

a. suicide pilot
b. sea battle that stopped the Japanese from nearing Australia
c. Japanese strategy of taking one island at a time
d. cry uttered by Japanese soldiers
e. punishment of Allied soldiers who had surrendered in the Philippines
f. sea battle that led to the destruction of four Japanese aircraft carriers
g. Allied strategy of taking one island at a time
h. sea battle that produced Japanese victory in Southeast Asia
i. sea battle that helped ensure retaking of the Philippines

The Atomic Bomb (pages 779–780)

Analyzing

Analyze the information in this lesson by answering the following questions.

1. Why did the United States develop the atomic bomb?

_____

_____

2. Why did Truman decide to use the atomic bomb?

_____

_____

Terms To Know

Define or describe the following key terms from this lesson.

Manhattan Project >

_____

_____

Potsdam Declaration >

_____

_____

The War Ends (page 780)

Responding

Read the lesson and write three sentences about the cost of the war.

_____

_____

_____

_____

_____

Terms To Know

Use the space below to define or describe the term from this lesson.

V-J Day >

_____

_____

Now that you have read the section, write the answers to the questions that were included in Setting a Purpose for Reading at the beginning of the section.

How did the United States plan to gain control of the Pacific region?

_____

_____

What role did the atomic bomb play in ending the war?

_____

_____

Chapter 27, Section 1
Cold War Origins

(pages 788–794)

Reason To Read

Setting a Purpose for Reading Think about these questions as you read:
- How did the United States attempt to stop the spread of communism?
- How did foreign policy change as a result of the Cold War?

Main Idea

As you read pages 788–794 in your textbook, complete this graphic organizer by listing important events in the Cold War.

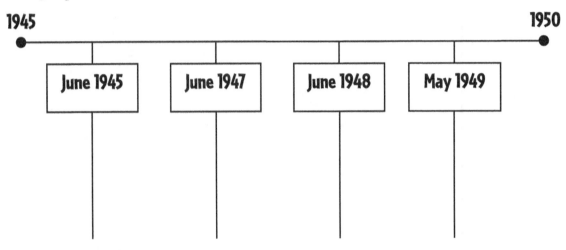

1945   **1950**

| June 1945 | June 1947 | June 1948 | May 1949 |

Sequencing Events

As you read, put the following events in the correct order by writing the number 1 through 7 in the space to the left. Use the number 1 for the event that occurred first, 2 for the next event, and so on.

_____ **A.** Roosevelt dies; Truman becomes president

_____ **B.** Marshall announces Marshall Plan

_____ **C.** NATO formed

_____ **D.** Soviets blockade West Berlin

_____ **E.** United Nations charter signed

_____ **F.** Truman announces Truman Doctrine

_____ **G.** Roosevelt, Churchill, Stalin meet at Yalta Conference

Wartime Diplomacy *(pages 788–790)*

Analyzing *Analyze the information in this lesson by answering the following questions.*

1. What issues divided the Allies as the war drew to a close?

_____

_____

2. What did the leaders agree to at Yalta?

_____

_____

Terms To Know *Define or describe the following key term.*

United Nations >
_____

_____

Soviet Expansion in Europe *(pages 790–791)*

Terms To Know *Read the following sentences. Choose the correct term from this lesson to complete the sentence by circling the term.*

1. By the late 1940s, the United States had developed a new policy toward the Soviet Union that was based on the idea of (containment, isolationism).

2. Churchill warned of the growing Soviet domination of country's behind what he called the ("communist curtain," "iron curtain").

3. In the (Marshall Plan, Truman Doctrine), the United States pledged to help nations threatened by communism and Soviet expansion.

 **Key Points**

 **Notes**

Academic Vocabulary

Read the sentence below. Put a checkmark in the space before the phrase that best explains what the academic vocabulary word sphere, *from this lesson, means in this passage.*

Churchill said that the countries within the "Soviet sphere" were largely being controlled by the Soviet Union.

_____ area _____ boundaries _____ territory

Crisis in Berlin *(pages 791–792)*

Connecting

Answer the following questions to connect the material in this subsection to material you read earlier.

1. Where had the Allies decided to divide Germany? How had they divided it?

   _____

   _____

2. What plan did the Allies announce in 1948? Why might Stalin fear this?

   _____

   _____

3. How did Stalin respond to this announcement?

   _____

   _____

4. How did Truman respond to this action?

   _____

   _____

Chapter 27, Section 1

 Key Points

 Notes

Terms To Know

Define or describe the following terms from this lesson.

Berlin airlift

_____

_____

_____

Berlin blockade

_____

_____

Two Armed Camps *(pages 792–794)*

Summarizing

As you read pages 792–794, write a one-sentence summary about the topic "The United States Rearms".

_____

_____

_____

Terms To Know

Define or describe the following key terms from this lesson.

cold war

_____

_____

_____

North Atlantic Treaty Organization

_____

_____

Academic Vocabulary

Use each of the following academic vocabulary words from this lesson in a sentence that reflects the meaning of the word.

mutual

_____

_____

_____

release

_____

_____

undergo

_____

_____

Section Wrap-up

Now that you have read the section, write the answers to the questions that were included in Setting a Purpose for Reading *at the beginning of the section.*

How did the United States attempt to stop the spread of communism?

_____

_____

How did foreign policy change as a result of the Cold War?

_____

_____

Chapter 27, Section 1

Chapter 27, Section 2
Postwar Politics

(pages 796–801)

Reason To Read

Setting a Purpose for Reading Think about these questions as you read:
- What economic problems did Americans face after World War II?
- What actions did President Truman and Congress propose to deal with the nation's problems?

Main Idea

As you read pages 796–801 in your textbook, complete this graphic organizer by identifying three measures that were part of Truman's Fair Deal.

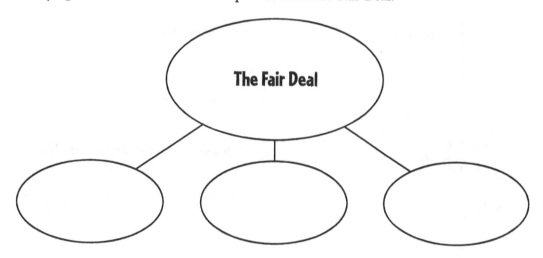

The Fair Deal

Sequencing Events

As you read, write the correct dates for each of these events:

_____ **Truman announces plan of domestic reforms**

_____ **Coal strike**

_____ **Congress passes Taft-Hartley bill**

_____ **Truman wins presidential election**

The Postwar Economy (pages 796–797)

Clarifying

Review pages 796–797 and answer these questions.

1. What contributed to inflation after World War II ended?

   _____

   _____

2. What happened to relations between businesses and unions after the war? What were the effects?

   _____

   _____

3. How did Truman address these problems?

   _____

   _____

Terms To Know

Define or describe the following term from this lesson:

> **consumer goods**

_____

_____

Truman Faces the Republicans (pages 797–800)

Questioning

Review pages 797–800 and write an important detail for each of these topics.

> **Government Reorganization**

_____

_____

_____

> **The Election of 1948**

_____

_____

_____

Terms To Know

Match the term from this lesson in the left column with the correct definition in the right column by writing the letter in the space to the left of the term.

_____ **1.** Central Intelligence Agency

_____ **2.** closed shop

_____ **3.** Fair Deal

_____ **4.** National Security Act

_____ **5.** Taft-Hartley bill

a. law that gave unions the right to organize

b. law that created the Department of Defense

c. workplace where only union members could work

d. group formed in 1947 to collect information on other lands

e. law that created the National Security Agency

f. Dewey's slogan for his domestic program

g. law that limited workers' rights

h. workplace closed to union members

i. Truman's slogan for his domestic program

A Fair Deal for Americans (pages 800–801)

Summarizing

Read the information on civil rights on pages 800–801. Then, write three sentences summarizing Truman's policies.

_____

_____

_____

_____

_____

Terms To Know

Define or describe the following term from this lesson.

desegregate

_____

_____

Now that you have read the section, write the answers to the questions that were included in Setting a Purpose for Reading *at the beginning of the section.*

What economic problems did Americans face after World War II?

_____

_____

What actions did President Truman and Congress propose to deal with the nation's problems?

_____

_____

Chapter 27, Section 3
The Korean War

(pages 802–805)

Reason To Read

Setting a Purpose for Reading Think about these questions as you read:
- What events led to the Korean War?
- How did America's war aims change during the war?

Main Idea

As you read pages 802–805 in your textbook, complete this chart by writing the date or event in the appropriate space.

Date	Event
June 25, 1950	
	UN forces capture Pyongyang
November 26, 1950	
	MacArthur relieved of command
July 27, 1953	

Sequencing Events

As you read, put the following events in the correct order by writing the number 1 through 4 in the space to the left. Use the number 1 for the event that occurred first, 2 for the next event, and so on.

_____ **A.** Cease-fire in Korea

_____ **B.** North Korea invades South Korea

_____ **C.** MacArthur dismissed from command

_____ **D.** American and Soviet troops divide Korea after Japanese forces leave

Conflict in Korea (pages 802–804)

Responding *As you read the lesson, respond to the following questions.*

1. How did Korea become divided in the first place?

_____

2. Why did North Korea invade the South?

_____

_____

3. What was the situation when MacArthur took command? What did he succeed in doing?

_____

_____

Terms To Know *Define or describe the following key term.*

38th parallel

_____

_____

American Leadership Divided (pages 804–805)

Identifying Cause and Effect *Read the section and then answer the questions to identify the causes and effects of actions in the late stages of the Korean War.*

1. Why did MacArthur propose attacking Chinese troops or even China itself?

_____

_____

2. Why did Truman reject that idea?

_____

_____

3. Why did Truman fire MacArtur?

_____

_____

Terms To Know

Define or describe each of the following key terms from this lesson.

demilitarized zone

_____

_____

stalemate

_____

_____

Section Wrap-up

Now that you have read the section, write the answers to the questions that were included in Setting a Purpose for Reading _at the beginning of the section._

What events led to the Korean War?

_____

_____

How did America's war aims change during the war?

_____

_____

Chapter 27, Section 4
The Red Scare

(pages 806–809)

Reason To Read

Setting a Purpose for Reading Think about these questions as you read:
- What effect did Cold War fears have on domestic politics?
- How did McCarthyism affect the nation?

Main Idea

As you read pages 806–809 in your textbook, complete this graphic organizer by explaining why these individuals are important.

	Historical significance
Alger Hiss	
Ethel Rosenberg	
Joseph McCarthy	

Sequencing Events

As you read, place the following events on the time line:
- **Senate censures McCarthy**
- **House Un-American Activities Committee begins hearings**
- **Chambers testifies that Hiss gave him secret papers in the 1930s**
- **Rosenbergs executed for spying**
- **McCarthy makes Wheeling speech**

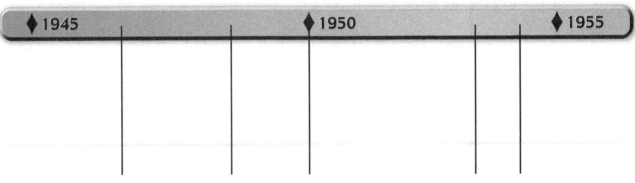

♦ 1945   ♦ 1950   ♦ 1955

Cold War Fears (pages 806–808)

Terms To Know

Read the following sentences. Choose the correct term from this lesson to complete the sentence by circling the term.

1. Film companies made (blacklists, "Red Lists") of people who would not be hired because their loyalty was suspicious.

2. Congress passed the (McCarran, McCarthy) Act, which required all organizations with links to the Communists to register with the government.

3. The (Patriotic Defense, Un-American Activities) Committee of the House staged public hearings that cast doubts on the loyalty of many Americans.

4. Many Americans feared (conversion, subversion) by Communists in the government.

5. One former government official was found guilty of (perjury, treason) for lying during an investigation.

Terms To Review

In the space available, define the following words you studied earlier.

espionage
(Chapter 23, Section 4)

_____
_____

Red Scare
(Chapter 24, Section 1)

_____
_____

sabotage
(Chapter 23, Section 4)

_____
_____

Key Points

Notes

McCarthyism (pages 808–809)

Determining the Main Idea

Write at least three details that support the main idea.

Main Idea ▷ From 1950 to 1954, the hunt for Communists in America was dominated by Senator Joseph McCarthy.

_____

_____

_____

Terms To Know

Choose the term from the list below that best completes each sentence and write the term in the space provided.

alleged   censure   blacklisted

1. McCarthy _____ that there were Communists through-out he government but he had no proof.

2. Once McCarthy lost popular support, the Senate voted to

_____ him.

Section Wrap-up

Now that you have read the section, write the answers to the questions that were included in **Setting a Purpose for Reading** *at the beginning of the section.*

What effect did Cold War fears have on domestic politics?

_____

_____

How did McCarthyism affect the nation?

_____

_____

Chapter 28, Section 1
Eisenhower in the White House

(pages 814–820)

Reason To Read

Setting a Purpose for Reading Think about these questions as you read:
• What beliefs and policies characterized the Eisenhower presidency?
• What foreign policy challenges did the Eisenhower administration face?

Main Idea

As you read pages 814–820 in your textbook, complete this graphic organizer by listing examples of actions the United States took to solve problems in world affairs.

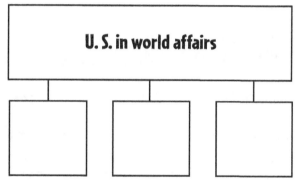

U. S. in world affairs

Sequencing Events

As you read, place the number representing each event in the appropriate circle on the time line:

1. **Suez crisis; Hungarian uprising**
2. **Geneva summit**
3. **U.S. launches** *Explorer*
4. **Soviet Union launches** *Sputnik*
5. **Eisenhower elected president**
6. **U-2 incident**
7. **French surrender after defeat at Dien bien phu**

1950   1955   1960

Key Points

Notes

Republican Revival (pages 814–815)

Scanning

Scan the lesson by reading the headings. Then write down two topics you think will be covered in this lesson.

_____

_____

_____

Terms To Review

In the space available, define the following word you studied earlier.

subversion
(Chapter 27, Section 4)

_____

_____

Domestic Policy (pages 815–816)

Evaluating

Read the lesson and then answer the questions.

1. What moderate financial policies did Eisenhower follow?

_____

_____

2. How did the creation of the interstate highway system stimulate the economy?

_____

_____

3. What moderate social policies did Eisenhower follow?

_____

_____

Terms To Know

Define or describe the following key terms from this lesson.

> **surplus**

_____

_____

_____

> **Federal Highway Act**

_____

_____

_____

> **Department of Health, Education, and Welfare (HEW)**

_____

_____

_____

Eisenhower and the Cold War (pages 816–818)

Interpreting

Interpret the information you read about Eisenhower's foreign policy by answering the following questions.

1. Why were Americans shocked by the Soviet launch of *Sputnik?*

_____

_____

2. What new approach to the Cold War did Dulles want?

_____

_____

3. What was the effect of the policy of massive retaliation on relations with the Soviet Union?

_____

_____

Terms To Know

Match the term from this lesson in the left column with the correct definition in the right column by writing the letter in the space to the left of the term.

____ **1.** arms race

____ **2.** Civil Defense Administration

____ **3.** conventional weapons

____ **4.** intercontinental ballistic missile

____ **5.** intermediate range ballistic missile

____ **6.** massive retaliation

____ **7.** National Aeronautics and Space Administration

____ **8.** Project Mercury

____ **9.** space race

____ **10.** *Vanguard*

a. non-nuclear weapons

b. competition to explore outside the earth

c. weapons that could reach targets many thousands of miles away

d. first successful U.S. satellite

e. competition to build more weapons

f. agency that taught people how to act in the event of a nuclear attack

g. policy of using nuclear weapons first, before an enemy could

h. weapons that could reach targets up to 1,500 miles away

i. policy of attacking instantly and with heavy force in response to a nuclear attack

j. U.S. satellite that exploded when launched

k. first program for putting an astronaut in space

l. agency put in charge of space exploration

m. agency that created an array of missiles to defend the U.S.

Foreign Policy Challenges *(pages 818–820)*

Sequencing

As you read, put the following events in the correct order by writing the numbers 1 through 6 in the spaces to the left. Use the number 1 for the event that occurred first, 2 for the next event, and so on.

____ **a.** French forced to surrender in Vietnam

____ **b.** Founding of Israel

____ **c.** Castro seizes power in Cuba

____ **d.** U-2 incident

____ **e.** Suez Canal crisis

____ **f.** Geneva summit

Chapter 28, Section 1

Terms To Know

Define or describe the following terms from this lesson.

domino theory _____
_____
_____

summit _____
_____
_____

peaceful coexistence _____
_____
_____

U-2 _____
_____

Academic Vocabulary

Circle the letter of the word that has the closest meaning to the boldfaced academic vocabulary word from this lesson.

"I can **conceive** of no greater tragedy than for the United States to become engaged in all-out war in Indochina."

a. detect   **b.** imagine   **c.** plan

Section Wrap-up

Now that you have read the section, write the answers to the questions that were included in Setting a Purpose for Reading *at the beginning of the section.*

What beliefs and policies characterized the Eisenhower presidency?

_____

_____

What foreign policy challenges did the Eisenhower administration face?

_____

_____

_____

Chapter 28, Section 2
1950s Prosperity

(pages 821–826)

Reason To Read

Setting a Purpose for Reading Think about these questions as you read:
- What factors helped the economy grow during the 1950s?
- How did the era's prosperity affect American society and culture?

Main Idea

As you read pages 821–826 in your textbook, complete this graphic organizer by describing three changes that occurred in American life as a result of the strong economy or the growth of technology.

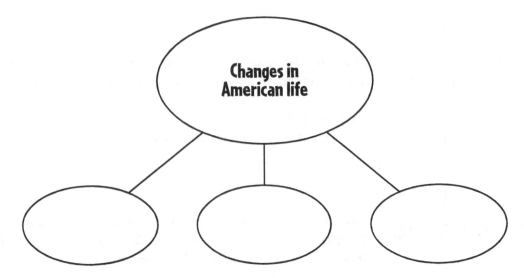

Sequencing Events

As you read, write the correct date for each of these events:

_____ **First Levittown built**

_____ **Polio vaccine first given to children**

_____ **IBM becomes leader in computer industry**

_____ **Elvis Presley bursts onto the scene**

 **Key Points**

 **Notes**

A Booming Economy *(pages 821–822)*

Monitoring Comprehension

Check your understanding of the information in this lesson by answering the following questions.

1. What prompted the growth of the economy after World War II?

_____

_____

2. What effect did this economic growth have on individual Americans?

_____

_____

Terms To Know

Read the following sentences. Choose the correct term from this lesson to complete the sentence by circling the term.

1. Economic growth meant that the average American enjoyed much higher (personal income, personal wealth).

2. That led to a better (gross personal product, standard of living), a measure of people's quality of life.

3. One new machine fueling business growth was the (automobile, computer).

Academic Vocabulary

In the spaces available, use the following academic vocabulary words in a sentence.

expert >

_____

_____

overall >

_____

_____

A Changing Nation (pages 822–826)

Questioning As you read each part of the lesson, ask yourself: what is an important detail? Write one of those details in each space below.

The Baby Boom >

_____
_____
_____
_____

Expanding Suburbs >

_____
_____
_____

A Nation on Wheels >

_____
_____
_____
_____

A Consumer Society >

_____
_____
_____
_____

An American Culture >

_____
_____
_____

Terms To Know Define or describe each of the following key terms from this lesson.

affluence >

_____
_____

generation gap >

_____
_____

Academic Vocabulary

Read the following sentence. In the space below, write in your own words the meaning of the boldfaced academic vocabulary word from this section.

Television became an important **source** for news, information, and entertainment in the 1950s.

_____

Section Wrap-up

Now that you have read the section, write the answers to the questions that were included in **Setting a Purpose for Reading** *at the beginning of the section.*

What factors helped the economy grow during the 1950s?

_____

_____

How did the era's prosperity affect American society and culture?

_____

_____

Chapter 28, Section 3
Problems in a Time of Plenty

(pages 828–831)

Reason To Read

Setting a Purpose for Reading Think about these questions as you read:
• Which groups did not share in the prosperity of the 1950s?
• Why did some people criticize American values of the period?

Main Idea

As you read pages 828–831 in your textbook, complete this graphic organizer by describing the economic problems these groups faced.

Kinds of workers	Economic problems
Small farmers	
Migrant farmworkers	
Factory workers	

Sequencing Events

From the list below, choose the correct year in which the Supreme Court decided the case *Brown* v. *Board of Education of Topeka, Kansas*. Circle the correct date.

1952   1954   1956   1958

Poverty *(pages 828–830)*

Comparing and Contrasting

Answer the following questions to compare and contrast the experience of some groups of Americans in the 1950s.

1. How did the situation of farmers compare to that of affluent Americans?

_____

_____

2. How did the lives of African American farmworkers in the South compare to those of Hispanic American farmworkers in the West?

_____

_____

3. What problems affected the urban poor?

_____

_____

Terms To Know

Define or describe the following key terms.

automation

_____

_____

ghetto

_____

_____

Terms To Review

Use each of the following terms, which you studied earlier, in a sentence that reflects the meaning of the term.

migrate
(Chapter 20, Section 2)

_____

_____

surplus
(Chapter 28, Section 1)

_____

Voices of Dissent (pages 830–831)

Evaluating *Review the information presented in this lesson, then answer these questions.*

1. Identify a social critic from the period.

_____

2. Summarize the critic's beliefs and opinions.

_____

_____

3. Do you think that these beliefs and opinions were valid? Why or why not?

_____

_____

Terms To Know *Define or describe the key term from this lesson listed below.*

materialism ➤
_____

_____

Section Wrap-up *Now that you have read the section, write the answers to the questions that were included in* **Setting a Purpose for Reading** *at the beginning of the section.*

Which groups did not share in the prosperity of the 1950s?

_____

_____

Why did some people criticize American values of the period?

_____

_____

Chapter 29, Section 1
The Civil Rights Movement
(pages 838–842)

Reason To Read

Setting a Purpose for Reading Think about these questions as you read:
- How did a Supreme Court decision help African Americans in their struggle for civil rights?
- Why did Dr. Martin Luther King, Jr., emerge as a leader?

Main Idea

As you read pages 838–842 in your textbook, complete this graphic organizer by describing the roles these people played in the civil rights movement.

	Roles
Linda Brown	
Rosa Parks	
Martin Luther King, Jr.	

Sequencing Events

Match the date in the left column with the correct event in the right column by writing the letter in the space to the left of the date.

_____ **1.** 1896

_____ **2.** 1954

_____ **3.** 1955

_____ **4.** 1957

a. Montgomery bus boycott

b. South abandons segregation

c. *Plessy v. Ferguson* makes segregation legal

d. integration of Central High School in Little Rock, Arkansas

e. *Brown v. Board of Education* makes school segregation illegal

Key Points Notes

Equality in Education (pages 838–840)

Scanning

Scan the lesson by reading the headings and looking at the map on page 839. Then write down three topics you think will be covered in this lesson. As you read, write down a fact about each topic.

_____

_____

_____

_____

_____

Terms To Know

Define or describe the following key terms.

Brown v. Board of Education of Topeka, Kansas ❯

_____

_____

integrating ❯

_____

_____

NAACP ❯

_____

_____

Gains on Other Fronts (pages 841–842)

Inferring

Read the section and then answer the questions to make inferences about what you read.

1. Why was Rosa Parks arrested for sitting in a certain area of a city bus?

_____

_____

2. Was the Montgomery bus boycott easy or difficult for the city's African Americans to carry out? Why?

_____

_____

3. How did Martin Luther King, Jr., become a leader of the civil rights movement?

_____

_____

Terms To Know

Define or describe the following key terms from this lesson.

civil disobedience

_____

_____

Southern Christian Leadership Conference

_____

_____

Academic Vocabulary

Circle the letter of the word or words that have the closest meaning to the underlined academic vocabulary word from this lesson.

1. The boycott organizers hoped the move would hurt the city bus system financially and force officials to <u>alter</u> their policies.

   a. apologize for   **b.** change   **c.** reverse

2. Parks belonged to the Montgomery <u>chapter</u> of the NAACP.

   a. part of a book   **b.** underground cell   **c.** unit of a larger group

Section Wrap-up

Now that you have read the section, write the answers to the questions that were included in **Setting a Purpose for Reading** *at the beginning of the section.*

How did a Supreme Court decision help African Americans in their struggle for civil rights?

_____

_____

Why did Dr. Martin Luther King, Jr., emerge as a leader?

_____

_____

Chapter 29, Section 2
Kennedy and Johnson

(pages 844–847)

Reason To Read

Setting a Purpose for Reading Think about these questions as you read:

- What were the goals for Kennedy's New Frontier?
- What new programs were created as part of the Great Society?

Main Idea

As you read pages 844–847 in your textbook, complete this graphic organizer by listing four programs that were part of the War on Poverty.

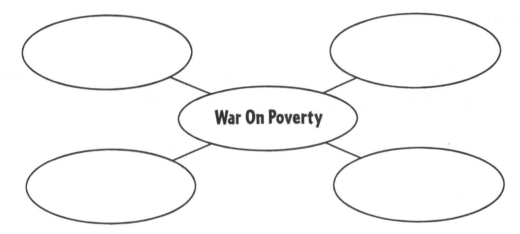

Sequencing Events

As you read, complete the chart by writing the event in the appropriate space on the chart.

Date	Event
November 1960	
January 20, 1961	
November 22, 1963	
July 1964	

Election of 1960 (pages 844–845)

Evaluating

Analyze the information about the presidential campaign of 1960 and answer the following questions.

1. Why were the televised debates a turning point in the 1960 election?

_____

_____

2. Do you think candidate debates are a good way for to form an opinion about candidates? Explain your answer.

_____

_____

Academic Vocabulary

Read the passage below. Put a checkmark in the space before the phrase that best explains what the academic vocabulary word stress, from this lesson, means in this passage.

Kennedy countered the concern over his being a Catholic by <u>stressing</u> that he believed that church and state should be separate.

_____ arguing   _____ emphasizing   _____ feeling pressured

The New Frontier (pages 845–846)

Responding

Review pages 845–846 and answer these questions.

1. What are domestic policies?

_____

_____

2. What were important domestic policies during the Kennedy administration?

_____

_____

3. What do you think are the two most important domestic issues the nation faces today?

_____

_____

Terms To Know

Match the term in the left column with the correct definition in the right column by writing the letter in the space to the left of the place.

____ **1.** New Frontier

____ **2.** Warren Commission

a. group investigating civil rights for Kennedy

b. group investigating Kennedy's assassination

c. Kennedy's civil rights program

d. Kennedy's domestic legislation program

Academic Vocabulary

Select the vocabulary term from the list below that best completes the sentence. Write your answer in the space provided.

available   reluctant   committed

Many representatives were _____ to spend as much money as Kennedy's programs would require, so Congress voted against them.

The "Great Society" (pages 846–847)

Analyzing

Review pages 846–847 and list two important facts about each of these topics.

The War on Poverty ▷ _____

_____

Civil Rights ▷ _____

_____

 **Key Points**

 **Notes**

Terms To Know

Match the term from this lesson in the left column with the correct definition in the right column by writing the letter in the space to the left of the term.

____ **1.** Civil Rights Act of 1964

____ **2.** Department of Housing and Urban Development

____ **3.** "Great Society"

____ **4.** Head Start

____ **5.** Job Corps

____ **6.** Medicaid

____ **7.** Medicare

____ **8.** poverty line

____ **9.** Upward Bound

____ **10.** Volunteers in Service to America

a. helped pay for health care of the elderly

b. helped poor students to attend college

c. minimum income needed to survive

d. agency that provided jobs to the poor

e. similar to the Peace Corps

f. new cabinet agency aimed to help cities rebuild

g. law guaranteeing voting rights of African Americans

h. slogan for Johnson's programs

i. provided preschool education for poor children

j. law banning discrimination in many areas of life

k. helped fund health care for poor people

l. what critics called Johnson's programs

m. new cabinet agency that funded housing

n. agency that provided job training to the poor

Section Wrap-up

Now that you have read the section, write the answers to the questions that were included in **Setting a Purpose for Reading** *at the beginning of the section.*

What were the goals for Kennedy's New Frontier?

_____

_____

What new programs were created as part of the Great Society?

_____

_____

Chapter 29, Section 3
The Struggle Continues
(pages 848–853)

Reason To Read

Setting a Purpose for Reading Think about these questions as you read:
- What actions did African Americans take in the early 1960s to secure their rights?
- What African American leaders emerged during this period?

Main Idea

As you read pages 848–853 in your textbook, complete this graphic organizer by describing the roles these people played in the civil rights movement.

	Roles
James Meredith	
Malcolm X	
Stokely Carmichael	

Sequencing Events

As you read, put the following events in the correct order by writing the number 1 through 6 in the space to the left. Use the number 1 for the event that occurred first, 2 for the next event, and so on.

_____ **A. March on Washington**

_____ **B. James Meredith enrolls in University of Mississippi**

_____ **C. Freedom Summer**

_____ **D. Freedom Riders try to take buses across state lines in South**

_____ **E. protest in Birmingham**

_____ **F. Congress passes Voting Rights Act**

The Movement Grows (pages 848–852)

Responding

Review the information on pages 848–852. Then, answer the questions that follow.

1. What did sit-ins accomplish?

_____

_____

2. What happened as a result of the Freedom Rides?

_____

_____

3. What happened regarding the integration of education in the early 1960s?

_____

_____

Terms To Know

Choose a term from this lesson from the list below to complete each sentence by writing the term in the correct space.

Congress of Racial Equality   Freedom Riders   sit-in

Freedom Summer   interstate   Voting Rights

Student Nonviolent Coordinating Committee

1. The _____ aimed to end segregation in bus transportation.

2. The Supreme Court ruled that _____ buses and bus stations had to be integrated.

3. Some students staged _____ to force stores to integrate.

4. With the _____ Act, Congress ensured that African Americans would have voting rights.

5. The _____ took the lead in challenging segregation in transportation.

Chapter 29, Section 3

Other Voices (pages 852–853)

 **Drawing Conclusions**

Read the section and then answer the questions to draw conclusions about what you read.

1. How did Malcolm X's ideas change?

_____

_____

2. What are two examples of violence that erupted because of African Americans' frustration and anger?

_____

_____

Terms To Know

Match the term from this lesson in the left column with the correct definition in the right column by writing the letter in the space to the left of the term.

____ 1. Black Panther Party

____ 2. Black Power

a. religious group also known as the Nation of Islam

b. group of young radicals

c. movement aimed at running African American candidates for office

d. movement of racial pride that urged African Americans to develop their own culture

Section Wrap-up

Now that you have read the section, write the answers to the questions that were included in Setting a Purpose for Reading *at the beginning of the section.*

Why was the March on Washington organized?

_____

_____

Why did some African American leaders criticize the goal of integration?

_____

_____

Chapter 29, Section 4
Other Groups Seek Rights
(pages 856–860)

Reason To Read

Setting a Purpose for Reading Think about these questions as you read:
- What steps did women and minorities take to improve their lives?
- What new leaders emerged?

Main Idea

As you read pages 856–860 in your textbook, complete this graphic organizer by describing the role each person played in the 1960s and 1970s.

	Roles
Phyllis Schlafly	
César Chávez	
Herman Badillo	

Sequencing Events

As you read, write the correct dates for each of these events.

_____ **Equal Pay Act passed**

_____ **National Organization for Women founded**

_____ **Workplace discrimination against women banned**

_____ **Sandra Day O'Connor named to Supreme Court**

Women's Rights *(pages 856–857)*

Determining the Main Idea

Write down the main idea of this section and at least three details that support that idea.

_____

_____

_____

_____

_____

_____

Terms To Know

Read the following sentences. Choose the correct term from this lesson to complete the sentence by circling the term.

1. Women who fought for their rights in the 1960s and 1970s were called (feminists, suffragists).

2. The (Equal Rights Amendment, Women's Rights Amendment) aimed to guarantee that women would have the same rights as men.

3. The (National Movement for Women's Rights, National Organization for Women) campaigned to gain rights for women in many areas.

4. According to the (Equal Pay Act, Workplace Equality Act), employers had to pay women the same as men for doing the same job.

Hispanic Americans *(pages 858–859)*

Questioning

As you read pages 868–859, ask yourself: what is an important detail about the farmworkers organizing? Write an important detail under the topic.

> **Farmworkers Organize**

_____

_____

_____

 **Key Points**

 **Notes**

Terms To Know

Define or describe the following key terms from this lesson.

Hispanic >
_____
_____
_____

La Raza Unida >
_____
_____
_____

The League of United Latin American Citizens >
_____
_____

Native Americans *(pages 859–860)*

Skimming

Skim the lesson by reading the text under each heading quickly to get a general idea of what it is about. Use one or two sentences to write that general idea in the spaces below.

Efforts to Organize

_____
_____

American Indian Movement

_____
_____

Americans With Disabilities

_____
_____

 **Key Points**

 **Notes**

Terms To Know

Define or describe the following key terms from this lesson.

American Indian Movement (AIM)

_____

_____

Indian Civil Rights Act of 1968

_____

_____

National Congress of American Indians (NCAI)

_____

_____

Academic Vocabulary

Write the correct form of the boldfaced academic vocabulary word from this lesson in the blank space to complete the sentence.

emphasis   emphasize

Native Americans increasingly came to _____ their own history, language, and culture in their schools in the 1960s.

Section Wrap-up

Now that you have read the section, write the answers to the questions that were included in **Setting a Purpose for Reading** *at the beginning of the section.*

What steps did women and minorities take to improve their lives?

_____

_____

What new leaders emerged?

_____

_____

Chapter 30, Section 1
Kennedy's Foreign Policy
(pages 866–870)

Reason To Read

Setting a Purpose for Reading Think about these questions as you read:
- How did the Kennedy administration handle challenges to foreign affairs ?
- What happened during the Cuban missile crisis?

Main Idea

As you read pages 866–870 in your textbook, complete this graphic organizer by describing the actions the Kennedy administration took in response to these crises.

Response to Crises	
Berlin Wall	**Cuban Missile Crisis**

Sequencing Events

As you read, place the following events on the time line:
- **Cuban missile crisis**
- **Kennedy and Khrushchev hold summit in Vienna**
- **Berlin Wall is started**
- **Bay of Pigs invasion fails**

◆ 1961	◆ 1962	◆ 1963

April
June
August
October

New Directions (pages 866–867)

Evaluating   *Read the section and then answer the questions to evaluate what you read.*

1. What approach did Kennedy take toward nuclear weapons?

_____

_____

2. What new military options did he develop and why?

_____

_____

3. How did he use non-military means to strengthen the position of the United States?

_____

_____

Terms To Know   *Match the term from this lesson in the left column with the correct definition in the right column by writing the letter in the space to the left of the term.*

_____ **1.** Alliance for Progress

_____ **2.** executive order

_____ **3.** flexible response

_____ **4.** Green Berets

_____ **5.** Peace Corps

a. special military unit trained to be ready to fight guerrilla fighters

b. new defense strategy that emphasized being able to strike anywhere in the world with nuclear weapons

c. special group formed to send volunteers to other countries to help people as teachers and advisers

d. mandate that Congress puts on the president

e. new defense strategy that emphasized special military units

f. rule issued by the president

g. new foreign policy plan for Western Europe

h. development plan aimed at Latin America

 **Key Points**

 **Notes**

Terms To Review

Read the sentence below. In the spaces that follow, explain the meaning of the vocabulary word you studied earlier.

promote
(Chapter 25, Section 2)

Kennedy hoped to **promote** economic development in Latin America.

_____

_____

Cold War Confrontations *(pages 867–869)*

Sequencing

As you read, put the following events in the correct order by writing the number 1 through 5 in the space to the left. Use the number 1 for the event that occurred first, 2 for the next event, and so on.

_____ **a.** Bay of Pigs invasion fails

_____ **b.** Communists build Berlin Wall

_____ **c.** Castro seizes power in Cuba

_____ **d.** Khrushchev tells Kennedy to pull troops out of Berlin

_____ **e.** CIA develops plan for attacking Castro at Bay of Pigs

Terms To Know

Define or describe the following key terms from this lesson.

Berlin Wall

_____

_____

exiles

_____

_____

Academic Vocabulary

In the space available, define the following academic vocabulary word.

intelligence

_____

_____

The Cuban Missile Crisis *(pages 869–870)*

Previewing   *As you read the section, answer the following questions.*

1. Look at the map on page 869. What does it show?

   _____

   _____

2. Look at the heading on page 870. What issue other than the Cuban missile crisis will be addressed in this section?

   _____

   _____

Terms To Know   *Use the spaces below to write a sentence using each of these key terms from this lesson.*

Apollo project

   _____

   _____

Cuban missile crisis

   _____

   _____

hot line

   _____

   _____

Academic Vocabulary   *Read the passage below. Put a checkmark in the space before the phrase that best explains what the academic vocabulary word* options, *from this lesson, means in this passage.*

When Kennedy learned of the Soviet missile bases being built in Cuba, he and his advisers discussed their different <u>options</u>.

_____ chances of survival

_____ opportunities for success

_____ possible courses of action

Now that you have read the section, write the answers to the questions that were included in **Setting a Purpose for Reading** *at the beginning of the section.*

Why did the Bay of Pigs invasion fail? How did Kennedy address the Berlin crisis?

_____

_____

What actions did Kennedy take during the Cuban missile crisis?

_____

_____

Chapter 30, Section 2
War in Vietnam

(pages 871–876)

Reason To Read

Setting a Purpose for Reading Think about these questions as you read:
• How did Vietnam become a divided country?
• Why did America increase its involvement in the Vietnam War?

Main Idea

As you read pages 871–876 in your textbook, complete this graphic organizer by filling in the main events that occurred after the Gulf of Tonkin Resolution.

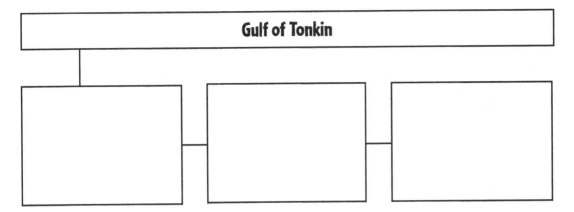

Gulf of Tonkin

Sequencing Events

As you read, put the following events in the correct order by writing the number 1 through 6 in the space to the left. Use the number 1 for the event that occurred first, 2 for the next event, and so on.

_____ **A.** Vietcong begin war against Diem

_____ **B.** Geneva Accords divide Vietnam

_____ **C.** Johnson begins escalation

_____ **D.** Officers carry out coup in South Vietnam

_____ **E.** Diem gains control of South Vietnam

_____ **F.** Gulf of Tonkin incident

The U.S. and Vietnam (pages 871–874)

Summarizing

As you read each subsection, write a one- or two-sentence summary.

The U.S. and Vietnam
_____
_____

The Geneva Accords
_____
_____

A Growing American Role
_____
_____

Terms To Know

Choose a term from this lesson from the list below to complete each sentence by writing the term in the correct space. You will not use all the terms.

Buddhists	coup	National Communist Front
National Liberation Front	revolution	Vietcong

1. The _____ attacked the U.S. supported government of South Vietnam.

2. Another name for that group is the _____ .

3. Attacks on _____ cost South Vietnam's government much support.

4. Army officers staged a _____ and overthrew it, with American support.

Academic Vocabulary

Write the correct form of the academic vocabulary word from this lesson in the blank space to complete the sentence.

globe   global   globalism

Kennedy viewed the U.S. role in Vietnam as part of the _____ conflict against communism.

The Conflict Deepens (pages 874–876)

Identifying Cause and Effect

As you read pages 874–876, answer the following questions to identify the causes and effects of actions in the Vietnam War.

1. What did McNamara think about the situation in Vietnam after his fact-finding mission?

_____

_____

2. What was the result of the Gulf of Tonkin Resolution?

_____

_____

3. Why did the United States find it difficult to fight the war?

_____

_____

4. Why did American troops grow frustrated as the war went on?

_____

_____

Terms To Know

Read the following sentences. Choose the correct term from this lesson to complete the sentence by circling the term.

1. A naval incident near North Vietnam led Congress to approve the (Gulf of Tonkin, North Vietnam) Resolution, which gave President Johnson broad powers to fight a war in Vietnam.

2. The next year, then, he began sending massive numbers of troops in a move called (acceleration, escalation).

3. American forces went out on (reconnaissance, search-and-destroy) missions aimed at finding and killing enemy troops.

4. Meanwhile, North Vietnam sent a steady stream of men and supplies over the (Ho Chi Minh, Liberation) Trail.

5. Both sides used (napalm, nuclear) weapons to start fires and destroy the thick jungle growth that enemy troops hid in.

6. The Americans also sprayed a plant-killer called (Agent Orange, Anti-Grow).

Academic Vocabulary

Use a dictionary to look up the following academic vocabulary word from this lesson and write the definition in your own words in the spaces available.

implicit

_____

_____

Section Wrap-up

Now that you have read the section, write the answers to the questions that were included in Setting a Purpose for Reading *at the beginning of the section.*

How did Vietnam become a divided country?

_____

_____

Why did America increase its involvement in the Vietnam War?

_____

_____

Chapter 30, Section 3
The Vietnam Years at Home

(pages 877–882)

Reason To Read

Setting a Purpose for Reading Think about these questions as you read:
• What factors contributed to the rise of the protest movement?
• How did Americans at home respond to the Vietnam War?

Main Idea

As you read pages 877–882 in your textbook, complete this graphic organizer by stating how you think people known as doves and hawks differed on these issues.

	The Draft	**Escalation**
Doves		
Hawks		

Sequencing Events

As you read, write the correct months from 1968 in which these events took place:

_____ **King assassinated**

_____ **Tet Offensive begins**

_____ **Nixon wins presidential election**

_____ **Robert Kennedy assassinated**

_____ **McCarthy has strong showing in New Hampshire primary**

_____ **Pueblo captured off North Korea**

_____ **Johnson announces new peace effort and decision not to seek reelection**

The Youth Protest (pages 877–878)

 **Responding** *As you read the section, respond to the following questions.*

1. What were the reasons people had for opposing the war in Vietnam?

_____

_____

2. What were the views of the two different groups that opposed the draft?

_____

_____

3. How did the public climate change during the course of the war?

_____

_____

Terms To Know *Match the term from this lesson in the left column with the correct definition in the right column by writing the letter in the space to the left of the term.*

_____ **1.** conscientious objector

_____ **2.** counterculture

_____ **3.** deferment

_____ **4.** dove

_____ **5.** generation gap

_____ **6.** hawk

_____ **7.** Pentagon

a. headquarters of the Defense Department
b. opponent of the war
c. growing gulf between older officers and younger enlisted men in the army
d. group that formed to counter the rising tide of antiwar protesters
e. secret group opposed to the war
f. person who opposed the war on moral grounds
g. supporter of the war
h. growing mistrust between older and younger adults
i. paper excusing someone from the draft
j. movement that rejected traditional American values

Terms To Review

In the space available, define the following word you studied earlier.

aspect
(Chapter 24, Section 4)

_____
_____

1968—Year of Crisis *(pages 879–880)*

Questioning

As you read each subsection, ask yourself: what is an important detail? Write one of those details in the spaces below.

The Tet Offensive

_____
_____
_____
_____

Impact Back Home

_____
_____
_____
_____

The President Responds

_____
_____
_____
_____

Terms To Know

Define or describe the following key terms from this lesson.

credibility gap

_____
_____
_____

Tet Offensive

_____
_____
_____

USS Pueblo

_____
_____

Academic Vocabulary

Read each sentence below. Put a checkmark in the space before the word or words that best explains what the bold-faced academic vocabulary word from this lesson means in this passage.

1. After **consulting** with his advisers, Johnson decided not to run for reelection.

   _____ asking the views of   _____ hiring   _____ polling

2. The Tet Offensive convinced one newspaper that the **prospect** of winning the war in Vietnam was not high.

   _____ difficulty   _____ possibility   _____ view

Violence Erupts *(pages 880–881)*

Sequencing

As you read, put the following events in the correct order by writing the number 1 through 5 in the space to the left. Use the number 1 for the event that occurred first, 2 for the next event, and so on.

_____ **a.** Martin Luther King, Jr., killed

_____ **b.** Violence erupts at Democratic convention

_____ **c.** Lyndon Johnson withdraws from presidential race

_____ **d.** Hubert Humphrey wins Democratic nomination

_____ **e.** Robert F. Kennedy assassinated

Terms To Review

In the space available, define the following word you studied earlier.

primary election
(Chapter 21, Section 2)

_____

_____

Election of 1968 (page 882)

Outlining   *Complete this outline as you read.*

I. The Wallace Candidacy

A. _____

_____

B. _____

_____

II. The "Silent Majority"

A. _____

_____

B. _____

_____

C. _____

_____

III. Nixon Wins

A. _____

_____

B. _____

_____

Terms To Know   *Define or describe the key term from this lesson shown below.*

"silent majority" >   _____

_____

Now that you have read the section, write the answers to the questions that were included in Setting a Purpose for Reading *at the beginning of the section.*

What factors contributed to the rise of the protest movement?

_____

_____

How did Americans at home respond to the Vietnam War?

_____

_____

Chapter 30, Section 4
Nixon and Vietnam

(pages 884–889)

Reason To Read

Setting a Purpose for Reading Think about these questions as you read:
- What steps did Nixon take to end the war in Vietnam?
- What were the costs of the Vietnam War?

Main Idea

As you read pages 884–889 in your textbook, complete this graphic organizer by identifying three strategies Nixon used to end the war.

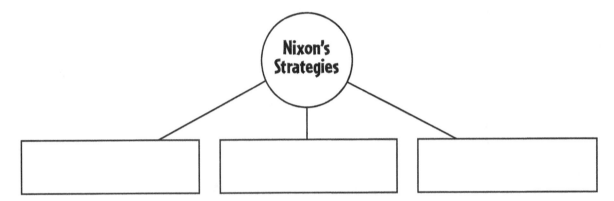

Sequencing Events

As you read, complete the chart by writing the date or the event in the appropriate place on the chart.

Date	Event
April 1970	
May 1970	
	U.S. resumes bombing of North Vietnam
January 1973	
	Saigon falls to North Vietnam

Key Points / Notes

A New Strategy (pages 884–885)

Synthesizing

Read the section on Nixon's strategy for Vietnam and then write at least three sentences describing the main points of the strategy.

_____

_____

_____

_____

_____

Terms To Know

Define or describe the following key term from this lesson.

Vietnamization >

_____

_____

Renewed Opposition at Home (pages 885–887)

Interpreting

Interpret the information you read about growing opposition to the war by answering the following questions.

1. Why did North Vietnam not agree to a peace plan?

_____

_____

2. What did critics say about Nixon's move into Cambodia after civil war erupted there?

_____

_____

3. Who did Nixon apparently hold responsible for the violence on college campuses?

_____

_____

Copyright © by The McGraw-Hill Companies, Inc.

Key Points

Notes

Terms To Know

Define or describe the following key term from this lesson.

martial law ›

_____

_____

"Peace Is at Hand" *(pages 888–889)*

Clarifying

As you read this section, answer the following questions to help you organize the information about the last years of the Vietnam War.

1. What military developments occurred in early 1972?

_____

_____

2. What condition did Nixon give up on, which helped the two sides near a peace agreement?

_____

_____

3. What were the terms of the peace agreement?

_____

_____

4. What happened after the United States withdrew from South Vietnam?

_____

_____

Terms To Review

Write two words that are related to each of the terms you studied earlier.

collapse
(Chapter 25, Section 2) ›

_____

_____

Key Points	Notes

unify
(Chapter 19, Section 1)

Legacy of the War (page 889)

Summarizing

Read the "Legacy of the War" on page 889. Then write a short summary of the information.

Terms To Know

Define or describe the following terms.

MIAs

Vietnam Veterans Memorial

Now that you have read the section, write the answers to the questions that were included in Setting a Purpose for Reading *at the beginning of the section.*

What steps did Nixon take to end the war in Vietnam?

_____

_____

What were the costs of the Vietnam War?

_____

_____

Chapter 31, Section 1
Nixon's Foreign Policy

(pages 896–900)

Reason To Read

Setting a Purpose for Reading Think about these questions as you read:

- How did Richard Nixon change U.S. political relations with the Soviet Union and China?
- What actions did the U.S. take regarding the Middle East and Latin America?

Main Idea

As you read pages 896–900 in your textbook, complete this graphic organizer by describing the goals of these strategies and policies.

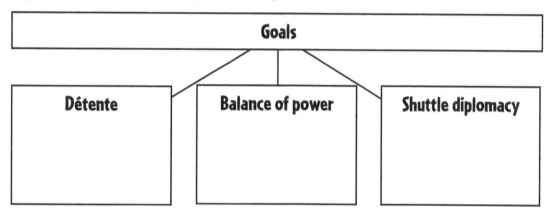

Sequencing Events

As you read, write the number next to the event on the appropriate place on time line:

1. **Arab oil embargo begins**
2. **Nixon visits Soviet Union**
3. **"Ping-Pong diplomacy" begins contact between U.S. and China**
4. **Nixon visits China**

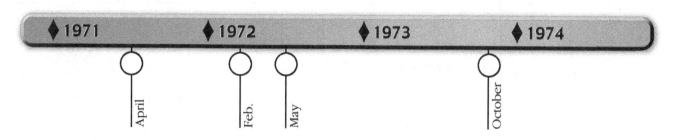

Easing the Cold War (pages 896–898)

Questioning

As you read pages 896–898, ask yourself: what is an important detail? Write one detail for each of the topics below.

Behind the Iron Curtain >

_____

_____

_____

Détente >

_____

_____

Academic Vocabulary

Read the sentence below. Put a checkmark in the space before the phrase that best explains what the academic vocabulary word ideology, *from this lesson, means in this sentence.*

Nixon and Kissinger believed in foreign policy based on national interests, not <u>ideology</u>.

____ economic principles

____ wishes

____ philosophy

The Middle East (pages 899–900)

Identifying Cause and Effect

Read the section and then answer the questions to identify causes and effects of issues in the Middle East.

1. What were the results of the Six-Day War of 1967?

_____

_____

2. What did some Arab states do out of anger at American support for Israel during the Yom Kippur War?

_____

_____

Chapter 31, Section 1

3. What did Kissinger's diplomacy produce?

_____

_____

Terms To Know

Use the following key terms from this lesson in a sentence.

shuttle diplomacy >

_____

_____

Yom Kippur War >

_____

_____

Latin America (page 900)

Summarizing

Read the lesson on relations with Latin America and then write three sentences summarizing the information.

_____

_____

_____

_____

_____

Section Wrap-up

Now that you have read the section, write the answers to the questions that were included in Setting a Purpose for Reading _at the beginning of the section._

How did Richard Nixon change U.S. political relations with the Soviet Union and China?

_____

_____

What actions did the U.S. take regarding the Middle East and Latin America?

_____

_____

Chapter 31, Section 2
Nixon and Watergate

(pages 901–908)

Reason To Read

Setting a Purpose for Reading Think about these questions as you read:
• How did Nixon struggle with domestic problems?
• How did the Watergate scandal affect politics?

Main Idea

As you read pages 901–908 in your textbook, complete this graphic organizer by listing three challenges Nixon faced during his presidency.

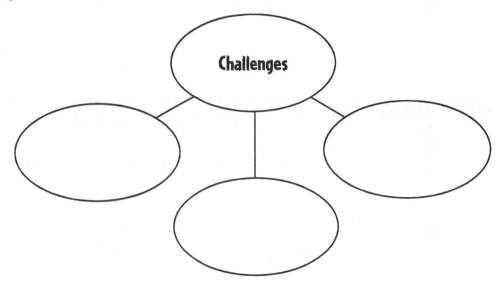

Sequencing Events

Match the date in the left column with the correct event in the right column by writing the letter in the space to the left of the date.

_____ 1. June 17, 1972

_____ 2. May 1973

_____ 3. October 1973

_____ 4. April 1974

_____ 5. August 5, 1974

_____ 6. August 8, 1974

a. Saturday Night Massacre

b. Nixon releases transcripts of taped conversations

c. Watergate break-in discovered

d. Nixon releases tapes under court order

e. Senate Watergate committee hearings begin

f. Nixon resigns

g. Nixon re-elected to second term

Nixon's Domestic Program (pages 901–903)

Summarizing

As you read the information on pages 901–903, write a short summary about these topics.

> **revenue sharing**

_____
_____
_____

> **affirmative action**

_____
_____
_____

Terms To Know

Match the term from this lesson in the left column with the correct definition in the right column by writing the letter in the space to the left of the term.

____ **1.** affirmative action

____ **2.** busing

____ **3.** deficit

____ **4.** Environmental Protection Agency

____ **5.** New Federalism

____ **6.** Occupational Health and Safety Administration

____ **7.** revenue sharing

____ **8.** stagflation

____ **9.** tight money policy

a. Nixon's slogan for his domestic programs

b. new agency intended to end workplace crime

c. combination of slow economic growth and rising prices

d. giving hiring preferences to minorities who had been excluded before

e. combination of low economic growth and low prices

f. spending more than the government takes in

g. steps taken to lead people to borrow more

h. transporting students to achieve integration

i. giving state money to the federal government

j. steps taken to push people to borrow less

k. new agency that focused on the workplace

l. giving federal money to state and local governments

m. new agency that tried to ensure clean air and water

Key Points

 **Notes**

The Watergate Crisis (pages 904–906)

Clarifying

As you read this section, answer the following questions to organize the information about the Watergate crisis.

1. What caused the Watergate crisis?

_____

_____

2. Why were the White House tapes important, and why could investigators not listen to them?

_____

_____

3. Why did Nixon finally release the tapes, and what did they reveal?

_____

_____

Terms To Know

Define or describe the following key terms from this lesson.

executive privilege >
_____

_____

impeachment >
_____

_____

Saturday Night Massacre >
_____

_____

Watergate >
_____

_____

A Time for Healing (pages 906–908)

Monitoring Comprehension

Check how well you understood what you read in this lesson by answering the following questions.

1. What major action did Ford take early in his presidency, and what effect did it have?

_____

_____

2. What economic problems did Ford face?

_____

_____

3. How did he try to solve them? How effective were those efforts?

_____

_____

Terms To Know

Define or describe the following terms from this lesson.

Helsinki Accords

_____

_____

pardon

_____

_____

under-employment

_____

_____

Terms To Review

In the space available, define the following word you studied earlier.

voluntary
(Chapter 25, Section 1)

_____

_____

 Key Points

 Notes

 Section Wrap-up

Now that you have read the section, write the answers to the questions that were included in Setting a Purpose for Reading *at the beginning of the section.*

How did Nixon struggle with domestic problems?

_____

_____

How did the Watergate scandal affect politics?

_____

_____

Chapter 31, Section 3
The Carter Presidency

(pages 910–914)

Reason To Read

Setting a Purpose for Reading Think about these questions as you read:
- How did President Carter emphasize human rights in foreign policy?
- What actions did Carter take to improve the economy?

Main Idea

As you read pages 910–914 in your textbook, complete this graphic organizer by listing three treaties that the Carter administration negotiated.

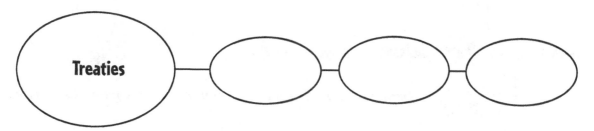

Sequencing Events

As you read, write the correct dates for each of these events:

_____ Carter presents National Energy Plan

_____ Camp David Accords announced

_____ Three Mile Island nuclear power plant accident

_____ SALT II treaty signed

_____ American hostages seized in Iran

_____ Soviet Union invades Afghanistan

_____ Refugees begin to leave Cuba in large numbers

The Election of 1976 *(pages 910–911)*

Analyzing *Analyze the information in this section by answering the following questions.*

1. How did Jimmy Carter capture the Democratic nomination?

_____

_____

2. How did Carter win the November election?

_____

_____

An Informal Presidency *(pages 911–912)*

Terms To Know *Define or describe the following key terms from this lesson.*

National Energy Plan >

_____

_____

trade deficit >

_____

_____

Academic Vocabulary *Read the passage below. Put a checkmark in the space before the phrase that best explains what the academic vocabulary word* exceed, *from this lesson, means in this passage.*

The value of the goods that Americans bought from abroad exceeded the value of goods American companies sold in other countries, a growing economic problem.

_____ did not equal   _____ fell below   _____ rose above

Foreign Affairs (pages 912–914)

Determining the Main Idea

Write down the main idea of this section in your own words.

_____

_____

_____

Terms To Know

Read the following sentences. Choose the correct term from this lesson to complete each sentence by circling the term.

1. Carter based his foreign policy on the idea of (civil liberties, human rights).

2. He objected to the (apartheid, integration) policy of the white government of South Africa, which denied rights to the majority black population.

3. Carter helped the leaders of Israel and Egypt reach a peace agreement called the (Camp David, White House) Accords.

4. Carter signed the (SALT II, SALT IV) treaty in an effort to limit nuclear weapons, but the Senate delayed ratifying it.

5. Late in his term, Islamic (Communists, fundamentalists) took control of Iran, leading to a serious crisis for the United States.

The Election of 1980 (page 914)

Evaluating

Read the section and then answer the questions to evaluate what you read.

1. What was Carter's position going into the election campaign? Why?

_____

_____

 Notes

2. What made Reagan an attractive candidate?

_____

_____

3. What was the result of the election?

_____

_____

Terms To Review

In the space available, define the following words you studied earlier.

obtain
(Chapter 25, Section 3)

_____

_____

Section Wrap-up

Now that you have read the section, write the answers to the questions that were included in **Setting a Purpose for Reading** *at the beginning of the section.*

How did President Carter emphasize human rights in foreign policy?

_____

_____

What actions did Carter take to improve the economy?

_____

_____

Chapter 32, Section 1
The Reagan Presidency
(pages 922–926)

Reason To Read

Setting a Purpose for Reading Think about these questions as you read:
- How did Ronald Reagan implement supply-side economics?
- How was Ronald Reagan active in foreign policy?
- How did the Soviet Union change?

Main Idea

As you read pages 922–926 in your textbook, complete this graphic organizer by providing three actions taken by Ronald Reagan.

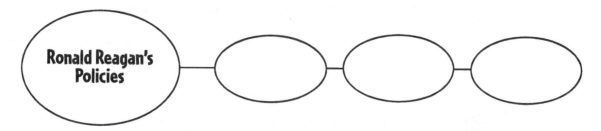

Sequencing Events

As you read, place the number representing each event in the appropriate circle on the time line.

1. **Reagan and Gorbachev sign International-Range Nuclear Forces Treaty**
2. **Congress lowers taxes and slashes domestic spending**
3. **Congress passed Gramm-Rudman-Hollings Act**
4. **Reagan wins reelection**

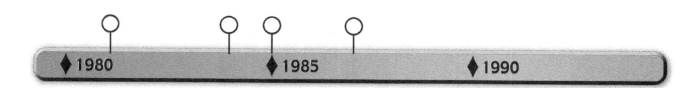

The Reagan Revolution (pages 922–924)

Interpreting   *Interpret the information you read about the Reagan revolution by answering the following questions.*

1. What conservative values did Reagan support?

_____

_____

2. What did Reagan's handling of the air traffic controller's strike reveal?

_____

_____

3. What conservative policies did Reagan put into place?

_____

_____

Terms To Know   *Define or describe the following key terms.*

deregulation

_____

_____

federal debt

_____

_____

Sunbelt

_____

_____

 **Key Points**

 **Notes**

Terms To Review

Read the passage below. Then in the spaces that follow, explain the meaning of the boldface term or academic vocabulary word you studied earlier.

Reagan cut taxes and also cut government spending on such programs as **welfare**. Because taxes were lower, the government collected less **revenue**.

welfare
(Chapter 25, Section 4)

_____

_____

revenue
(Chapter 21, Section 3)

_____

_____

Reagan's Foreign Policy *(pages 924–925)*

Outlining

As you read pages 924–925, complete this outline on the Reagan administration's foreign policy.

I. Military Buildup

   A. _____

   B. _____

II. Latin America

   A. _____

   B. _____

   C. _____

III. The Middle East

   A. _____

   B. _____

Copyright © by The McGraw-Hill Companies, Inc.

Terms To Know

Match the term from this lesson in the left column with the correct definition in the right column by writing the letter in the space to the left of the term.

_____ **1.** contras

_____ **2.** Sandinistas

_____ **3.** Strategic Defense Initiative

a. Communist rebels who seized government of Nicaragua

b. those opposed to American involvement in Central America

c. rationale for attacking Communists in Central America

d. anti-Communists who received aid from United States under Reagan

e. Communist rebels in Grenada

f. antimissile defense system

Reagan's Second Term *(pages 925–926)*

Responding

As you read the section, respond to the following questions.

1. Why did Reagan win such an overwhelming victory in the 1984 election?

_____

_____

2. How did Gorbachev change Soviet society?

_____

_____

Terms To Know

Read the following sentences. Choose the correct term from this lesson to complete the sentence by circling the term.

1. The (Iran-Contra, Lebanon-Contra) scandal arose out of the desire of some on the Reagan administration to help the contras and win the release of American hostages in Lebanon.

2. Gorbachev's policy of (glasnost, perestroika) led to a dramatic opening of Soviet society.

 **Key Points**

 **Notes**

3. With (glasnost, perestroika), he tried to achieve better economic growth by letting local people make economic decisions.

4. Reagan and Gorbachev signed a(n) (Intermediate-Range Nuclear Forces, Short-Range Missile) treaty aimed at reducing both countries' stockpiles of certain nuclear weapons.

 **Section Wrap-up**

Now that you have read the section, write the answers to the questions that were included in Setting a Purpose for Reading *at the beginning of the section.*

How did Ronald Reagan implement supply-side economics?

_____

_____

How was Ronald Reagan active in foreign policy?

_____

_____

How did the Soviet Union change?

_____

_____

Chapter 32, Section 2
The Bush Presidency

(pages 928–933)

Reason To Read

Setting a Purpose for Reading Think about these questions as you read:
- How did the Soviet Union collapse?
- How did George Bush use the military overseas?
- How did George Bush have difficulty domestically?

Main Idea

As you read pages 928–933 in your textbook, complete this graphic organizer by providing three key events leading to the fall of communism.

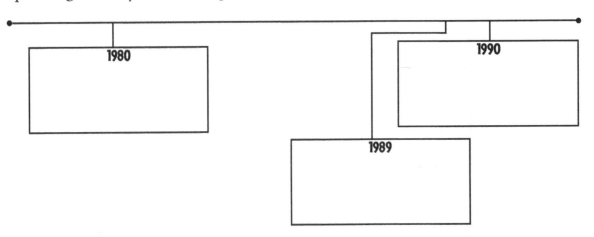

Sequencing Events

Match the date in the left column with the correct event in the right column by writing the letter in the space to the left of the date.

_____ 1. 1980

_____ 2. June 3, 1989

_____ 3. Nov. 9, 1989

_____ 4. Aug. 1991

_____ 5. Dec. 1991

a. coup in Soviet Union fails

b. Berlin Wall opened

c. Soviet Union breaks up

d. Chinese government cracks down on democracy protestors

e. Solidarity union formed in Poland

f. George H. W. Bush elected to second term

A New World Order (pages 928–930)

Connecting
Write three details that support the main idea.

Main Idea > During the Bush presidency, many changes in world affairs took place.

_____

_____

_____

Terms To Know
Define or describe each of the following key terms from this lesson.

Solidarity >

_____

_____

Strategic Arms Reduction Treaty (START) >

_____

_____

Academic Vocabulary
In the space available, define the following academic vocabulary word from this lesson.

successor >

_____

_____

A New Foreign Policy (pages 931–932)

Reviewing
Review pages 931–932 and list an important fact about each of these events.

The Persian Gulf War >

_____

_____

Operation Desert Storm >

_____

 **Key Points**

 **Notes**

Terms To Know

Define or describe each of the following key terms from this lesson.

envoy ⟩ _____
_____

Operation Desert Shield ⟩ _____
_____

Operation Desert Storm ⟩ _____
_____

Tiananmen Square ⟩ _____
_____

Academic Vocabulary

Read the following sentences. In the space below, write in your own words the meaning of the boldfaced academic vocabulary word from this lesson.

After 100 hours of ground fighting, President Bush **suspended** all military action.

_____

Domestic Issues (pages 932–933)

Summarizing

As you read pages 932–933, write a one-sentence summary about each of these topics.

Savings and Loan Scandal ⟩ _____
_____

Economic Downturn ⟩ _____
_____

Key Points **Notes**

Terms To Know

Use the spaces below to write a sentence using the following term from this lesson.

bankruptcy

_____

_____

Section Wrap-up

Now that you have read the section, write the answers to the questions that were included in Setting a Purpose for Reading *at the beginning of the section.*

How did the Soviet Union collapse?

_____

_____

How did George Bush use the military overseas?

_____

_____

How did George Bush have difficulty domestically?

_____

_____

Chapter 32, Section 3
A New Century
(pages 936–944)

Reason To Read

Setting a Purpose for Reading Think about these questions as you read:
- Why was President Clinton impeached by Congress?
- Why did the election of 2000 trigger controversy?

Main Idea

As you read pages 936–944 in your textbook, complete this graphic organizer by describing three domestic programs of the 1990s.

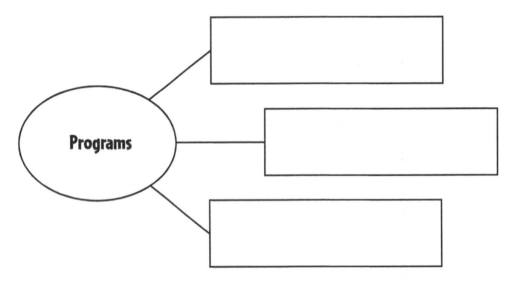

Sequencing Events

As you read, put the following events in the correct order by writing the number 1 through 7 in the space to the left. Use the number 1 for the event that occurred first, 2 for the next event, and so on.

_____ **A.** Brady Bill passed, signed into law

_____ **B.** federal budget reaches surplus

_____ **C.** Bush signs tax cut into law

_____ **D.** Clinton impeachment trial

_____ **E.** crime bill passes

_____ **F.** George W. Bush elected president

_____ **G.** Republicans write Contract with America

The Clinton Administration (pages 936–939)

Scanning

Scan the lesson by reading the headings. Then write down three topics you think will be covered in this lesson.

_____

_____

_____

_____

Terms To Know

Define or describe the following key terms from this lesson.

budget surplus

_____

_____

deficit spending

_____

_____

grassroots

_____

_____

gross domestic product

_____

_____

incumbents

_____

_____

line-item veto

_____

_____

perjury

_____

_____

Academic Vocabulary

Read the following sentences. In the space below, write in your own words the meaning of the **boldfaced** *academic vocabulary word from this lesson.*

As Starr learned of other possible cases of wrongdoing by President Clinton, he expanded the **scope** of his investigation.

_____

_____

Foreign Policy *(pages 939–940)*

Clarifying

As you read this section, answer the following questions to clarify the information about foreign policy under the Clinton administration.

1. What were the arguments for and against NAFTA?

_____

_____

2. Did the peace plan generated in late 1993 lead to peace in the Middle East? Explain your answer.

_____

_____

Terms To Know

In the spaces below, write a sentence using each of the following key terms from this lesson.

ethnic cleansing >
_____

_____

North American Free Trade Agreement (NAFTA) >
_____

_____

A New President for a New Century (pages 940–942)

Questioning

As you read pages 940–942, ask yourself: what is an important detail? Write one detail for each of the following topics.

The Election of 2000

_____
_____
_____

Cabinet and Advisers

_____
_____
_____

President Bush's First Term

_____
_____

Academic Vocabulary

Write the correct form of the boldfaced academic vocabulary word from this lesson in the blank space to complete the sentence.

select   selected   selection

Gore wanted hand recounts done only in _____ counties in Florida.

Looking to the Future (pages 943–944)

Questioning

As you read each subsection, ask yourself: what is an important detail? Write one detail about each of the following topics.

A Changing Society

_____
_____

Environmental Challenges

_____
_____

Terms To Know

Choose a term from this lesson from the list below to complete each sentence by writing the term in the correct space. You will not use all the terms.

air pollution   global warming   terrorism

Internet   nitrogen

ozone   telecommunications

1. Scientists disagree on whether or not _____ is affecting the environment.

2. The United States and several other nations took steps to fix one environmental problem, the decline in the _____ layer.

3. The rise of the _____ has allowed millions around the world to connect with each other by computer.

4. A growing problem is _____, the use of violence by groups to achieve political aims.

Academic Vocabulary

Read the following sentence. In the space below, write in your own words the meaning of the **boldfaced** *academic vocabulary word from this lesson.*

Governments took steps to stop making chemicals that were damaging the **layer** of ozone in the earth's atmosphere, which protects people from harmful rays from the sun.

_____

_____

Now that you have read the section, write the answers to the questions that were included in Setting a Purpose for Reading *at the beginning of the lesson.*

Why was President Clinton impeached by Congress?

_____

_____

Why did the election of 2000 trigger controversy?

_____

_____

Chapter 32, Section 4
The War on Terrorism

(pages 945–951)

Reason To Read

Setting a Purpose for Reading Think about these questions as you read:
• How did Americans respond to terrorism?
• What actions did the government take to fight terrorism?

Main Idea

As you read pages 945–951 in your textbook, complete this graphic organizer by explaining how Americans responded to the events of September 11, 2001.

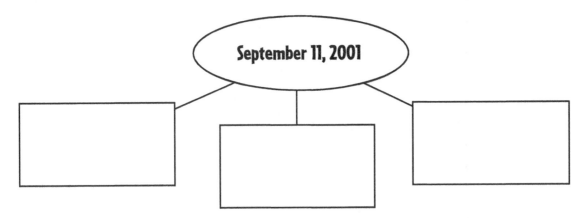

September 11, 2001

Sequencing Events

As you read, place the number representing each event in the appropriate circle on the time line.

1. Soviet Union invades Afghanistan

2. 9/11 attacks on the World Trade Center and Pentagon

3. First attack on World Trade Center

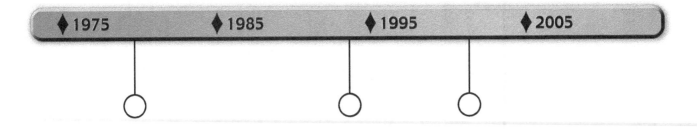

1975   1985   1995   2005

The Terrorist Threat (pages 946–947)

Monitoring Comprehension

Check how well you understood what you read in this section by answering the following questions.

1. How do the views of Muslim fundamentalists differ from those of most Muslims?

_____

_____

2. What terrorist attacks did al-Qaeda carry out against the United States before September 11, 2001?

_____

_____

Terms To Know

Choose a term from this lesson from the list below to complete each sentence by writing the term in the correct space. You will not use all the answers.

al-Qaeda	USS *Alabama*	Baath	Buddhists
USS *Cole*	mullahs	Muslims	Taliban

1. A small number of _____, followers of Islam, came to adopt extremist views that threatened the United States and many other countries.

2. A group called the _____ took control of the government of Afghanistan and allowed terrorists to set up training camps there.

3. Those terrorists belonged to an organization called

_____ .

4. This group carried out a bombing of a U.S. naval ship called the

_____ .

Key Points

Notes

Academic Vocabulary

Read the following sentence. In the space below, write in your own words the meaning of the boldfaced academic vocabulary word from this lesson.

Fundamentalists like bin Laden believe any action is **justified** to remove Western ideas from Muslim society.

_____

_____

Terms To Review

Use each of the following terms, which you studied earlier, in a sentence that reflects the meaning of the term.

fundamentalist
(Chapter 31, Section 3)

_____

_____

_____

identify
(Chapter 19, Section 4)

_____

_____

A New War Begins (pages 947–950)

Responding

As you read pages 947–950, answer the following questions.

1. How did people across the nation respond to the terrorist attacks of September 11?

_____

_____

2. What steps did the government take to improve security?

_____

_____

3. What steps did the administration take to combat terrorism abroad?

_____

_____

Terms To Know

Match the term from this lesson in the left column with the correct definition in the right column by writing the letter in the space to the left of the term.

____ **1.** anthrax

____ **2.** counter-terrorism

____ **3.** Homeland Security

____ **4.** Northern Alliance

____ **5.** USA Patriot Act

a. group that joined with the United States in Afghanistan

b. law passed in 2001 to strengthen efforts to find and block terrorists

c. animal disease carried by mosquitoes

d. deadly gas

e. agency created to protect Americans from terrorism

f. collective name for efforts to fight terrorism

g. law passed in 2001 to pay tribute to those killed in September 11 attacks

h. agency created in Afghanistan in wake of war there

i. animal disease that might be used as weapon

Academic Vocabulary

Read the passage below. Put a checkmark in the space before the phrase that best explains what the academic vocabulary word prior, *from this lesson, means in this passage.*

The new counter-terrorism law gave law enforcement officials the right to search a suspect's home or office without giving <u>prior</u> notice.

_____ formal _____ previous _____ public

Widening the War on Terror (pages 950–951)

Responding

As you read pages 950–951, answer these questions.

1. What are weapons of mass destruction? _____

_____

2. Why did President Bush order military force against Iraq?

_____

_____

_____

Key Points

Notes

Academic Vocabulary

Use each of these academic vocabulary terms in a sentence that reflects the meaning of the term.

regime

_____
_____
_____

nuclear

_____
_____
_____

Terms To Review

Read the sentence below. In the spaces that follow, explain the meaning of the academic vocabulary word decade *you studied earlier.*

The war on terrorism began during the first <u>decade</u> of the twenty-first century.

decade
(Chapter 18, Section 2)

_____
_____

Section Wrap-up

Now that you have read the section, write the answers to the questions that were included in Setting a Purpose for Reading *at the beginning of the lesson.*

How did Americans respond to terrorism?

_____
_____

What actions did the government take to fight terrorism?

_____
_____